AZ
HANDBOOK

UK Government & Politics

Paul Fairclough

Editor:
Eric Magee

DIGITAL EDITION

PHILIP ALLAN
UPDATES

Philip Allan Updates, an imprint of Hodder Education, an Hachette UK company, Market Place, Deddington, Oxfordshire OX15 0SE

Orders

Bookpoint Ltd, 130 Milton Park, Abingdon, Oxfordshire OX14 4SB
tel: 01235 827720
fax: 01235 400454
e-mail: uk.orders@bookpoint.co.uk

Lines are open 9.00 a.m.–5.00 p.m., Monday to Saturday, with a 24-hour message answering service. You can also order through the Philip Allan Updates website: www.philipallan.co.uk

ISBN 978-0-340-99111-4

First published 2010

Impression number   5 4 3 2 1
Year 2015 2014 2013 2012 2011 2010

Typeset by Macmillan, India

Printed by Antony Rowe Ltd, Chippenham, Wiltshire.

Environmental information

Hachette UK's policy is to use papers that are natural, renewable and recyclable products and made from wood grown in sustainable forests. The logging and manufacturing processes are expected to conform to the environmental regulations of the country of origin.

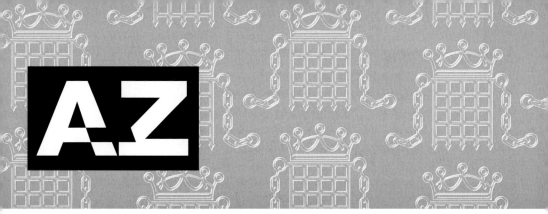

Contents

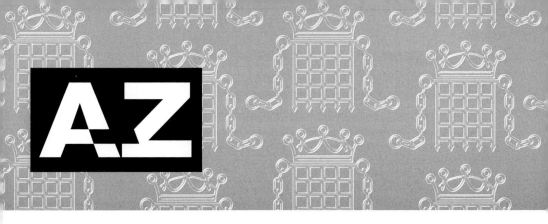

How to use this book

The *A–Z UK Government and Politics Handbook* is an alphabetical textbook designed for ease of use. Each entry begins with a one-sentence definition. This helps the user to add precision to the completion of reports or case studies.

Entries are generally developed in line with the relative importance of the concept identified. For example, *disclaim* is dealt with in a single line, whereas a core political term such as *insider group* receives nearly half a page. The latter would provide sufficient material to allow you to enhance an essay piece – and many entries also benefit from the use of examples or tips that will help you illustrate your answers fully.

The study of government and politics can be developed further by making use of the cross-referenced entries. For example, the entry for *Tony Blair* refers the reader to *prime minister* and *New Labour* as well as to a number of other entries. Cross-referenced entries are identified by the use of bold italics. The use of cross-referencing has been limited to important, linked terms. Therefore essay or project writing should benefit from following the logical pathway indicated by italicised entries.

Government and politics students have always had difficulties with the language of the subject. This stems from several factors:
- in the absence of a GCSE in government and politics, most students have been denied the opportunity to become familiar with key political terms prior to beginning their sixth form studies in the subject
- media commentators – and some writers – use, adapt or invent phrases (such as 'quasi-federalism' or 'sofa-government'), some of which prove temporary, while others become established as part of mainstream political vocabulary
- popular textbooks and the three main examination boards use different terms for essentially similar concepts (e.g. 'sectional group' and 'interest group')

The *A–Z UK Government and Politics Handbook* is a political glossary offering a single solution to these problems. Providing full coverage of all three main GCE AS specifications, the handbook is also a valuable reference/revision companion.

To aid the revision process, carefully selected lists are provided at the back of the book. Those facing AS examinations can use the lists to make the best use of the handbook during their revision time. The revision recommendations are split into units, for ease of use. Separate lists are provided for the three main AS specifications (AQA, OCR and Edexcel). You can also use the website that accompanies this handbook to access revision lists specific to your exam board unit.

In addition, the 'Hints for exam success' section at the back of the book provides general guidance on revision technique as well as lists of revision dos and don'ts.

A–Z Online

This digital edition of the *A–Z UK Government and Politics Handbook* includes free access to a supporting website and a free desktop widget to make searching for terms even quicker. Log on to **www.philipallan.co.uk/a-zonline** and create an account using the unique code provided on the inside front cover of this book.

Once you are logged on, you will be able to:
- search the entire database of terms in this handbook
- print revision lists specific to your exam board
- get expert advice from examiners on how to get an A* grade
- create a personal library of your favourite terms
- expand your vocabulary with our word of the week

You can also add the other *A–Z Handbooks (digital editions)* that you own to your personal library on A–Z Online. We hope that the *A–Z UK Government and Politics Handbook* will prove to be an invaluable resource, fully relevant from the first to the last day of your UK government and politics course.

Acknowledgements

My thanks go to Katie Blainey at Philip Allan Updates for her support and to the various editors who worked on the original manuscript and flagged up omissions; in particular Lesley Butland and Eric Magee. Also I am grateful for the support and patience of my wife Clare, my daughters Adele and Felicity and my son Douglas.

Paul Fairclough

A and others v. Secretary of State for the Home Department (2004): a landmark legal case in which the *indefinite detention* of terrorist suspects was ruled incompatible with Article 4 of the *Human Rights Act (1998)*. See *declaration of incompatibility*.
- The case was heard before the Appellate Committee of the House of Lords (see *Law Lords*).
- The indefinite detention of terrorist suspects had originally been authorised under the *Anti-terrorism, Crime and Security Act (2001)*.

Abortion Act (1967): the *Act of Parliament* that legalised abortion in Great Britain.
- It allowed for an abortion up to the 28th week of pregnancy, where two doctors agreed that it was necessary.
- The law did not apply in Northern Ireland and was subsequently amended by the *Human Embryology and Fertilisation Act (1990)*.

> **TIP:** An excellent example of a successful *Private Members' Bill*.

abstention: where people opt not to participate in a given activity. It is usually referred to in the context of *electoral turnout*.

access points: those points within the political system where individuals and groups may seek to apply pressure and thereby influence policy makers. Often referred to as points of leverage. See also *insider group*.

> **TIP:** Access points exist not only at the national level (e.g. *Number 10*, *Parliament*, the *civil service*) but also at *subnational* (e.g. local and regional government) and supranational (e.g. the *European Commission*) levels.

accountability: the principle that those holding public office should be answerable for their performance in post. It is:
- closely linked to the concept of *scrutiny* (or oversight)
- made easier by the use of the *recall election* device in many US states

Example

MPs are held accountable by their constituents at election time. The UK government is also held accountable by *Parliament* as it is drawn from the *legislature* (see *fusion of powers*).

Act of Parliament: a piece of *statute law* created when a *bill* completes its passage through *Parliament* and receives the *royal assent*. It is the end result of the *legislative process* or passage of legislation.

Act of Union: commonly referring to the parliamentary *statute law* of 1707 under which England and Scotland formed Great Britain. It may also refer to the Act of 1800 under which Great Britain and Ireland joined to form the *United Kingdom*.

active citizenship: the idea that there needs to be a better balance between *citizens' rights* and their responsibilities within society. It is

- closely associated with the Conservative administrations of the 1980s and 1990s under Margaret Thatcher and John Major
- characterised by policies such as the *Citizen's Charter*, local Neighbourhood Watch schemes and Michael Howard's suggestion that people should 'walk with a purpose', i.e. always be on the lookout for crimes being committed

activist: an individual who takes an active role in politics, i.e. beyond simply voting:

- often associated with involvement in *political parties*, *pressure groups* or other forms of political protest
- often prefixed by the word *grassroots* when referring to local activism

ad hoc: Latin phrase meaning created for a particular purpose – as opposed to being permanent. Commons *standing committees* are said to be ad hoc as they are established to look at a particular piece of legislation.

Adam Smith Institute: a right of centre *think-tank* established in the UK in 1981.

- It was originally founded in the USA in 1978.
- It is named after the philosopher and economist Adam Smith (1723–90).
- It is closely associated with the *neo-liberal* or *New Right* ideas adopted by *Margaret Thatcher's* Conservative administrations in the 1980s.

Adams, Gerry (1948–): President of *Sinn Fein* and leading figure in the Northern Ireland peace process. See *Good Friday Agreement (1998)*.

Addington, Henry: *prime minister* (Tory), 1801–04.

additional member system (AMS): a *hybrid electoral system*.

- Under the AMS, a proportion of seats in the *legislature* is awarded under a *majoritarian electoral system* with the remainder (the 'additional members') being allocated on a more proportional basis, often as a *top-up*.
- These additional members are normally elected under a *party list system* employing the *d'Hondt Formula*.

Example

A variant of the AMS system (*first-past-the-post* with a top-up) is used in elections to the *Scottish Parliament*, the *Welsh Assembly* and the *Greater London Assembly*. The Jenkins Report recommended another variant of AMS, known as *AV plus,* for use in elections to the Westminster Parliament. Germany and New Zealand also use AMS.

---

adjournment debate: a *debate* initiated by a *backbencher* in the *House of Commons* during the final 30 minutes of a day's business in the chamber. Such debates are often used to raise issues of interest to the member or to his or her constituents.

adversarial politics: the instinctive antagonism between the two main Westminster parties, similar to so-called 'yah-boo' politics. The theory was used by Professor S. E. Finer and commonly applied to UK politics in the 1970s.

> **TIP:** Adversarial politics is generally contrasted with the *consensus politics* of the 1950s and 1960s (see *postwar consensus*).

advisor: see *special advisor*

affiliated: most often used where an individual or a group is formally linked to a *political party*, without holding regular membership. Most *trade unions* and many other organisations are affiliated to the *Labour Party*.

> **Example**
> Many socialist societies, such as the *Fabian Society* and the Cooperative Society, are affiliated to the Labour Party. Such organisations helped to found the party, along with the trade unions, at the start of the twentieth century. Their affiliate status means that they retain a degree of input into the development of party policy and the election of party officials such as the leader.

> **TIP:** The *block vote* held by such affiliated organisations at the Labour *party conference* has long been a contentious issue.

affirmative action: a form of positive discrimination that is:
- designed to allow for an *equality of outcome*
- closely associated with strategies to address the issue of racial inequality in the USA

See also *women-only shortlists*.

agencification: the process of transferring the responsibility for delivering some government services to free-standing agencies (see *executive agency*). It is associated with the Next Steps Programme (see *Ibbs Report (1988)*), introduced by *Margaret Thatcher* in the 1980s.

agency: see *executive agency*

agency capture: where an agency falls under the control or influence of those it is supposed to be regulating. It is sometimes referred to as 'clientelism'.

agenda: a list of things to be done or discussed at a meeting. See *cabinet agenda* and *agenda-setting*.

agenda-setting: the process by which a government's priorities are established.
- The individuals and institutions that comprise the *core executive* play a crucial role determining the direction of government.
- The *media* are also said to play an important role in shaping the political agenda.

Aitken, Jonathan (1942–): a former Conservative MP (1974–97), defence minister (1992–94) and chief secretary to the *Treasury* (1994–95), who was convicted of perjury in 1999 and sentenced to 18 months in prison. Aitken was found to have lied under oath during a libel case he brought against the *Guardian* newspaper in 1997. The original case involved an article published in 1995, relating to Aitken's supposed links with arms dealers and leading Saudis.

He later led a policy group on prison reform for *Iain Duncan Smith*'s *Centre for Social Justice*. See also *sleaze*.

Al Fayed, Mohamed (1929–): the owner of Harrods and a key figure in the *cash for questions* scandal.

alienation: a sense of disaffection with established institutions and practices, and often associated with *abstention* and low *turnout*.

alignment: a long-established and enduring relationship between certain groups of voters and a particular *political party*.
- High levels of alignment in the 1950s and 1960s went hand in hand with the idea of *electoral stability*.
- A process of *dealignment* since the 1970s led to greater *electoral volatility*.

> **TIP:** It is important that you are able to distinguish between *partisan alignment* and *class alignment*. Though the latter was one facet of the former, the two terms are completely analogous.

all-women shortlists: see *women-only shortlists*

alternative vote system (AV): a *majoritarian electoral system* that results in fewer *wasted votes* and greater *voter choice* than *first-past-the-post*.
- AV is a preferential system, with voters ranking candidates in order of preference within each single-member constituency.
- A candidate securing more than 50% of first preference votes is duly elected.
- Where no candidate wins outright on the basis of first preference votes, the worst-performing candidates are eliminated in turn, with their votes being transferred according to their second choices until a candidate breaks through the 50% barrier.

Example

Although this system has not been used in the UK, it is similar to the *supplementary vote (SV)* system used in the London mayoral election. The *Jenkins Commission* also favoured a variant of AV (known as *AV plus* or AV top-up) for use in elections to the Westminster Parliament.

> **TIP:** Although AV is said to be fairer because it reduces *wasted votes*, enhances *voter choice* and provides the victorious candidate with a stronger personal *mandate*, it does not necessarily produce results that are any more *proportional*. Indeed, the *Essex model* suggested that Labour's Commons majority would have been even bigger in 1997 under AV than it was under *first-past-the-post*.

amendment: a formal change made to a *bill* during the *legislative process*. The governing party's Commons majority and the control exercised by the government *whips* allow it to secure the changes it desires, whilst limiting the number of amendments that can be made by *opposition* parties or *backbenchers*.

AMS: see *additional member system (AMS)*

Amsterdam, Treaty of (1997): An *EU* treaty that extended the *co-decision procedure* into most areas of EU policy. It also confirmed the incorporation of the *Social Chapter* (previously a protocol) into EU treaties, following the UK's decision to give up the opt-out negotiated by *John Major*. The treaty also extended the *Council of Ministers'* use of *qualified majority voting* into 11 additional areas of policy.

anarchism: a political philosophy that holds that the existence of the *state* is both unnecessary and unhelpful. From the Greek meaning 'no government' or 'no ruler'.

Anglo-Irish Agreement (1985): an agreement between the UK and the Republic of Ireland that sought to bring about an end to the troubles in Northern Ireland. It was signed by the then UK prime minister, *Margaret Thatcher* and the Irish Taoiseach, Garret FitzGerald. See also *Downing Street Declaration* and *Good Friday Agreement (1998)*.

annual conference: see *party conference*

anonymity: the principle that UK *civil servants* should be able to conduct their business in private without being held publicly and personally responsible for the work they do.
- Anonymity is one of the three traditional principles of the UK *civil service*, the others being *impartiality* (neutrality) and *permanence*.
- It is linked to the *role responsibility* aspect of *individual ministerial responsibility*, i.e. the notion that the *secretary of state* is directly responsible and accountable for all that goes on in his or her *department*.

> **TIP:** The principle of anonymity has been undermined by two key developments: the rise of high-profile special *advisors*; and the process of *agencification*.

Anti-Poll Tax Federation: a *pressure group* that coordinated the activities of the many *Anti-Poll Tax Unions* established in England, Scotland and Wales. See *poll tax*.

Anti-Poll Tax Unions: local organisations established to campaign against the *poll tax* in the late 1980s and early 1990s. See also *Anti-Poll Tax Federation*.

Anti-terrorism, Crime and Security Act (2001): the *Act of Parliament* that gave the police and security services wide-ranging powers to deal with the threat posed by terrorism. It included the powers to freeze the assets of suspected terrorists and detain non-British terrorists indefinitely pending deportation.

> **TIP:** The indefinite detention of foreign terrorist suspects was ultimately ruled incompatible with the *Human Rights Act (1998)*. See also *A and others v. Secretary of State for the Home Department (2004)* and the *Prevention of Terrorism Act (2005)*.

apathy: a state of being passive or indifferent, often linked to low *turnout* in elections.

> **TIP:** Low turnout does not necessarily equate to political apathy as citizens may simply be engaged in other forms of political *participation*, e.g. *pressure group* activity.

appeal court: any court that has the power to review and correct judgments handed down by an inferior (i.e. lower) court. See *Court of Appeal* and *Supreme Court*.

Appellate Committee of the House of Lords: see *Law Lords*

Ashdown, Paddy (1941–): MP for Yeovil (1983–2001) first as a Liberal and later as a Liberal Democrat. He was leader of the *Liberal Democrats* between 1989 and 1999.
- Ashdown worked behind the scenes to forge closer links with New Labour ahead of the 1997 general election.
- The parties' shared interest in constitutional reform resulted in the Liberal Democrats being given seats on the *Joint Cabinet Committee on Constitutional Reform* in the wake of Labour's victory.
- In 2007 Gordon Brown was said to have offered Lord Ashdown a role in his 'government of all the talents'.

Asquith, Herbert Henry: *prime minister* (Liberal), 1908–16.

asymmetrical bicameralism: see *bicameralism*

Athenian democracy: a form of *direct democracy* practised in classical Athens. It is said to have originated in c500 BC where the city-state's 40 000 adult free men or citizens had the right to attend forum meetings at which certain policies could be approved or rejected by means of a vote

attack-ads: negative *campaign* advertisements designed to discredit the character or policies of one's opponent.
- Attack-ads are common in US election campaigns, where *candidates* are permitted to buy up the slots of television or radio airtime time set aside for commercial advertising in order to run political ads against their opponent.
- They are less of an issue in the UK, where political advertising on television and radio is prohibited, aside from the scheduled *party political broadcasts*.

attitude cause group: a *pressure group* that seeks to change people's attitude towards a particular cause. See *sectional/cause group typology* and *cause group*.

Attlee, Clement Richard: *prime minister* (Labour), 1945–51.

authority: the right to take a particular course of action. The German sociologist Max Weber (1864–1920) identified three sources of authority:
- traditional authority (based on established traditions and customs)
- charismatic authority (based upon the abilities and personalities of individual leaders)
- legal-rational authority (granted as a result of a formal process such as an election).

Example

In the UK the doctrine of *parliamentary sovereignty* states that only *Parliament* has the authority to make and unmake UK laws. This legal-rational authority is legitimised through free and fair elections. The governing party's authority to try to carry its policies through into law is based upon the *mandate* it has secured in the preceding election.

TIP: It is important to be able to distinguish between authority and power. While those in authority will generally possess a degree of power, this is not always the case, as power and authority may be held independently of one another. A bomb-wielding terrorist may have power without authority; a teacher might have authority without genuine power; and an officer in a tactical firearms unit may have power and authority.

AV: see *alternative vote system (AV)*

AV plus: a *hybrid electoral system* where a proportion of seats would be awarded under the majoritarian *alternative vote system (AV)* and the remainder would be distributed proportionally under an open *regional list system*.

- The *Jenkins Report (1998)* recommended this system for use in elections to *Westminster*.
- The proportional element of the system (the 'plus') would see seats distributed as a *top-up* using the *d'Hondt formula*. This would benefit parties that had fared badly under the majoritarian AV system used in the *constituency* contests.
- As with *AMS* in Scotland and Wales, voters would cast two votes: one transferable vote for the person they wanted to represent them in their constituency; and one non-transferable vote for the party they wanted to support in their region.

AV top-up: see *AV plus*.

A–Z Online

Log on to A–Z Online to search the database of terms, print revision lists and much more. Go to **www.philipallan.co.uk/a-zonline** to get started.

backbench rebellion (or revolt): see *rebellion (backbench)*.

backbencher: an *MP* who does not hold front bench responsibilities as a government minister, shadow minister or party spokesperson.
- The term relates to the position of the benches where such MPs sit in the *House of Commons*.
- Backbenchers are often dismissively referred to as *lobby fodder*.

Back to basics: a political campaign focusing on law and order, the family and education.
- It was launched by *John Major*'s Conservative administration in 1993.
- Widely taken as a call for a moral crusade, the campaign was derailed amid the allegations of *sleaze* that hit the party between 1993 and its defeat at the 1997 *general election*.

backwoodsmen: referring to those absentee Conservative *hereditary peers* who attended the *Lords* only to vote down radical proposals passed through the *Commons* by successive Labour *governments*.

Bagehot, Walter (1826–77): author of *The English Constitution* (1867), founder of the *National Review* and later editor of *The Economist*.
- Bagehot drew a distinction between the efficient elements of the *constitution* (i.e. those that held real power) and those that were dignified (i.e. essentially ceremonial).
- For Bagehot, the *cabinet* was the 'efficient secret' of the English constitution. It was, as he put it, 'a hyphen which joins, a buckle which fastens' the *legislature* to the *executive*. The *prime minister* was merely *primus inter pares*.

Baldwin, Stanley: *prime minister* (Conservative), 1923, 1924–29 and 1935–37.

Balfour, Arthur James: *prime minister* (Conservative), 1902–05.

ballot: a vote called on a particular issue or in the election of an individual to public office. Also used as shorthand for the *ballot paper* and as an alternative way of referring to the act of voting, i.e. casting a ballot.

ballot bill: a *Private Members' Bill* that MPs qualify to introduce by having their names drawn randomly in a ballot.
- Those MPs wishing to introduce a ballot bill put their names into the hat at the start of the *parliamentary session*.
- The first 20 names drawn have some chance of introducing their chosen legislative proposal, though the limited time available means that normally only a handful of proposals receives serious consideration.
- Such bills are discussed in time set aside on 13 Fridays in each parliamentary session.

Example
The *Abortion Act (1967)* began life as a private member's ballot bill introduced by the Liberal *backbencher* David Steel. Though he was a relatively inexperienced MP at the time, having been a member for only 18 months, Steel was successful in the private member's ballot and saw his proposal enacted into law with *cross-party* support.

> **TIP:** MPs often put their names into the ballot without having settled on the legislative cause they will adopt if successful. As a result, those whose names are drawn early in the ballot are often subject to considerable lobbying from pressure groups that already have a proposal drafted.

ballot box: a locked box in which voters place their completed ballot papers at the polling station. It is an essential feature of the *secret ballot* system adopted in the UK as a result of the Ballot Act (1872).

ballot paper: the slip of paper on which on which voters register their choice of candidate or party at an election.
- Ballot papers were traditionally issued at the polling station on election day to those whose names appeared on the *electoral register*.
- The move towards *postal voting* means that many voters now receive their ballot papers directly by mail in advance of the election.
- Ballot papers that have been defaced, filled in incorrectly or left blank are recorded as *spoilt ballots*.

bandwagon effect: the theory that voters are more likely to vote for parties that are doing well in the polls, thereby further increasing that party's lead. See also *boomerang effect*.

> **TIP:** The fear that opinion polls may serve to shape as well as reflect public opinion has led countries such as France to ban such polls in the days leading up to an election.

Bank of England: the state-owned UK central bank.
- The bank manages the *Consolidated Fund*.
- In 1997, the incoming Labour Government gave the Bank control over the UK's base interest rate. The Bank's Monetary Policy Committee meets monthly to set the interest rate, with a view to keeping inflation within upper and lower limits established by the government.

Bell, Martin (1938–): the former BBC correspondent and *independent MP* for the *constituency* of Tatton (1997–2001).
- Bell was elected to *Parliament* in 1997 when running as an *independent* anti-corruption *candidate* against the sitting Conservative Party MP *Neil Hamilton*. See *cash for questions*.
- He ran against the sitting Conservative MP Eric Pickles in the Brentwood and Ongar *constituency* but was defeated.

Benn, Tony (1925–): long-serving MP, former Labour *minister* and political writer, thinker, orator and activist.

- Benn first became an MP in 1950 but was disqualified from retaining his seat when he inherited the title of 2nd Viscount Stangate in 1960.
- He campaigned for the right to *disclaim* his peerage and was permitted to do so following the *Peerages Act (1963)*. He subsequently reclaimed his seat in the *Commons* when the sitting MP stood down in order to allow a *by-election*.
- He was a minister in the Labour governments of the 1960s and 1970s.
- He retired from the Commons at the 2001 *general election* but remained active in politics, e.g. becoming president of the *Stop the War Coalition*.

Bentinck, William (Duke of Portland): *prime minister* (Whig), 1783 and 1807–09.

Better Quality Services: a central government initiative aimed at improving the quality of public services and encouraging *public–private partnerships*. It was introduced by *New Labour* in 1998 and was a successor to John Major's *Citizen's Charter*.

Beveridge Report (1942): the wartime report, chaired by William Beveridge, that identified a range of social problems facing the nation and laid the foundations for the creation of the *welfare state*.

bias: a predisposition towards a particular point of view. Contrast with impartiality or neutrality. See *judicial neutrality*.

bicameralism: the practice of having a *legislature* comprising two chambers.

- A second chamber is said to allow for a more careful examination of legislative proposals and more effective *scrutiny* (or *oversight*) of the *executive*.
- Some countries operate under a *unicameral legislature*.

Example

The UK operates under a system of asymmetrical bicameralism, where the *House of Commons* holds far greater power than the *House of Lords*; the latter serving largely as a revising chamber. The USA practises balanced bicameralism, with the House of Representatives and the Senate sharing co-equal legislative power.

bilateral meetings: meetings between the *prime minister* and a single *cabinet* colleague. See also *sofa government*.

- In the modern era, decisions have increasingly been taken in such meetings and in *kitchen cabinets* as opposed to cabinet proper. This is one of the factors that is said to have undermined *cabinet government*.
- Bilateral meetings were used extensively by *Tony Blair* during his time in office.

Bilderberg Group: a regular meeting of over 100 leading figures in the fields of politics, economics and the media. The secrecy surrounding such meetings and the fact that they are by invitation only have led to accusations that the group is part of a *New World Order*.

bill: a legislative proposal that has begun its passage through *Parliament*.

- A bill becomes a law – also known as an *Act of Parliament* or a *statute* – once it has passed through the *Commons* and the *Lords* and received the *royal assent*.
- Most bills originate with the government. See also *government bill*, *Private Members' Bill*, *private bill* and *public bill*.

Bill of Rights: a single authoritative document setting out the rights available to citizens.

- The USA probably has the most famous Bill of Rights (comprising the first ten amendments to the US Constitution).
- The UK has traditionally not had a formal Bill of Rights but the **European Convention on Human Rights (1950)** was incorporated into UK law under the **Human Rights Act (1998)** (see also **negative rights** and **positive rights**).
- Critics of the Human Rights Act argue in favour of a properly codified and entrenched Bill of Rights, either for England or for the UK as a whole (see **codified constitution** and **entrenchment**).

bipartisan: *cross-party* cooperation. See also **adversarial politics**.

Example

The Conservative and Labour Parties took a bipartisan approach to the **Good Friday Agreement (1998)**, with proposals relating to the future of Northern Ireland being discussed largely on their merit rather than on an adversarial basis.

Birmingham Six: the six men sentenced to life imprisonment in 1975 for a series of pub bombings in Birmingham in 1974.
- The men were said to be members of the **IRA**.
- The **Court of Appeal** eventually freed them in 1991 as a result of doubts over the forensic evidence used to convict them.
- Their case is often cited as a notable **miscarriage of justice**.

Black Wednesday: 16 September 1992, the day when the falling value of the pound on the currency markets forced the Conservative government to withdraw from the European *Exchange Rate Mechanism (ERM)*.
- The manner in which the **incumbent** Conservative government reacted to the crisis was said to have contributed to the party's losing its reputation for economic competence.
- The crisis was said to have cost the government in excess of £3 billion, most of which had been spent trying to halt the slide of the UK currency.

Blackstone, William (1723–80): an English judge and author of the four-volume *Commentaries on the Laws of England*. Blackstone famously summed up the doctrine of parliamentary sovereignty when stating that '[Parliament] can, in short, do every thing that is not naturally impossible'.

Blair, Tony (1953–): *prime minister* (Labour), 1997–2007.
- Blair was the Labour MP for Sedgefield (1983–2007) and leader of the **Labour Party** (1994–2007).
- He continued the process of party modernisation begun by previous Labour leaders **Neil Kinnock** and **John Smith** (see **New Labour**). This involved weakening the links between Labour and the **trade unions** and reforming **Clause IV** of the party's 1918 Constitution.
- Blair was closely associated with developing the **third way**, an approach said to fall between **conservatism** and **socialism**.
- His leadership brought unprecedented electoral success for the party, including its biggest ever victory (in 1997) and the completion of a second full term in office for the first time in the party's history.
- Critics accused Blair of adopting an overly **presidential** style during his time as **prime minister**. He was said to favour **bilateral meetings** and **sofa government** over more formal institutions such as the **cabinet**.

Blairism: the political ideology of the former Labour leader and prime minister *Tony Blair* and those who share his outlook. See also *third way*.

Blair's Babes: referring collectively to the 101 female Labour MPs elected to the *Commons* at the time of the 1997 *general election*, and closely associated with the Labour Party's use of *women-only shortlists* ahead of that election. It is seen by some as a dismissive and patronising term.

block vote: where trade unions and other organisations affiliated to the *Labour Party* were permitted to cast a single vote equal to the total number of members they claimed to represent.
- The vote could be cast by the union leader without having to consult individual members.
- It could be used at the *party conference* when voting on policy proposals and when choosing a party leader.

> **TIP:** Labour's move towards *one member, one vote (OMOV)* under *John Smith* and *Tony Blair* limited the block vote, though it was still seen in the selection of Frank Dobson, rather than *Ken Livingstone*, as the official Labour candidate in the 1999 election for *Mayor of London* and in some votes at conference.

Bloody Sunday: 30 January 1972, referring to the deaths of 14 civilians shot by the British Army's Parachute Regiment in Derry, Northern Ireland. It was the subject of the Saville Inquiry, established by *Tony Blair* in 1998 and due to report, finally, in 2010.

BNP: see *British National Party (BNP)*.

boomerang effect: where a strong performance in the *opinion polls* for a particular party ultimately results in that party losing support.
- It may occur where people vote in sympathy for parties that are doing badly in the polls, perhaps because they see them as the underdogs.
- It is also likely to result from people failing to turn out and vote where they see that their preferred party is well ahead in the polls. See also *bandwagon effect*.

borough council: referring either to the historic name by which some *district councils* are still known or to the London Boroughs.

bottom-up: where power resides or the impetus for change comes from the *grassroots* level. See also *top-down*.

Boundary Commissions: The Boundary Commissions Act (1992) requires the four national Boundary Commissions of England, Northern Ireland, Scotland and Wales to review the existing constituency boundaries periodically, in line with demographic changes.
- This process normally takes place every decade or so on the basis of data collected in the census.
- Though the commissions are guided by the general principle that parliamentary constituencies should consist of a roughly equal number of voters (around 70,000 at present), other factors, including the natural desire to avoid constituencies that are overly disparate or too geographically large, are also taken into consideration.
- The result of this process is that the numbers of voters within a constituency may vary from around 55,000 to well over 100,000.

Bow Group: a liberal-leaning faction in the *Conservative Party*. Established in 1951.

Brent Spar: an offshore oil platform that became the subject of a high-profile *Greenpeace* campaign after Shell UK made plans to dispose of it at sea.
- The UK *government* had granted Shell UK permission to dump the 14,500 tonne Brent Spar oil platform in the North Atlantic.
- *Greenpeace* opposed the decision. It was also looking for a symbol that could be used to focus the attention of a planned European environmental summit.
- Greenpeace *activists* boarded the Spar and turned it into a floating TV station broadcasting directly to the world's media.
- Shell eventually abandoned its plan to dump the Spar at sea.

British National Party (BNP): A *right-wing* nationalist party founded in 1982, following a split in the *National Front*. It opposes immigration and favours voluntary repatriation of non-indigenous peoples.
- The party has achieved some success in *local elections* and in the 2008 elections to the *Greater London Assembly*, where its candidate, Richard Barnbrook, secured one of the 25 seats available.
- It achieved a major breakthrough in the 2009 elections to the *European Parliament*, securing two seats: one in the Yorkshire and the Humber region and the other in North West England.
- It generally performs poorly in *general elections*, securing only 0.7% of the popular vote in 2005.

broadsheet: a content-heavy newspaper traditionally printed on A2-size paper, though also published in more compact formats in recent years. Contrast with *tabloid*. Titles include the *Guardian, The Times, Daily Telegraph* and *Independent.*

Brown, Gordon (1951–): *prime minister* (Labour), from 2007. Labour MP for Dunfermline East (1983–2005) and Kirkcaldy and Cowdenbeath (from 2005). Labour Leader from 2007. Chancellor of the exchequer (1997–2007).

Bruges Group: a *Eurosceptic Conservative Party faction* named after a famously abrasive speech against further *European integration* delivered by *Margaret Thatcher* at a 1988 summit at Bruges.

Budget: the government's annual plans for government spending and taxation, prepared by the *chancellor of the exchequer* and presented to *Parliament* for its approval.

bureaucracy: the unelected part of *government* and the structures and processes that govern its operation. See *civil service* and *government department*. The term 'bureaucratic' is also often used in criticism of processes that are overly long or requiring excessive volumes of paperwork.

Burke, Edmund (1729–97): a long-serving *Whig* MP and author of *Reflections on the Revolution in France* (1790) and closely associated with the concept of *representative democracy*.

Burkean model: see *Burke, Edmund (1729–97)*, *representative democracy* and *trustee model*.

Butskellism: referring to the *postwar consensus*, more specifically to the way in which the Labour chancellor of the exchequer Hugh Gaitskell and his Conservative successor in the post Rab Butler both accepted the need to adopt *Keynesianism*.

by-election: an *election* in a single parliamentary constituency or council ward occurring between regular elections, generally resulting from the death, resignation or disqualification from office of the incumbent. In 1997 the High Court ruled that there would have to be a by-election in Winchester after Liberal Democrat candidate Mark Oaten's victory by just two votes in the general election was contested.

Example

On 6 November 2008, a by-election was held in the Glenrothes constituency, following the death of the incumbent Labour MP John MacDougall. The Labour **candidate**, Lindsay Roy, held the seat for the party in a **campaign** that saw the prime minister **Gordon Brown** break with tradition and travel to Scotland to take part in the by-election campaign.

cabinet: the leading committee of *government*, chaired by the *prime minister* and comprising the *secretaries of state* who head up each *government department* along with other key individuals.
- The size of the cabinet can vary, though there are only 23 paid positions.
- In theory the cabinet is the supreme decision-making body in government but its position is said to have been undermined by the rise of a more *presidential* prime minister favouring the greater use of *bilateral meetings*.

cabinet agenda: the ordered list of items to be discussed at the weekly *cabinet* meeting. The *prime minister* controls the cabinet agenda and can also largely determine who is permitted to speak, and when, once the meeting is under way.

cabinet committee: a subset of the *cabinet*, chaired by the *prime minister*, or someone of his choosing, and focusing on a particular area of policy.
- The prime minister has considerable control over the number, scope, composition and operation of cabinet committees. Some cabinet committees are permanent (see example below) others are **ad hoc**.
- Cabinet committees were first established under *Maurice Hankey*, who was appointed to the post of Secretary to the *war cabinet* by *George Lloyd* in 1916.
- *John Major* was the first *prime minister* to publish details about the structure and composition of cabinet committees as part of his commitment to *open government*.

> **Example**
>
> The cabinet committees that operate on a permanent basis are grouped together into categories such as foreign and defence policy, domestic/home affairs and economic policy. An example of a permanent committee would be the Energy and the Environment Committee (EE). *Ad hoc* (or miscellaneous) committees are established to deal with specific issues or concerns, e.g. the Olympics Committee (MISC 25).

cabinet government: the traditional view that *cabinet* is the key decision-making body within the *government* with the *prime minister* acting only as *primus inter pares* (first amongst equals). See also *collective responsibility*. *Walter Bagehot* described cabinet as the 'efficient secret' of the English *constitution*.

> **TIP:** A decline in the number and length of cabinet meetings under *Tony Blair*, along with his willingness to make key decisions outside cabinet in bilateral meetings (e.g. the decision to hand control over interest rates to the Bank of England), led some to question the notion of cabinet government.

cabinet minister: a senior member of the *government* appointed by the *prime minister* and in most cases holding ultimate responsibility for a government *department* as *secretary of state*.

Cabinet Office: the *civil service* body that supports and coordinates the work of *cabinet*. It is headed by the *cabinet secretary*, a senior *civil servant*. See also *Hankey, Maurice (1877–1963)*.

> **TIP:** The reorganisation of the Cabinet Office and the *Prime Minister's Office* under *Tony Blair* led some to herald the rise of a de facto *prime minister's department*.

Cabinet Office Briefing Room A (COBRA): see *Civil Contingencies Committee*.

cabinet secretary: A senior *civil servant* who heads up the *Cabinet Office* and reports directly to the *prime minister*.

Callaghan, James: *prime minister* (Labour), 1976–79. See also *winter of discontent*.

Cameron, David (1966–): MP for Witney (from 2001) and Leader of the *Conservative Party* (from 2005). Cameron was a former *special advisor* to the Conservative chancellor of the exchequer Norman Lamont (see *Black Wednesday*) and was credited with modernising the *Conservative Party* and restoring its electoral fortunes. See *New Tories*.

campaign: a collective term describing the various methods, strategies and set-piece events by which a political party seeks to appeal to voters at the time of an election.
- *General election* campaigns officially last for 17 working days from the point at which *Parliament* is dissolved to *polling day*. In reality, most parties are engaged in almost continuous campaigning, albeit at a far lower intensity.
- At a constituency level, *grassroots* activists engage in *canvassing*. The national party makes use of mailshots, *party election broadcasts*, rallies and billboard advertising campaigns.
- In recent general elections the major parties have turned to professional consultants when planning their campaigns, e.g. Australian consultant Lynton Crosby ran the Conservatives' 2005 campaign. See also *focus groups* and *pollsters*.

> **TIP:** Some still see the campaign and other *short-term factors* (see *recency model*) as less important than *long-term factors* (see *primacy model*) in shaping voting behaviour.

Campaign for Nuclear Disarmament (CND): an *attitude cause group* that favours unilateral nuclear disarmament and opposes the building of new nuclear power stations. CND is best known for the Aldermaston March, an annual event dating from 1958. These mass marches finish at the site of the Atomic Weapons Establishment near Aldermaston.

Campbell, Alastair (1957–): one of Tony Blair's closest *special advisors*. He served first as *press secretary* and later as *Director of Communications and Strategy* and was part of Blair's inner circle. See also *spin doctor* and *sofa government*.

Campbell, Sir Menzies (1941–): *Liberal Democrat* MP for the constituency of North East Fife (from 1987) and one-time leader of the party (2006–07). Commonly referred to as Ming Campbell, he resigned as the Liberal Democrat leader in 2007 and was succeeded by *Nick Clegg*.

Campbell-Bannerman, Sir Henry: *prime minister* (Liberal), 1905–08.

candidate: an individual seeking election to public office.

> **TIP:** In the UK, candidate selection is still largely in the hands of the main *political parties*. Anyone wishing to stand as an *independent* candidate in the general election must put down a *deposit* of £500, which is forfeited in the event of failing to secure 5% of the vote in the *constituency*.

candidate-centred campaigns: campaigns that focus on the image and personality of the *candidate* as opposed to his or her intellectual abilities, policies or record in office. They are closely associated with the decline of *long-term factors* in *voting behaviour*, with the rise of the *mass media* and with the emergence of *catch-all parties*.

candidate selection: see *candidate*, *internal party democracy* and *primary election*

Canning, George: *prime minister* (Tory), 1827.

canvassing: where local *party activists* go from door to door in an effort to assess (i.e. canvass) the strength of support and win over *floating voters*.

capitalism: an economic system in which the control of the means of production is retained by an economic elite, i.e. the bourgeoisie. See also *Karl Marx* and *communism*.

card vote: where the delegates representing *affiliated* organisations at the Labour *party conference* would once cast their *block vote* by holding up a card displaying the number of members on behalf of whom they were voting.

career politician: see *professional politician*

case law: see *common law*

cash for honours: see *cash for peerages*

cash for peerages: the 2006–07 scandal and subsequent police investigation into the question of whether Lord Levy and other senior figures in the *Labour Party* had been seeking to 'sell' seats in the *House of Lords* in return for donations to the party. No criminal charges were brought against those accused.

cash for questions: a 1994 scandal surrounding the allegation that a number of Conservative MPs, most notably *Neil Hamilton*, had accepted monies and other benefits in kind to table *parliamentary questions*. See also *Mohamed Al Fayed* and *Ian Greer Associates*.

- The payments received by those accused had not been declared in the *Register of Members' Interests*.
- The scandal contributed to the allegations of *sleaze* that dogged the Conservatives in the run-up to the 1997 general election.
- Hamilton ultimately lost his Tatton seat to the former BBC journalist *Martin Bell* who ran as an independent anti-corruption candidate.
- The *Nolan Committee* was established in the wake of the scandal.

catch-all party: a *political party* that moves way from its core *ideology* and policies in order to broaden its electoral appeal. See *New Labour* and *ideology*.

cause group: also known as a promotional group, this is a *pressure group* that seeks to advance an idea or cause that is not of direct benefit to its members only. Contrast with *sectional group*.

- Cause groups form part of the *sectional/cause group typology*, which classifies groups according to their aims.
- They can be subdivided into *attitude cause groups*, *political cause groups* and *sectional cause groups*.

Example

The *Royal Society for the Protection of Birds (RSPB)* has become one of the most visible UK cause groups in recent years. Its membership stood at 1.2 million in 2009, more than the sum of the memberships of all the main UK political parties.

Cavendish, William (Duke of Devonshire): *prime minister* (Whig), 1756–57.

CBI: see *Confederation of British Industry (CBI)*

census: a survey of the UK population conducted every ten years.
- The first UK census was taken in 1801.
- The census plays a crucial role in allowing the *government* to plan policy and direct resources to where they are needed.
- It also provides the evidence upon which parliamentary *constituencies* are laid out by the *Boundary Commissions*.

central government: the UK government based mostly at Westminster, with other central government offices located in various other parts of the country. See *unitary state* and *devolution*.

Central Office: the administrative heart of the *Conservative Party* located in Smith Square, London. It is led by the Conservative *party chairman* and manages the day-to-day organisation of the party, including membership, finances and the oversight of election campaigns.

Centre for Policy Studies: a right wing *think-tank* established by *Margaret Thatcher* and Keith Joseph in 1974 and said to have been central to the development of *Thatcherism*.

Centre for Social Justice: a right-of-centre *think-tank* that seeks to target poverty by forging links with voluntary groups and charitable institutions.
- Founded by former Conservative Party leader *Iain Duncan Smith*.
- Associated with two major reports: *Breakdown Britain* (2006), which outlined the problems facing the country; and *Breakthrough Britain* (2007), which suggested a range of remedies.

Chamberlain, (Arthur) Neville: *prime minister* (Conservative), 1937–40.

champagne socialist: a pejorative term referring to individuals who champion the benefits of *socialism* while not applying the basic tenets of the *ideology* to their everyday life, implying a degree of hypocrisy.

chancellor of the exchequer: the senior *cabinet* member who heads the *Treasury*, delivers the *Budget* and is responsible for overseeing the government's economic policy. *Gordon Brown* was chancellor of the exchequer between 1997 and 2007 before becoming *prime minister*.

Charter 88: a *political cause group* that advocated a range of *constitutional reforms*.

- The group's name came from the fact that it published a charter, a list detailing its demands, in 1988.
- These demands included a *codified constitution* for the UK, a *Bill of Rights* and a *freedom of information* act.
- Charter 88 also called for *electoral reform* and the creation of a more democratic second chamber without *hereditary peers*.
- In 2007 Charter 88 became part of a group called Unlock Democracy.

> **TIP:** Charter 88 had a major influence on the development of *New Labour* thinking ahead of the 1997 *general election*. Many of the reforms the group called for were included in the party's 1997 *manifesto* and most ultimately found their way on to the *statute* books, albeit in a diluted form in some cases. See *constitutional reform*.

Charterism: see *Service First*

checks and balances: a system of forced cooperation in which the various branches of government check and limit one another.

- Checks and balances are an essential feature of the *separation of powers* enshrined in the US *constitution*.
- They are less obvious under the UK system where the *executive* is drawn from the *legislature* and there is a tendency towards *executive dominance*. See also *fusion of powers* and *elective dictatorship*.

Example

In the USA the president has the right to recommend policies to Congress when delivering his state of the union address, but he must rely on Congress to pass the necessary *legislation*. Congress in turn can initiate its own legislation but the president can in effect kill any bill with his *veto*, unless both the House of Representatives and the Senate can secure the two-thirds majority needed to override that veto. Even when *bills* do make it into law – and only around 3% do – the US Supreme Court has the power to strike them down, either in part or in their entirety, where they are judged to have violated the US constitution.

chief executive: see *head of government*

chief of staff: the individual charged with the task of coordinating the various elements that comprise the *Prime Minister's Office* and liaising between the *prime minister* and other elements within the *core executive*. The emergence and growth of the role during Tony Blair's time as prime minister was seen by many as an example of the Americanisation of the UK executive and the emergence of a presidential prime minister. Jonathan Powell served as Blair's chief of staff.

chief whip: in respect of each party, the *MP* or *peer* who leads the team of *whips* charged with the task of ensuring that those taking the *party whip* do as the party requests them to do on key votes. The government's chief whip in the *Commons* is present at meetings of *cabinet*. MP Nick Brown held the post of Labour chief whip between 1997 and 1998. He was appointed to the post for a second time in 2008.

Churchill, Sir Winston Leonard Spencer: *prime minister* (Conservative), 1940–45 and 1951–55.

churn: where significant *electoral volatility* is masked by the fact that the headline *swing* is small.

- The way in which swing is calculated tends to give the impression that voters are moving in a single direction, e.g. a 3% swing from Labour to the Conservatives in 2005.
- This means that it is possible for there to be no swing at all where the millions of voters moving from one party to another are cancelled out by an identical number moving in the opposite direction.

> **TIP:** Those who believe that *long-term factors* are at the heart of explaining *voting behaviour* often take low levels of swing to support their view, because one would expect greater electoral volatility if the election was determined largely by *short-term factors*. The presence of churn offers the possibility that the electorate may still be volatile even where the headline swing is negligible – as it was in 2001 (at 1.8%).

citizen: an individual formally recognised as a full 'member' of a *state* and therefore entitled to the various *rights* associated with *citizenship*, e.g. full voting rights.

- Citizenship carries responsibilities as well as rights, e.g. citizens can be conscripted into the armed forces in times of war.
- By changing what was an Economic Community into the *European Union*, the *Maastricht Treaty* developed the concept of European Union citizenship. This means that UK citizens also have the right to live and work in other EU countries as well as holding limited voting rights when resident in one of those states.

Citizen's Charter: an initiative aimed at providing certain guarantees regarding the quality of publicly provided services.

- Launched by *John Major* in 1991.
- Often seen as Major's 'big idea'.
- Charter marks were awarded in recognition of particularly high levels of service.
- It was replaced by New Labour's *Service First* initiative in 1998.

citizens' jury: a panel of *citizens* convened to hear evidence and deliver their verdict on a government proposal or a specific policy area. They are used widely outside the UK, most notably in the USA and Germany, and were championed by the prime minister *Gordon Brown* in 2007 as a means of enhancing *political participation*. They are similar in many respects to the *focus groups* used by the main UK political parties.

> **TIP:** Such 'juries' do not have final say on a given policy. Their feedback is considered by a panel of specialists and, ultimately, those politicians serving in government posts.

citizens' rights: see *rights*

citizenship: a status granted to an individual by the *state* or acquired by virtue of being born within a particular state's jurisdiction. Citizenship affords the individual certain *rights* and carries with it certain responsibilities. See *citizen* and *active citizenship*.

Civil Contingencies Committee: a UK *cabinet committee* that coordinates the government's response to events such as acts of domestic terrorism and natural disasters.
- The committee meets in Cabinet Office Briefing Room A and is therefore more commonly known by the acronym of that facility, i.e. COBRA.
- COBRA is generally chaired by the Home Secretary.

> **Example**
>
> COBRA met on 7 July 2005 in order to coordinate the response to the terrorist attacks on London. See *7/7*. The then prime minister *Tony Blair* flew down from Scotland, where he had been chairing the G8 summit, to attend the COBRA meeting.

civil disobedience: the act of refusing certain orders given by the *state*, without resorting to physical violence. It is closely associated with the approach of non-violence adopted by political leaders such as Mahatma Gandhi in India and Martin Luther King Jr in the USA.

> **Example**
>
> The campaign against the *poll tax* saw widespread civil disobedience. Many thousands refused to register for the tax, others refused to pay and then failed to attend court when issued with a summons. Many local *Anti-Poll Tax Unions* used non-violent protest as a way of preventing their local *councils* from setting the level at which the tax would be charged. The scale of civil disobedience made it impossible for the courts to process all the cases arising. See *Anti-Poll Tax Federation*.

civil law: laws relating to disputes between two or more individuals, between an individual and an organisation or between different organisations. It is commonly concerned with issues arising from legal contracts of one sort or another. Contrast with *criminal law*.

civil liberties: the essential freedoms enjoyed by individuals in a *liberal democracy*. They are similar to *rights*. The ability to exercise such freedoms may be limited in times of war or other national emergency, e.g. an immediate terrorist threat.

> **Example**
>
> The civil liberties generally said to exist in a *liberal democracy* include the *freedom of speech*, the freedom of assembly and the right to *petition* the government for *redress of grievances*.

civil rights: see *rights*

civil servant: an unelected bureaucrat working within the *civil service*. See *senior civil service* and *mandarins*.
- The widest possible definition of the term encompasses a wide range of public employees, including teachers and police officers.

- Attention is generally focused on those who work at the higher levels of the *civil service*, much of which is based in *Whitehall*.

civil service: the bureaucratic element of *government* comprising the *civil servants* who work in *government departments* and other *agencies* established by the *executive*. It is often referred to simply as *Whitehall*.

- The civil service is said to be based upon three core principles: *anonymity*, *impartiality* and *permanence*.
- A process of *agencification* has seen many tasks previously discharged by the core civil service placed under the control of *executive agencies* (see *Next Steps Programme*).

Civil Service Code: the document that sets out the core values under which *civil servants* should operate.

- Traditionally, the Code stressed the importance of the traditional civil service principles of *impartiality* and *anonymity* (see also *permanence*).
- The version of the Code produced in 2006 highlighted integrity, honesty, objectivity and impartiality – with no mention of anonymity.

Clarke, Kenneth (1940–): leading Conservative MP for Rushcliffe and former *chancellor of the exchequer* (1993–97).

- Clarke served in various government positions throughout the 18 years the *Conservative Party* was in office between 1979 and 1997.
- This included spells as Home Secretary (1992–93), Secretary of State for Education and Science (1990–92) and Secretary of State for Health (1988–90).
- He was president of the *Tory Reform Group* from 1997 and stood unsuccessfully for the leadership of the party in 1997, 2001 (see below) and 2005.
- He was a keen *Europhile* in a party that became increasingly *Eurosceptic* in the 1990s.

Example

Clarke's defeat at the hands of *Iain Duncan Smith* in the 2001 Conservative Party leadership contest highlighted one of the problems inherent in the system introduced by the outgoing party leader *William Hague*. Clarke made it through to the final *ballot* of party members largely because some of the MPs that had backed Duncan Smith in earlier ballots transferred their support to Clarke in the last round. Such tactical voting was designed to ensure that Michael Portillo, Duncan Smith's biggest rival for the leadership, would not make it through to the final run-off: Duncan Smith's supporters knew that their man would have a far better chance of beating the Europhile Clarke in a ballot of party members, than he would in defeating Portillo (an experienced and charismatic fellow Eurosceptic).

class: see *social class*

class alignment: a long-term correlation between *social class* and *voting behaviour*. See also *class dealignment*.

- Class alignment is where the majority of *working class* voters consistently support the *Labour Party* and those in the *middle class* consistently support the *Conservative Party*.

- It was seen as a major influence on **voting behaviour** in the period between 1945 and the mid-1970s. In the 1960s, Peter Pulzer concluded that 'class is the basis of British party politics; all else is embellishment and detail'.

<blockquote>
TIP: It is important to be able to distinguish between class alignment and *partisan alignment*. Though the former may contribute to the latter, other factors involved in the *socialisation* of an individual may also help to establish a strong bond with a particular *political party*, e.g. gender, education and upbringing.
</blockquote>

class dealignment: a decline in **class alignment**.
- Said to have occurred since the mid-1970s.
- Accompanied by and probably resulting from the rise of **short-term factors** (see **recency model**) and parallel changes in the UK class system (see also **old working class**, **new working class** and **embourgeoisement**).
- Class dealignment has resulted in greater electoral **volatility**. See also **floating voters**.

<blockquote>
TIP: Although the period since the 1970s is said to have been characterised by class dealignment, there is still a clear correlation between *social class* and voting, as show in the table below.
</blockquote>

class voting: where people vote for the natural party of their social class. See **class alignment**.

Class and voting at general elections

Social class	Conservative			Labour			Liberal Democrats		
	2005	2001	1997	2005	2001	1997	2005	2001	1997
AB	37	40	43	28	33	30	29	21	21
C1	36	33	35	32	40	37	23	21	19
C2	33	29	28	40	47	52	19	17	13
DE	25	28	21	48	49	58	18	17	15

classical liberalism: an early form of **liberalism** that favoured minimal state intervention.
- Emerged in the nineteenth century.
- Classical liberals stressed the importance of freedom, toleration and equality.
- They believed that self-reliance and self-improvement had a bigger part to play than the state in improving the lives of those from less privileged backgrounds.

<blockquote>
TIP: Classical liberals believed that a free market and free trade would best meet the needs of the people in the long run. The failure of the market to deliver – particularly in respect of the terrible working conditions and poor life chances suffered by those on lower incomes – led to the development of new or *progressive liberalism* in the twentieth century. See also *neo-liberalism*.
</blockquote>

Clause IV: the section of the **Labour Party**'s 1918 Constitution that committed the party to a path of wealth redistribution and nationalisation. Clause IV was amended in 1995 as part of the modernisation programme introduced under **Tony Blair**. See **New Labour**.

Clegg, Nick (1967–): Liberal Democrat MP for Sheffield Hallam from 2005 and elected leader of the party in December 2007.

- Clegg had previously served one term as an **MEP** representing the East Midlands region (1999–2004).
- He defeated Chris Huhne to become leader.
- He replaced Vince Cable, who had served as caretaker leader in the wake of **Sir Menzies Campbell**'s resignation in October 2007.

Clegg's early leadership of the Liberal Democrats was marked by a number of controversial public statements. The morning after his election he admitted that he did not believe in God, when questioned on Radio 5-Live's breakfast programme. In a subsequent interview for *GQ* magazine in 2008, he admitted to having slept with 'no more than 30 women'; a comment that resulted in his being nicknamed 'Cleggover' in some sections of the press. Clegg proved an effective performer at **Prime Minister's Questions**. He also looked to modernise the party's policies.

Climate Change Camp: referring to the protest camps established at a number of environmentally sensitive sites, most notably that close to the site of the Kingsnorth Power Station in Kent in the summer of 2008. See also **Greenpeace**.

closed list system: a list system where the order of the names on each party's list is predetermined by the party itself, i.e. with no input for voters on polling day. See **party list system** and **open list**.

Example

A closed list system is used in UK elections to the **European Parliament**. Each party draws up a list of **candidates** in each of the regions and candidates are then elected from these lists in proportion to the votes cast for each party in each region. For example, Caroline Lucas was at the top of the Green Party's list in the South East England region in the 2009 European Election and was duly elected when the party secured enough votes to win one of the ten seats available in that region.

CLP: see **Constituency Labour Party**

coalition government: where two or more parties combine to form a **government**. See also **minority government**.

- Coalition governments are usually formed where no party holds an overall majority in the Commons (see **hung parliament**).
- **Proportional electoral systems** are more likely to result in coalition government than **majoritarian electoral systems**.

Example

Coalition governments are common in other parts of Europe (e.g. Germany) and have also been seen in Scotland in the wake of **devolution**. A coalition government of sorts (a government of national unity) was in place during the Second World War.

COBRA: see *Civil Contingencies Committee*

co-decision procedure: a procedure in the *EU*, where legislative power is shared between the *European Parliament* and the *Council of Ministers* in some areas of *policy*.

- The procedure was introduced under the *Treaty of Maastricht* and extended under the *Treaty of Amsterdam*.
- It effectively granted the *European Parliament* a veto in some areas of policy.

codified constitution: a single authoritative document setting out the rules that govern the relationship between the state and its citizens and between the constituent parts of the state. See also *constitution* and *uncodified constitution*. Codified constitutions are generally entrenched (see *entrenchment*).

Example

The US Constitution is codified. It was drawn up at the Philadelphia Convention (1787) and came into force in 1789, having been ratified by the various states.

collective decision making: see *cabinet government*, *collective responsibility* and *primus inter pares*

collective responsibility: the *convention* under which members of the UK *cabinet* are required to stand publicly by those decisions made privately within cabinet. See *cabinet government*.

- Those who do not wish to operate under this convention are expected to resign their cabinet posts and argue their case as *backbenchers*.
- Collective responsibility is intrinsically linked to the idea of *collective decision making*.

Example

In March 2003, the Leader of the House of Commons, **Robin Cook**, stood down from his seat in cabinet in order to speak out against the decision to go to war in Iraq. Clare Short also opposed military action but was persuaded to stay in cabinet with the promise that she would be involved in the reconstruction after the war. This is an example of an 'agreement to differ', where a prime minister keeps a minister in cabinet in spite of his or her dissent. A prime minister can also suspend collective responsibility. Harold Wilson suspended collective responsibility in 1975 so that cabinet ministers could be involved in the 'yes' and 'no' campaigns that accompanied the nationwide referendum on continued UK membership of the EEC.

TIP: Some argue that the decline of the cabinet as a collective decision-making body has undermined the doctrine of collective responsibility, as it is hard to require *ministers* to stand by decisions made elsewhere. See also *cabinet government*, *bilateral meetings* and *cabinet committees*.

Commission: see *European Commission*

commissioner: in the *EU*, a member of the *European Commission*. In 2009 the European Commission consisted of 27 individuals, with each EU member state having the right to appoint a single commissioner.

Committee of Permanent Representatives (COREPER): an organisation of civil servants, sent from EU member states, that undertakes the technical work on policy proposals before they are discussed in the EU's *Council of Ministers*.
* COREPER coordinates the work of over 250 individual committees of civil servants.
* COREPER I deals with most social issues as well as some aspects of economic policy.
* COREPER II deals with political issues and external relations, i.e. foreign policy.

Committee of Selection: the *House of Commons* committee responsible for assigning MPs to *standing committees* and *select committees*. The committee comprises senior MPs from each party and is supposedly non-partisan.

> **TIP:** Although in theory impartial, recent years have seen the committee accused of politicking, e.g. its unsuccessful attempt to block the reappointment of independent-minded Labour *backbencher* Gwyneth Dunwoody as chair of the Transport select committee in 2001.

Committee of the Whole House: where the committee stage of a bill in the *Commons* or the *Lords* is conducted on the floor of the chamber, thus allowing all members the opportunity to participate.
* It is used in the passage of the *Budget* and in the case of proposals for major *constitutional reform*.
* It is more common in the *Lords* where there has traditionally been less pressure on the chamber's calendar.

Committee on Standards in Public Life: established in the wake of the *cash for questions* scandal, and charged with the task of investigating outside payments to MPs. It was initially chaired by Lord Nolan and resulted in the publication of the *Nolan Report (1995)*.

committee stage: the stage of the *legislative process* when a *bill* is subject to detailed consideration, most often in a *standing committee* (see also *Committee of the Whole House*).
* It takes place after the *second reading*.
* The government can normally amend *legislation* at this stage as standing committees reflect the strength of the parties in the chamber itself.
* The party *whips* routinely look to control their members within the committee.
* The government can also impose a *guillotine* on proceedings in order to ensure the speedy passage of a *bill* through a committee.

Common Agricultural Policy (CAP): the *EU* scheme of agricultural subsidies that has traditionally accounted for around half of the Union's annual expenditure.
* The policy was originally introduced as a means of regulating the supply of agricultural produce and thereby guaranteeing both farmers and consumers a fair price for the goods they produced or purchased.
* The enormous cost of the policy and its tendency to result in surplus produce (e.g. the 'butter mountains' and 'wine lakes' of the 1980s) led to widespread criticism.
* Reform of the CAP is expected to result in a 30% cut in the costs of the scheme by 2013.

common law: collectively referring to the body of legal *precedent* resulting from the rulings of senior judges. Sometimes referred to as *case law* or *judge-made law*, it is an important source of the UK's *constitution*.

Commons: see *House of Commons*

communism: an ideology advocating equality and the collective ownership of the means of production. See *Karl Marx*.

community charge: see *poll tax*

Comprehensive Spending Review: a *Treasury*-led exercise that serves to plan the strategic objectives of each government *department* and its projected spend over a three-year period.

Compton, Spencer (Earl of Wilmington): *prime minister* (Whig), 1742–43.

compulsory competitive tendering: the practice of outsourcing the delivery of certain public services to private companies on the basis of the interested parties submitting sealed bids.
- These bids, known as tenders, outline the sum that will be payable if the company is awarded the contract to provide the services in question.
- There is an assumption that, with all other things being equal, the contract would normally go to the company submitting the lowest bid.

compulsory voting: a legal requirement for all eligible voters to cast a ballot at a given election.
- It is in force in a number of countries, including Australia.
- Some argue that the adoption of compulsory voting in the UK election would improve *turnout*.

> **TIP:** Countries that operate under a system of compulsory voting generally experience turnout in excess of 90%. The turnout at the 2007 elections to the Federal Parliament of Australia was 95%.

Confederation of British Industry (CBI): a *peak group* representing the interests of major UK companies.
- The CBI has traditionally had close links with the *Conservative Party* in the same way that the *Labour Party* was historically linked to the peak group representing *trade unions*: the *TUC*.
- *New Labour* made an effort to reach out to the CBI. In 1999, *Tony Blair* became the first serving prime minister to address the CBI conference.

conference: see *party conference*

consensus politics: characterising a broad agreement between politicians of all mainstream parties across a range of policies. See also *postwar consensus* and *adversarial politics*.

conservatism: a loose *ideology* that favours pragmatism, while at the same time seeking to preserve the **status quo**.
- It is closely associated with the *Conservative Party* in the UK (see *one-nation Tories* and *wets*).
- Contrast with *Thatcherism* and *neo-liberalism* ideology (see also *dries*).

Conservative Association: the main local unit of the *Conservative Party* operating at *constituency* level.

- Conservative associations play a key role in selecting Conservative **candidates**, raising funds and organising election campaigns (see **canvassing**).
- Representatives of Conservative associations attend the **party conference**.
- They are also consulted on policy under the **Fresh Future** initiative.

Conservative Party: emerging from the *Tory Party* in the mid-nineteenth century, the Conservative Party has been the party of government in the UK for most of the twentieth century.

- It is associated with pragmatism as opposed to a more ideological approach, though this tradition came under threat under the leadership of **Margaret Thatcher** in the 1980s. See **conservatism**, **one-nation Tories** and **Thatcherism**.
- Historically the party of the middle class, it was successful in attracting the support of significant numbers of **working class** voters in the 1980s.

Consolidated Fund: a *government* bank account used to pay the salaries of *judges* and certain other officials. The fund, managed by the **Bank of England**, receives all government tax revenues.

> **TIP:** Judges' salaries are classified as standing services and are therefore paid from the fund automatically. The fact that the payment of such salaries is not part of the regular budgetary planning process means that politicians are unable to manipulate judges' salaries as a way of controlling them. See also *judicial independence*.

constituency: a geographical area returning a single *MP* to *Parliament*.

- The term may also refer to those voters traditionally supporting a particular **political party**, i.e. a party's natural constituency.
- The term **ward** is generally used in place of constituency when referring to elected offices at **local government** level. See also **single-member constituency**, **multi-member constituency** and **Boundary Commissions**.

Constituency Labour Party: the local unit of *Labour Party* organisation comprising those party members residing in the parliamentary **constituency** in question.

- The CLP plays a key role in selecting **candidates** for elections to **Westminster**, though it can select only candidates from the approved list and their nominees are still subject to approval by the party's **National Executive Committee (NEC)**.
- It can deselect its **MP** as a candidate for subsequent elections if it is unhappy with the incumbent's performance in post.
- CLPs send delegates to the annual **party conference**, where they can have an input into making party **policy**.
- Collectively, CLPs control one third of the votes in the **electoral college** that elects the leader of the party.

> **TIP:** The local *activists* who control many CLPs tend to be more *left wing* than many of those in office at national level. In the past this has had the potential to result in embarrassing arguments at the annual party conference, though such events have been more carefully stage-managed in recent years.

constituent: an individual residing in a particular parliamentary **constituency** and represented by the **MP** returned by that constituency in an **election**.

constitution: a body of rules that defines the manner in which a **state** or society is organised. See also **codified constitution** and **uncodified constitution**.

- A constitution establishes the relationship between the **state** and its **citizens**, and between the various institutions that constitute the state.
- It may also refer to the collected rules and procedures governing the operation of other organisations, including most **political parties** and some **pressure groups**, e.g. **Clause IV** of the **Labour Party**'s 1918 constitution.

constitutional: that which is operating within the framework of rules established by a **constitution**.

Constitutional Council: a body charged with the task of considering proposals for **constitutional reform**. It was established by the prime minister **Gordon Brown** in 2009 as, in effect, a new **cabinet committee**.

constitutional democracy: see **liberal democracy**

constitutional government: where **government** functions according to rules established in a **constitution**. It is often used to refer to a system in which the **executive** branch is subjected to effective **scrutiny**.

constitutional monarchy: a monarchy whose role and powers are limited, both by the rules established under a **constitution** and by the presence of other more powerful **state** institutions.

- In the UK the monarch's powers have been limited both by **statute** and by **convention** since the seventeenth century, e.g. see **Glorious Revolution (1689)**.
- Most of the powers formally held by the monarch are now exercised by the **prime minister**. See **royal prerogative**.
- The monarch essentially acts as ceremonial **head of state**.

constitutional reform: a fundamental change to the relationship between the institutions that comprise the **state**, or between the state and its **citizens**. **New Labour's** first decade in power (1997–2007) saw a range of constitutional reforms including **devolution**, **Lords Reform (1997–2010)**, the **Human Rights Act (1998)**, the **Freedom of Information Act (2000)** and the creation of a new UK **Supreme Court** under the **Constitutional Reform Act (2005)**.

Constitutional Reform Act (2005): a piece of **statute law** that addressed a number of key areas relating to the organisation and independence of the **senior judiciary** in the UK.

- The Act built on proposals officially unveiled in 2003 and earlier heralded in Labour's 2001 general election **manifesto**.
- It enhanced **judicial independence** in four major ways: first, by legally requiring ministers to respect that very concept; second, by reducing the power associated with the office of **Lord Chancellor** and placing many of its responsibilities into the hands of the **Lord Chief Justice**; third, by establishing a fully independent **Judicial Appointments Commission**; and fourth, by creating a new UK **Supreme Court**. See also **separation of powers**.

Constitutional Renewal Bill (2008): a somewhat disparate *bill* that offered a number of small-scale constitutional changes. The bill:
- was supposed to follow on from the *Governance of Britain Green Paper (2007)*
- passed over some of the more intractable areas of *constitutional reform* such as *Lords Reform (1997–2010)* and *electoral reform*
- brought forward fairly minor proposals in six areas: the legal status of protests in the vicinity of Parliament; the role of the Attorney General; the judicial appointments process; the treaty power and the war power; the core values of the civil service (which had been subject to consultation back in 2004) and the flying of the union flag (Union Jack) on public buildings

constitutionalism: the principle that those who hold political office must operate according to the rules established in a *constitution*. Another term for *constitutional government*.

consultation: a process whereby government *departments* engage in a dialogue with those individuals and groups likely to be affected by a particular policy proposal. See also *Green Paper*, *White Paper* and *insider group*.

consumer voting model: see the *supermarket voting model* of voting behaviour.

contempt of court: a court order finding an individual guilty of failing to follow instructions issued by the court or acting in a manner that is likely to affect adversely the outcome of a trial. It is often associated with limitations on the freedom of the *press* to publish details of a case in advance of a trial or while the trial is under way. See also *judicial independence*.

contracting out: the act of subcontracting the delivery of some aspect of public service (e.g. waste disposal) to a third party. Also referred to as outsourcing. See also *compulsory competitive tendering*.

control order: a form of house arrest introduced under the *Prevention of Terrorism Act (2005)*. It was brought in after the *indefinite detention* of foreign terrorist suspects allowed under the *Anti-terrorism, Crime and Security Act (2001)* was declared incompatible with Article 4 of the *Human Rights Act (1998)*.

convention: a long-established and generally accepted constitutional practice.
- The doctrine of *collective responsibility* and the *Salisbury Doctrine* are both well-known constitutional conventions.
- Conventions have no legal standing. What *authority* they have rests largely upon how long they have existed.

convergence criteria: the four main economic tests that an *EU* member state was required to meet before it could apply to adopt the *euro*. The criteria related to the nation's inflation rate, budget deficit, official interest rate and membership of the *Exchange Rate Mechanism (ERM)*.

Cook, Robin (1946–2005): *Labour Party* foreign secretary (1997–2001) and Leader of the Commons (2001–03) who resigned from *cabinet* in 2003 in protest at the decision to go to war in Iraq. See also *collective responsibility*.

cooperation procedure: a style of cooperative decision making involving the main *EU* institutions. Established under the *Single European Act (1986)* and subsequently superseded by the *co-decision procedure*.

COPA-COGECA: a *Eurogroup* representing farming interests across the various EU member states. See also *peak group*.

- The UK-based *National Farmers' Union (NFU)* is a member of COPA-COGECA.
- COPA-COGECA dates from 1962 when COPA (the Committee of Professional Agricultural Organisations) and COGECA (the General Confederation of Agricultural Cooperatives) underwent a partial merger.
- In 2005, COPA-COGECA had 69 member organisations and represented some 11 million farmers EU-wide.

core executive: The network of high-ranking individuals, institutions and advisory bodies that operate at the heart of central government, developing and overseeing the execution of government policy. R. A. W. Rhodes saw the core executive as 'the complex web of institutions, networks and practices surrounding the prime minister, cabinet, cabinet committees and their official counterparts, less formalised ministerial "clubs" or meetings, bilateral negotiations … interdepartmental committees [and] coordinating departments' such as the Cabinet Office, the Treasury, the Foreign Office, the law officers, and the security and intelligence services.

> **TIP:** Some argue that changes made to the *Prime Minister's Office* and the *Cabinet Office* under Tony Blair created a *prime minister's department* in all but name. Such changes, when taken alongside the rise of *bilateral meetings* and so-called *sofa government*, marked a significant shift in power within the core executive.

core insiders: *pressure groups* that work closely with government and are consulted regularly across a range of policy areas. See *insider groups* and *insider/outsider typology*.

COREPER: see *Committee of Permanent Representatives (COREPER)*.

corporatism: an approach to governmental decision making that stressed the importance of cooperation between business interests and trade unions. Often referred to as *tripartism*.

- Corporatism is closely associated with the *National Economic Development Council (NEDC)* that operated between 1962 and 1992.
- It was an approach rejected by *Margaret Thatcher* who famously described the National Union of Mineworkers as the 'enemy within' at the time of the *miners' strike (1984–85)* and who introduced a raft of anti-union legislation in the 1980s.

council: an elected unit of *local government*. See *borough council*, *county council* and *district council*.

Council of Europe: the *intergovernmental* body responsible for producing the *European Convention on Human Rights (1950)*. See also *Human Rights Act (1998)*.

> **TIP:** Not to be confused with the *Council of Ministers* or the *European Council*, both of which are *EU* institutions: the Council of Europe is not directly linked to the EU.

Council of Ministers: historically the *EU*'s most important decision-making body, holding both *executive* and *legislative* power:

- comprising one representative from each member state; the actual membership changing in line with the issues being discussed
- known as the *European Council* when the premier of each member state attends

- originally operated on the basis of unanimity but EU enlargement and integration since the *Single European Act (1986)* has resulted in the introduction and extension of *qualified majority voting*
- the rise of the *co-decision procedure* has seen the Council share some of its legislative power with the *European Parliament*

council tax: the property-based local tax introduced in place of the community charge (see *poll tax*) in 1993.

councillor: an individual elected to public office at *local government* level.
- Those eligible may seek election as councillors to *parish, borough, district, metropolitan district, county* or *unitary authority* authorities.
- Most councillors represent an area known as a *ward*.

counter-terrorism: see *Anti-terrorism, Crime and Security Act (2001)*, the *Prevention of Terrorism Act (2005)* and *Civil Contingencies Committee*.

county council: a unit of elected *local government* taking broad responsibility in the areas of education, roads, waste management, the fire service and the police, e.g. Essex County Council. Councillors are elected quadrennially.

court: a state-established institution charged with the task of adjudicating in the case of disputes arising under the law.

Court of Appeal: the highest UK *appeal court* below the level of the UK *Supreme Court*.
- It is divided into two divisions – the Criminal Division and the Civil Division – the former hearing appeals relating to criminal cases heard in the crown court, with the latter reviewing civil cases on appeal from the high court and county courts.
- The judgements of the Court of Appeal are crucial because they can set legal *precedent* (see *common law*).

Cranborne Compromise: the 1999 deal that saw 92 of the 700 or so hereditary peers retain their right to sit and vote in the transitional chamber after the *House of Lords Act (1999)* came into effect.
- The compromise was negotiated by the Conservative Leader in the Lords, Viscount Cranborne, supposedly behind the back of the then conservative leader *William Hague*.
- The compromise was enshrined in law by means of the *Weatherill Amendment*.

Criminal Justice and Public Order Act (1994): a piece of *statute law* that gave the authorities the power to deal with a number of forms of antisocial behaviour. It was widely seen as an attempt to clamp down on New Age travellers, squatters and those engaged in *direct action*, including hunt saboteurs.

criminal law: relating to those offences considered serious enough for the state to take the lead in prosecuting. Most cases under criminal law can result in a period of incarceration (i.e. imprisonment). Contrast with *civil law*.

crossbencher: an *independent* member of the *House of Lords*, i.e. one who does not take the whip of any political party. So-called because such peers sit on the benches between and at right angles to the two front benches, looking out across the space between.

Crossman, Richard (1907–74): a Labour *cabinet minister* in the late 1960s, editor of the *New Statesman* and author of *Diaries of a Cabinet Minister*. Crossman is often associated with advancing the idea of **prime ministerial government**. His diaries were also said to be the inspiration for the acclaimed BBC TV series **Yes Minister**.

cross-party: bipartisan. Contrast with **adversarial politics**.

Currie, Edwina (1946–): a former Conservative *junior minister* for Health, who resigned in 1988. Currie was forced to resign after she had publicly stated that most of the UK's egg production was infected with salmonella.

> **TIP:** An excellent example of a minister resigning under the *role responsibility* strand of individual ministerial responsibility.

Do you need revision help and advice?

Go to pages 180–196 for a range of revision appendices that include plenty of exam advice and tips.

Dalyell, Tam (1932–): see *West Lothian question*

dark green: see *ecologism*

Davies, Ron (1946–): a former Secretary of State for Wales and who resigned in 1998 following what he referred to as a 'moment of madness' on Clapham Common. His comment referred to his being mugged by a man he had first met on the Common, a well-known meeting place for gay men (Davies subsequently announced that he was bisexual). This was seen as an example of the *personal responsibility* strand of *individual ministerial responsibility*.

dealignment: the breakdown of the long-term and consistent inclination to vote for a particular *political party* observed in the *electorate*. See also *class dealignment* and *partisan dealignment*.

debate: see *parliamentary debate*

declaration of incompatibility: see *Human Rights Act (1998)* and *judicial review*

decommissioning (of arms): the act of 'putting arms beyond use' in Northern Ireland under the *Good Friday Agreement (1998)*.

deference: routinely submitting to another's *authority* or the authority of those in power collectively. See *political culture*.

deindustrialisation: a process by which industry declines or is actively downgraded within a country, commonly used with reference to the decline of heavy industry in the UK since the 1960s.

delegate model: a model of representation where an individual is sent to a meeting or *party conference* with clear instructions as to how to vote on a particular issue and represent the views of those who have sent him or her. It is often contrasted with *representative democracy* or the *trustee model*.

> **Example**
>
> The *Labour Party* annual conference traditionally operated on the basis of delegates sent from *Constituency Labour Parties*, *trade unions* and other *affiliated* organisations.

delegated legislation: laws or regulations enacted by government *ministers* under the authority granted to them in a piece of parliamentary *statute law*. See also *Order in Council* and *secondary legislative powers*. It commonly involves the minister in question 'filling in the details' where Parliament has provided the broader legal framework within which policy will be administered.

Delors Plan: the push towards *European integration* developed by the two-term President of the *European Commission*, Jacques Delors.

- Delors led the Commission between 1985 and 1995.
- The plan was widely seen as a roadmap to a more *federal* Europe with the *Single European Act (1986)* and the *Treaty of Maastricht* representing major landmarks on that journey.

democracy: derived from the Greek *demokratia*; a compound of *demos* (meaning 'the people') and *kratos* (meaning 'power'). Literally, therefore, democracy is 'rule by the people' or 'people power'.

- Some argue that the word *demos* could just as easily be defined as 'the mob', which would leave democracy as 'mob rule' or 'mobocracy'.
- A distinction is commonly drawn between *representative democracy* and *direct democracy* (see also *delegate model*, *trustee model* and *pluralist democracy*).

democratic deficit: where the *power* to make key decisions is taken away from elected institutions and placed in the hands of those who are not directly accountable to the public (see *accountability*).

- The phrase is often used when criticising the way in which power has been transferred from the UK *Parliament* to European institutions under the *Treaty of Rome*. The extension of the *co-decision procedure* has helped to ease such concerns, to a degree at least.
- The growth in the number of government *quangos* is also said to have contributed to a democratic deficit.

Democratic Unionist Party (DUP): a Protestant, *unionist* party operating in Northern Ireland, founded by *Revd Ian Paisley* in 1971. The DUP initially opposed the *Good Friday Agreement (1998)*, though ultimately went into government with *Sinn Fein* in 2007.

demonstration: a rally, march or other public protest against a particular policy or government position.

Demos: an independent *think-tank* that became closely associated with *New Labour* after 1997. Established in 1993.

denationalisation: see *privatisation*

department: a unit of *government* concerned with developing and administering *policy* in a particular field. Since the 1980s, much of the work of government departments has been transferred to semi-independent *agencies* (see *agencification* and *Next Steps Programme*).

Example

In July 2009, the *Home Office* was headed by Alan Johnson MP, a leading *cabinet* member. There were also five other *ministers* working in the department below cabinet rank: two ministers of state (David Hanson MP and Phil Woolas MP); and three other ministers (Alan Campbell MP, Meg Hillier MP and Lord West of Spithead).

departmental select committees: those parliamentary committees that scrutinise the work of individual government **departments** in the UK. See also **non-departmental select committees.**

- Originally established in 1979, there were 16 departmental select committees operating in 2009.
- They are supposed to operate on a non-partisan basis.
- Departmental select committees have the right to call witnesses as part of their investigations but they do not have the legal power of **subpoena**, i.e. they cannot force those they call to attend.

Example

The Transport Select Committee has the task of scrutinising the policies, administration and expenditure of the Department for Transport. It also has **oversight** of the various executive **agencies** and other bodies that administer some aspects of the Department's work, e.g. the Driver and Vehicle Licensing Agency (DVLA).

dependency culture: where high levels of government benefits and other support, far from helping recipients, result in their developing a kind of learned helplessness.

deposit: a sum of £500 paid in advance by **candidates** seeking **election** to **Westminster** and forfeited if they fail to secure 5% of the **votes** cast in the **constituency** in which they are standing.

- A deposit is also required of those seeking election to other major elected offices, e.g. to the **European Parliament** or the **Scottish Parliament**.
- Prior to 1985, the deposit was only £150 but the threshold was far higher at 12.5%.
- The deposit is supposed to deter those candidates who have little realistic chance of electoral success.

deregulation: the removal or rationalisation of government regulations with a view to establishing a **free market**. It is closely associated with the **neo-liberal** approach to economic policy adopted by **Margaret Thatcher**'s Conservative administrations in the 1980s.

derogation: a process by which a country is exempted, perhaps temporarily, from observing a law or regulation it had previously agreed to abide by. It is a means by which the UK government can effectively suspend certain articles in the **European Convention on Human Rights (1950)**, incorporated into UK law under the **Human Rights Act (1998)**.

Example

Under Article 15 of the European Convention on Human Rights, national governments are permitted to derogate some articles of the Convention in times of emergency. Part 4 of the UK's **Anti-terrorism Crime and Security Act (2001)**, which permitted **indefinite detention** of foreign terrorist suspects, was passed only after the government opted to derogate Article 5 of the Human Rights Act (1998) on the grounds that there was a 'public emergency threatening the life of the nation'. This phrase met the requirements for derogation set out in Article 15.

deselection: the process by which the constituency party of the sitting **MP** replaces the incumbent as its official **candidate** for the next **election**.

Example

Frank Cook, the Labour MP for Stockton North, was deselected by his **Constituency Labour Party** in January 2008. He had represented the constituency in the Commons since 1983.

deviant voting: where electors (deviant voters) vote against the natural party of their **social class**. See **working-class Tories**. It is closely associated with theories of **class dealignment** and the rise of **short-term factors** (see **recency model**) over **long-term factors** (see **primacy model**) influencing **voting behaviour**.

devolution: a process by which **Westminster** delegates power to another tier of **government**, whether **subnational** or **supranational**.
- Devolution commonly refers to the creation of devolved institutions in Scotland, Wales, London and Northern Ireland following **New Labour**'s victory in the 1997 **general election**.
- The term is occasionally also used in reference to the transfer of power to the **EU**.
- Plans for devolution to English regional assemblies were abandoned after the 'no' vote in the **North East referendum (2004)**.

d'Hondt formula: the mathematical formula under which seats are distributed to political parties under the **party list** element of the **additional member system (AMS)** (or other hybrid system).

$$THE\ D'HONDT\ FORMULA:\quad \frac{\text{Total votes won by the party}}{\text{Seats already won}} + 1$$

Dicey, A. V. (1835–1922): a lawyer and constitutional theorist best known for his seminal work *An Introduction to the Study of the Law of the Constitution* (1885). The book has long been regarded as a **work of authority**. Dicey was regarded as an authority on the **rule of law**.

differential swing: where the quoted national percentage **swing** in an **election** masks significant differences by **constituency** or region.

Example

At the 2005 **general election** the Labour vote fell by 5.5% nationally (compared to 2001) with the Conservatives gaining 0.6%; a national swing of 3.05% from Labour to the Conservatives. In the constituency of Enfield Southgate, however, the figure was 8.7%.

differential turnout: where the quoted national percentage **turnout** in an **election** masks significant differences by **constituency** or region.

Example

The 2005 **general election** saw a national turnout of 61.5%. The highest turnout in a single parliamentary constituency was recorded in West Tyrone (at 80.2%). The lowest came in Liverpool Riverside (41.4%).

digital democracy: see *e-democracy*

Diplock courts: a type of court operating under a single judge without a jury.

- They were introduced in Northern Ireland in 1972 as a way of addressing the problems associated with jury intimidation in many high-profile terrorism cases, and abolished in 2007.
- Lord Diplock proposed them in a report considering alternatives to internment (a form of *indefinite detention*).

direct action: forms of political protest that move beyond traditional pressure group methods and may involve a degree of *civil disobedience*, illegality or even violence. It is said to have gained in popularity as groups adopting more conventional methods have failed to achieve their goals (see also *outsider groups*).

Example

In October 2007, six *Greenpeace* activists scaled and then lowered themselves down the 200-metre chimney at the coal-fired Kingsnorth power station in Kent, painting the word 'Gordon' down its length. In September 2008, the campaigners were cleared of causing £30,000 of damage to the chimney, having successfully argued that the immediate risk of climate change legitimised their protest.

direct democracy: where decisions are taken directly by the people as opposed to their elected representatives. See also *representative democracy*. Direct democracy is said:

- to have originated in classical Athens c500 AB, where the city-state's 40,000 free men had the right to attend forum meetings at which certain policies could be approved or rejected
- still to exist in a pure form in New England town meetings
- to be impractical in modern states with large populations, though an element of direct democracy can still be provided through devices such as *referendums* and *initiatives* and propositions in many states

direct rule: referring to the practice of administering the government of Northern Ireland directly from *Westminster*. See also *unitary state* and *devolution*.

- The power-sharing arrangements and devolved institutions established under the *Good Friday Agreement (1998)* were supposed to herald the end of direct rule.
- Direct rule was restored between 2002 and 2007 in response to an upsurge in paramilitary violence.

Director of Communications and Strategy: a senior *special advisor* to the *prime minister*. See also *spin doctor*.

- The post was famously held by *Alastair Campbell* from 2000 until his resignation in 2003.
- Campbell had previously served as Tony Blair's *press secretary* (1997–2000).
- Some saw the emergence of this post and that of *chief of staff* as part of a process of Americanisation within the UK core executive.

disclaim: the act of giving up one's peerage under the *Peerages Act (1963)*. See *Benn, Tony (1925–)*.

disengagement: see *apathy*

Disraeli, Benjamin (Earl of Beaconsfield): *prime minister* (Conservative), 1868 and 1874–80.

dissolution: the device by which a parliamentary session is ended and a *general election* is called. A dissolution is granted by the *monarch* at the request of the incumbent *prime minister*.

district council: a unit of elected *local government* holding responsibility for local planning decisions, leisure facilities, housing and refuse collection. Councillors are elected every four years. An example is Oadby and Wigston District Council in Leicestershire.

divine right: the belief that the power of the monarch comes directly from God.

division: a formal vote in the *Commons* or the *Lords*. During a division *MPs* or *peers* physically leave their seats in their chamber and walk through either the 'aye' or the 'no' lobby to cast their vote (see *division lobbies*).

division lobbies: the areas on either side of the *House of Commons*' and the *House of Lords*' chambers where *MPs* and *peers* pass in order to record their votes in a *division*.

doctrine: a coherent set of beliefs or principles under which individuals operate. See also *ideology* and *Salisbury Doctrine*.

'dodgy dossier': see *weapons of mass destruction*

dominant ideology model: the notion that there exists a shared set of values and beliefs within any society that will shape the way in which individuals view individual political parties. See also *political culture*. It is associated with *elites theory*.

dominant-party system: a system under which many political parties exist but only one has a realistic chance of winning an election and forming a government.

> **Example**
>
> Japan operated under a dominant-party system between 1955 and 1993, with the Liberal Democratic Party providing 15 consecutive prime ministers during that period.

Donorgate: see *Political Parties, Elections and Referendums Act (2000)*

double jeopardy: the principle that individuals should not be put on trial for the same offence on two or more occasions. The Criminal Justice Act (2003) effectively removed double jeopardy where new evidence comes to light.

Douglas-Home, Sir Alec: *prime minister* (Conservative), 1963–64.

Downing Street: the road housing the official residences of the prime minister (at Number 10), the chancellor of the exchequer (at Number 11), the chief whip's Office (at Number 9) and the offices of many other key individuals within the *core executive*.

Downing Street Declaration: see the *Good Friday Agreement (1998)*

dries: a *Conservative Party* faction fully subscribing to the *neo-liberal*, *New Right* agenda set out by *Margaret Thatcher* from the mid-1970s. See *Thatcherism*, *one-nation Tories* and *wets*.

Droop formula: see *quota*

Drummond, Stuart (1973–): the directly elected Mayor of Hartlepool, first elected in 2002 when standing as H'Angus the Monkey, the Hartlepool Football Club mascot – a job he held at the that time.

- Initially a joke candidate, Drummond had promised to provide free bananas for schoolchildren – his only major *campaign* pledge and one he failed to deliver once in office..
- He gave up the role of H'Angus following his election and was subsequently re-elected in 2005 and 2009.

Duncan Smith, Iain (1954–): the Conservative MP for Chingford (1992–97) and later Chingford and Woodford Green (1997 onwards). Former *Conservative Party* leader (2001–03). Founder and Chair of the *Centre for Social Justice*.

- Duncan Smith was the the first Conservative leader to be elected by a ballot of all party members, part of an electoral mechanism introduced by former leader *William Hague*.
- His leadership came to an abrupt end when he lost a vote of confidence held amongst fellow Conservative MPs.

DUP: see *Democratic Unionist Party (DUP)*

A–Z Online

Log on to A–Z Online to search the database of terms, print revision lists and much more. Go to **www.philipallan.co.uk/a-zonline** to get started.

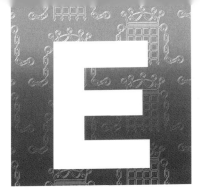

early day motion: in effect a form of parliamentary petition, where an **MP** tables a **bill** for debate in the **Commons** and other MPs can add their name to it. There is rarely time in the parliamentary calendar for such bills to be discussed.

Example

The Labour **backbencher** Michael Meacher tabled early day motion 178 in the wake of the 2005 **general election**. It was signed by 412 MPs:

That this House agrees with the Government's Chief Scientific Adviser that climate change is a threat to civilisation; welcomes the cross-party agreement in favour of major cuts in greenhouse gas emissions, and particularly in carbon dioxide emissions, by 2050; believes that such a long-term target will best be met through a series of more regular milestones; and therefore notes the Climate Change Bill that was presented by a cross-party group of honourable Members in the final days before the general election, and hopes that such a Bill will be brought forward in this Parliament so that annual cuts in carbon dioxide emissions of 3 per cent can be delivered in a framework that includes regular reporting and new scrutiny and corrective processes.

ecologism: an **ideology** of the environment and conservation, often taken as similar to environmentalism.
- Ecologism is seen as being at the more ideologically militant end of the environmentalist spectrum (sometimes referred to as 'dark green') with mainstream environmentalism being less of an ideology and more of a lifestyle choice (so-called 'light green').
- Whereas environmentalism focuses on managing the way in which contemporary human existence affects the environment (i.e. dealing with the symptoms of the problem), ecologism stresses the need for a fundamental change in the way in which human societies operate and how they interact with the non-human world.

economic competence: see **Black Wednesday**

economical with the truth: a euphemism for lying or at the very least deceiving someone by holding back some or all of what one knows.
- MPs are not permitted to accuse other members of lying in **Commons** debates.
- The use of this phrase is one way in which members have tried to circumvent this procedural rule.

e-democracy: the greater use of the internet, mobile phones and other electronic media as a means of enhancing the operation of existing political institutions and processes.

It addresses the decline in some forms of **political participation** by making it far easier for **citizens** to engage with decision makers and shape the political agenda (see **agenda-setting**). e-democracy involves devices such as online **petitions** and blogs. See also **new media**.

Eden, Anthony: *prime minister* (Conservative), 1955–57

EDM: see *early day motion*

EEC: see *European Economic Community (EEC)*

election: a means by which **citizens** can select public officials by casting a **vote** (or votes) indicating their preference(s). Elections are a key feature of the democratic state.

Example

UK citizens can vote in a range of elections (e.g. **general elections**, **local elections**, regional elections and elections to the **European Parliament**). EU citizens resident in the UK are permitted to vote in local elections and elections to the European Parliament.

---

election manifesto: see *manifesto*

elective dictatorship: describing the way in which the **power** and **authority** of **Parliament** is concentrated in the hands of any party leader who possesses and can control a sizeable majority in the **House of Commons**.

- The phrase was coined by Lord Hailsham in a lecture given in 1976.
- It is another term for ideas of executive dominance.

TIP: Lord Hailsham accepted that the *uncodified* basis of the UK *executive* inevitably created a tendency towards executive dominance: governments commanding large Commons majorities are able to circumvent parliamentary procedure; the work of the majority party's *whips* and the imposition of *guillotines* on parliamentary *debate* allow governments to force through bills; the Lords' power to block government initiatives is limited by the *Parliament Act (1911)* and the *Parliament Act (1949)*, and by the *Salisbury Doctrine*; and the powers of *scrutiny* held by UK *standing committees* and *departmental select committees* are weak in comparison to those exercised by US standing committees.

Lord Hailsham's chief concern was that this executive dominance had become embodied in the singular figure of the *prime minister* – as opposed to the collective body of the *cabinet*.

---

electoral college: a body involved in the indirect election of a public official.

Example

Legally speaking, it is the 538-member US Electoral College that has the task of electing the US president. Regular voters are simply electing the individuals who will represent their state in the Electoral College. An electoral college system is also used in the election of **Labour Party** leaders in the UK. This electoral college comprises three groups, each carrying one third of the total college vote: the **trade unions** and other **affiliated** organisations; ordinary members, through their **Constituency Labour Party**; and the **Parliamentary Labour Party**, along with elected Labour members of the **European Parliament**.

---

electoral mandate: see *mandate*

electoral reform: any change to the system under which elections are conducted. Criticisms of the *first-past-the-post* system used in elections to *Westminster* have led to calls for electoral reform. See also the *Jenkins Commission*.

electoral register: a list containing the names of all those entitled to vote in a constituency.

- The register is compiled in each constituency each year, well ahead of the regular election season in May.
- Householders are legally required to complete the official registration form in respect of those living at the property who are eligible to vote, or who will be within the life of the register.

electoral stability: where *voting behaviour* remains fairly predictable and constant from one election to the next. See also *churn*.

- Electoral stability is closely associated with voting models that stress the importance of *long-term factors* (see *primacy model*) such as *social class* and *socialisation*.
- It is often linked to low levels of *swing*.
- It is said to have declined as a result of the twin processes of *partisan dealignment* and *class dealignment*.

Contrast with *electoral volatility*

electoral system: a mechanism by which voters are translated into seats in a *legislature* or an individual is returned to a singular office. See also *majoritarian electoral system*, *proportional electoral system* and *hybrid electoral system*.

- The *first-past-the-post* or *simple plurality* system was once used in all major UK elections and is still used in most local elections in England and Wales and in elections to *Westminster*.
- A number of other systems were employed in other elections after New Labour came to power in 1997. See *party list system*, *single transferable vote (STV)*, *additional member system (AMS)* and *supplementary vote (SV)*.

electoral turnout: see *turnout*

electoral volatility: usually referring to uncertainty in *voting behaviour* resulting from large numbers of voters switching their allegiance between *political parties* as a result of *short-term factors* (see *recency model*).

- Since the relative stability of *voting behaviour* in the 1950s, electoral volatility, linked to *class dealignment* and *partisan dealignment*, has increased.
- Electoral volatility is often measured in terms of the percentage *swing* recorded between one election and the next.

> **TIP:** Even where the recorded swing is relatively small, there can still be consider-able electoral volatility. This is because the quoted percentage reflects only the net movement of voters between one party and another and may therefore disguise significant movements of voters in opposite directions that cancel one another out (see *churn*).

electorate: those individuals entitled to *vote* because they qualify under the *franchise* and appear on the *electoral register*.

elites theory: the belief that modern societies are dominated by an elite that uses its privileged position to benefit its own members while at the same time excluding others from the key decision-making processes.

- The theory is closely associated with the work of American sociologist Charles Wright Mills and his seminal book *The Power Elite* (1956).
- Contrast with *pluralist theory*. See also *New World Order* and the *Bilderberg Group*.

elitism: the tendency to defer to the ideas of a small group who share a common socio-economic background. See *elites theory*.

embourgeoisement: a process by which those in the *working class* come to see themselves as *middle class* and cast their *ballots* accordingly at election time. See *social class*, *class voting*, *old working class* and *new working class*. It is closely linked to the decline of the Labour Party in the 1980s and early 1990s and with the rise of so-called *deviant voting*.

EMU: see *European Economic and Monetary Union (EMU)*

enabling authority: the local council as a facilitator rather than simply a service provider, involving the provision of public services through both public and private organisations and businesses.

English Democrats: a minor English *political party* that campaigns in favour of the creation of a devolved English parliament along the lines of the *Scottish Parliament*. The party has achieved limited electoral success, though in 2009 the English Democrats party candidate, Peter Davies, was directly elected as mayor of the Metropolitan Borough of Doncaster. See also *West Lothian question* and *English votes for English laws*.

English votes for English laws: the idea that only those *MPs* representing English constituencies at *Westminster* should be permitted to vote on bills directly affecting England. See *West Lothian question* and *devolution*.

enlargement: see *EU enlargement*

entrenchment: where *laws* or constitutional provisions are afforded greater protection from arbitrary change than regular *statutes*. Entrenchment is made difficult under the UK system because of the doctrine of *parliamentary sovereignty*.

> **TIP:** The use of *referendums* as a means of legitimising major constitutional changes, such as the creation of the *Scottish Parliament*, could be said to provide a degree of entrenchment, as it would be difficult for *Parliament* to reverse such changes without a further referendum. A degree of entrenchment could also be achieved by adding a measure to the list of things exempted from the provisions of the *Parliament Act (1911)* and the *Parliament Act (1949)*, thereby requiring the *Lords* as well as the *Commons* to approve a measure before it could become law.

environmentalism: see *ecologism*

equality of opportunity: the absence of any formal barriers to social mobility – a 'level playing field'.

equality of outcome: a facet of *social justice* concerned with ensuring that those less able to take advantage of the opportunities available (see *equality of opportunity*) are not disadvantaged. Whereas equality of opportunity could be seen as fairly passive, equality of outcome generally involves some form of social engineering, e.g. **affirmative action**. Conservatives generally stress equality of opportunity whereas socialists prefer to speak in terms of equality of outcome.

Erskine May: referring to *Parliamentary Practice*, a **work of authority** first published in 1844.

Essex model: referring to a 'rerun' of the 1997 **general election** conducted by academics from the Universities of London and Essex under a number of alternate **electoral systems**. The research was based upon a sample of 8,000 voters.

Example: the findings of the Essex model

The table shows the number of Commons seats that main parties might have won in 1997 under various different electoral systems.

Party	FPTP	AV	SV	List	STV	AMS
Conservative	165	110	110	202	144	203
Labour	419	436	436	285	342	303
LibDem	46	84	84	110	131	115
SNP/PC	10	10	10	46	24	20
Others	19	19	19	18	18	18
Majority	179	213	213	−89	25	−27

ethnicity: referring to race and culture.

EU: see *European Union (EU)*

EU enlargement: the ongoing expansion of the 'European project' from a **European Economic Community (EEC)** of six members in 1957 to a **European Union** comprising 27 member states by January 2007. The process of enlargement has necessitated a reworking of the Union's main institutions. See also **qualified majority voting** and **Lisbon, Treaty of (2007)**.

euro: the single European currency operating within the **Eurozone**. It was established along lines set out in the **Treaty of Maastricht** and came into circulation in 2002.

TIP: Note that not all EU member states have adopted the euro. In 1992, the then prime minister *John Major* secured a UK opt-out from the *European Economic and Monetary Union (EMU)* when negotiating the Maastricht Treaty; as did Denmark. Other states have failed to meet the *convergence criteria* or are not eligible because they have only recently become EU member states. In 2009, only 16 of the 27 EU member states were in the Eurozone.

eurocrat: an EU-level civil servant. See **European Commission** and **Committee of Permanent Representatives (COREPER)**.

Euro-elections: see *European elections*

Eurogroup: a pressure group operating at *EU* level.

- Eurogroups are *peak groups* representing likeminded pressure groups from the various EU member states.
- Eurogroups tend to form in those areas of policy where the level of EU regulation makes it impossible for groups to focus simply on *access points* within their own country.
- They often work closely with the European Commission and with the *Committee of Permanent Representatives (COREPER)*.

Example

Although the *National Farmers' Union (NFU)* in the UK has its own permanent office in Brussels, it is also a member of the Eurogroup *COPA-COGECA*, which represents over 11 million farmers EU-wide.

Euroland: see *Eurozone*

European Central Bank: an *EU* institution responsible for determining the level at which the interest rate is set within the *Eurozone*.

European Commission: a key *EU* institution that holds significant *executive* powers within the Union as well as the right to develop proposals for EU policy and impose punishments where states fall foul of EU laws and regulations.

- In 2009, the Commission comprised 27 *commissioners*, one per EU member state.
- The *European Parliament* has oversight of the Commission. The Parliament controls the budget and can also force the resignation of the Commission, as it did in 1999.

European Communities Act (1972): the *Act of Parliament* under which the UK joined the *European Economic Community (EEC)* from 1 January, 1973.

European Community: the forerunner of the *European Union*, the latter coming into existence following the *Treaty of Maastricht*. See also *European Economic Community (EEC)*.

European constitution: see *Lisbon, Treaty of (2007)*

European Convention on Human Rights (1950): a treaty extending a range of *rights* to the *citizens* of those countries that become signatories to the Convention.

- The treaty was the product of the *Council of Europe*, an *intergovernmental* organisation that is not part of the EU. The ECHR therefore does not have the power of EU law.
- Cases under the ECHR can be heard in the *European Court of Human Rights* or in UK courts, since the *Human Rights Act (1998)* came into force in October 2000. This Act incorporated the ECHR into UK law.

European Council: a body comprising the heads of government of all *EU* member states and the president of the *European Commission*. It meets biannually.

European Council of Ministers: see *Council of Ministers*

European Court of Human Rights: a final court of appeal for cases arising under the *European Convention on Human Rights (1950)*. It is not an *EU* institution, despite being based in Strasbourg. The highest EU court is the *European Court of Justice*.

European Court of Justice: the supreme court of the *EU*, based in Luxembourg.
- The court is concerned with interpreting and applying EU law.
- It hears cases against states accused of violating EU law and adjudicates in disputes between member states.
- The court's power is rooted in the fact that EU law is superior to national law under the *Treaty of Rome*.

European currency: see *euro*

European Economic and Monetary Union: the roadmap towards the creation of a single European currency, established under the *Treaty of Maastricht* and involving the creation of a *single European currency* under the control of a *European Central Bank*.
- It resulted in the establishment of a *European Central Bank* as well as the *euro*.
- *John Major* successfully negotiated an opt-out, as did Denmark. This meant that neither country sought to adopt the *euro* in the first wave.

See also *convergence criteria*.

European Economic Community (EEC): a European trade organisation established under the *Treaty of Rome* (1957) by West Germany, France, Italy, Belgium, the Netherlands, and Luxembourg. It became the *European Union* in 1993.
- The EEC was founded with the twin aims of preventing renewed hostilities on the European mainland and providing stability in the supply and price of agricultural produce.
- The UK joined the EEC on 1 January 1973, following the passing of the *European Communities Act (1972)*. The UK's entry had been negotiated by the then Conservative Party prime minister, *Edward Heath*.

European elections: held every five years across the various EU member states in order to select those who will sit as members of the European Parliament (MEPs). Since 1999, British elections to the *European Parliament* have taken place under a closed regional *party list system*. European elections in Northern Ireland take place under the *single transferable vote (STV)* system.

European Free Trade Association (EFTA): established in 1960 as 'half-way house' for those states who wanted to improve trade with other European states, without formally joining the *European Economic Community (EEU)* (now *EU*).
- Several states have used membership of EFTA as a stepping stone to joining the EU (formerly EEC), e.g. the UK and Sweden.
- By 2009, EFTA had only four remaining member states: Iceland, Liechtenstein, Norway, and Switzerland.

European integration: see *integration*

European law: a law established under the authority of the *European Union (EU)* or *European Community* that preceded it. Under the *Treaty of Rome* European law is superior to UK law and the national laws of other EU member states.

European Parliament: an *EU* institution that was once little more than a debating chamber but now shares legislative power with the *Council of Ministers* under the *co-decision procedure*.
- Following the 2009 European elections, the Parliament consisted of 736 *MEPs* elected across the 27 member states.

- Seats are apportioned between member states in broad proportion to population. The UK had 72 seats in 2009, Germany had 99 and Malta had just 5.
- The European Parliament plays a key role in the scrutiny of the *European Commission* and the *European Council of Ministers*. In 1999, the Parliament forced the resignation of the Commission amid allegations of corruption.
- MEPs tend to sit in ideological, transnational party groupings in the Parliament chamber – as opposed to national groupings. Labour Party MEPs sit with the Party of European Socialists.

European Union (EU): a multi-national European organisation established under the *Treaty of Maastricht*, consisting of 27 member states in 2009.

- The EU grew out of the *European Community*, which itself had developed from the *European Economic Community (EEC)* established under the *Treaty of Rome*.
- Whereas these organisations focused largely on trade and economic policy, the European Union was always intended to have an input into social and foreign policy.
- The EU combines some elements that are *supranational* with others that are intergovernmental.
- The EU's main institutions are the *Council of Ministers*, the *European Commission*, the *European Parliament* and the *European Court of Justice*. The *European Court of Human Rights* is not an EU institution.

Europeanisation: the emergence of a common European identity or *political culture*, aside from the national identities of the states that make up the continent. Some see Europeanisation as going hand in hand with European integration and *enlargement* – with the end goal being a *federation* of a United States of Europe.

Europhile: one who broadly favours further European *integration* and *enlargement*. The former Conservative chancellor of the exchequer *Kenneth Clarke*'s reputation as a Europhile was said to have been a key factor in his losing all three of the party leadership races that he contested.

Europhobe: see *Eurosceptic*

Eurosceptic: an individual who questions the benefits of UK membership of the European Union.

- Eurosceptics tend to oppose further EU integration and enlargement, arguing that such processes undermine *parliamentary sovereignty* and make it difficult for the government to act in the national interest.
- This position is associated with some on the right of the *Conservative Party*. See also *Bruges Group* and *No Turning Back Group*.

Euroscepticism: the position taken by *Eurosceptics*.

Eurozone: collectively referring to the territories of those *EU* member states that have adopted the *euro*.

Exchange Rate Mechanism (ERM): a mechanism for managing changes in the relative value of the various European currencies ahead of the introduction of the European single currency or *euro*.

- The UK was famously forced to withdraw from the ERM on *Black Wednesday*.

- A successful period within the ERM was subsequently established as one of the four key *convergence criteria* that had to be met by those countries wanting to adopt the euro.

executive: the branch of *government* charged with the task of executing and administrating the laws enacted by the *legislature*. The UK executive comprises the *prime minister* and *cabinet*; other *government ministers*; *civil servants* working within government *departments* and *agencies*; and other individuals and bodies operating within the *core executive*. See also *separation of powers* and *fusion of powers*.

Example

The USA operates under a singular executive, with the *constitution* vesting all executive power in the hands of the president. The UK is traditionally said to operate under a collective executive with the prime minister sitting in cabinet as *primus inter pares* (first among equals). The greater concentration of executive power in the hands of the prime minister in recent years is said to have resulted in the rise of a more *presidential prime minister*.

executive agency: a quasi-autonomous body that holds responsibility for administering an aspect of government policy or regulating some area of government activity.
- Such agencies are an office of government that is subordinate to but sufficiently independent of its parent *Whitehall* department to allow it to carry out certain key administrative functions.
- They are often associated with the process of *agencification* that began with the *Next Steps Programme*.
- Some argue that the way in which the delivery of government services has been transferred to such agencies has undermined *role responsibility* within cabinet and brought the *civil service* principles of *anonymity* and *permanence* into question.
- Although such agencies are in theory simply administering rather than making policy, their chief executives are often high-profile, public figures with a high degree of operational independence.

Example

By the time that *New Labour* came to power in 1997, it was estimated that three-quarters of UK civil servants were working for agencies, as opposed to the civil service proper. New Labour continued this process of agencification. By 2006, there were said to be over 270 agencies. The Ministry of Defence is served by a number of agencies, ranging from the Defence Vetting Agency (which conducts background checks on potential employees) to Service Children's Education (which manages the education of the children of service personnel posted overseas).

executive democracy: see *elective dictatorship*

executive dominance: see *elective dictatorship*

exit poll: a poll conducted retrospectively, often as *voters* are leave *polling stations* having cast their *ballot*.

- Exit polls are often said to be more accurate than regular **opinion polls**: first, because they take place after the act of voting; and second, because they generally involve far larger and more accurate samples.
- Exit polls provide the detailed data upon which **psephologists** base their analysis of the **voting behaviour** of various different groups within the **electorate**.

See also **opinion polls**.

expressive voting: voting as an emotional, as opposed to a rational, act. Contrast with **instrumental voting**, the **rational choice model** and **consumer voting model**.

Are you studying other subjects?

The A–Z Handbooks (digital editions) are available in 14 different subjects. Browse the range and order other handbooks at **www.philipallan.co.uk/a-zonline**.

Fabian Society: a left-leaning *think-tank* that played a part in forming the *Labour Party*. It was established in 1884 by *socialists* George Bernard Shaw, Sidney Webb and Beatrice Webb. It is an *affiliated* organisation of the Labour Party.

faction: an organised group of likeminded individuals operating within a larger group. The term is commonly used when referring to groupings within the main UK political parties.
- *Conservative Party* factions have included the *Monday Club*, the *Bruges Group*, the *No Turning Back group* and the *Bow Group*.
- *Labour Party* factions have included the *Tribune Group* and, until the 1980s, the *Militant Tendency*.

See also *affiliated*.

factionalism: the presence of a number of competing *factions*.

Factortame case: a case in which the *European Court of Justice* established the *precedent* that UK courts could suspend UK *statute law* where it appeared to violate *European law*.
- The case took its name from a Spanish-owned fishing company, Factortame Limited, which challenged the legality of the Merchant Shipping Act (1988) under European law.
- Under this ruling, UK courts can suspend *Acts of Parliament* that appear to violate EU law until the European Court of Justice is able to make a final determination as to their legality. UK courts cannot themselves strike down an Act of Parliament, because of the doctrine of *parliamentary sovereignty*.

Falklands factor: referring to the role played by the *Falklands War* as a pivotal *short-term factor* in the *Conservative Party's* landslide victory in the 1983 *general election*.

Falklands War: the conflict between the UK and Argentina that followed the Argentine invasion of the Falkland Islands and South Georgia in 1982.

far left: see *communism*

far right: see *fascism*

fascism: a radical nationalist ideology that favours an authoritarian approach to government.
- Fascism is most closely associated with Hitler's Nazi Party (in power in Germany 1933–45) and Benito Mussolini's National Fascist Party (in government in Italy 1922–43).
- In the UK it is often used with reference to Oswald Mosley's British Union of Fascists, which existed from 1932 until it was banned in 1940.
- The term is applied pejoratively to modern right-wing parties such as the *British National Party (BNP)*.

fat cats: a derogatory term applied to those wealthy individuals who donate money to *political parties* or individual *candidates*. See also *smoke-filled rooms*.

Fathers 4 Justice: a fathers' rights *pressure group* established by marketing consultant Matt O'Connor in 2000.

- Fathers 4 Justice is a *sectional group* and an *outsider group*.
- The group's tactic of getting members dressed as superheroes to scale major public buildings – including the Palace of Westminster and Buckingham Palace – attracted considerable media coverage.

federalism: a form of government under which sovereign power is divided between a central government and a number of regional authorities, often referred to as states.

- Under a federal system the central and the various state governments tend to operate within separate spheres of authority.
- Federalism generally involves a degree of entrenchment, where neither the central nor the various state governments can take significant powers from one another without a formal *amendment to the constitution*.
- The USA operates under a federal system. The central government in Washington DC takes the responsibility for defence and major economic policy, and the 50 state governments control many areas of social policy. See also *unitary state*.

feminism: an *ideology* originally associated with a desire to achieve gender equality and establish legal rights for women. It is increasingly concerned with celebrating the contribution made by women and challenging gender-based stereotypes.

filibuster: a device whereby a legislator or group of legislators talk at length, often on totally unrelated matters, in order to stop a debate moving through to a formal vote on a bill or other measure.

- Filibusters are more common in the US Senate, though they have also been seen in the UK.
- Government can overcome this tactic in the *House of Commons* by the use of the *guillotine*, a device that cuts short *debate* through the imposition of time limits.
- The term is derived from the Spanish word for pirate.

Example

In April 2007, Liberal Democrats Simon Hughes and Norman Baker led a five-hour filibuster that effectively killed a Private Members' Bill attempting to exempt MPs from the Freedom of Information Act (2000).

Financial Management Initiative (1982): a policy that looked to bring greater accountability and efficiency to the work of the *civil service*.

- The policy originated with Derek Rayner, the head of *Margaret Thatcher*'s Efficiency Unit.
- It focused on the importance of clear departmental objectives and the measuring of performance against those objectives.
- It also paved the way for the process of *agencification* ushered in under the *Ibbs Report (1988)*.

First Lord of the Treasury: see *prime minister*

first minister: the formal title used to refer to the chief executives of the devolved institutions in Scotland, Wales and Northern Ireland. They are not directly elected but drawn from their respective *legislatures*.

first-past-the-post: an *electoral system* used in elections to *Westminster*.

- Often referred to as the *simple plurality* system, as a candidate needs to secure only one vote more than the nearest rival in order to be elected in a *single-member constituency*.
- The system was used in virtually all other elections in the UK before 1997.
- It is widely criticised for its tendency to result in large numbers of *wasted votes* and for its lack of *proportionality*. See also *electoral reform*.

first reading: the first stage in the *legislative process*, where a *bill* is formally introduced in the *Commons* (or the *Lords*) and a vote is taken on whether or not the proposal should proceed to a *second reading*.

Fitzroy, Augustus Henry (Duke of Grafton): *prime minister* (Whig), 1768–70.

Five Giants: the ills that the *Beveridge Report (1942)* argued needed to be defeated: want; disease; ignorance; squalor; and idleness.

fixed elections: the practice of holding *elections* at fixed intervals.

- In the UK the *prime minister* can call a *general election* at a time of his or her choosing, as long as *Parliament* is dissolved within five years of the previous election. This means that the premier can potentially schedule the contest to his or her party's political advantage.
- The USA operates under a system of fixed elections, e.g. the House of Representatives is elected on the same day every two years – along with one-third of the Senate. The US president is elected on the same day every leap-year.

fixed terms: where politicians are elected to serve terms of a predetermined length.

- In the UK there is an upper limit on the length of an MP's term – the maximum of five years that can elapse between one general election taking place and the next one being called.
- There is no lower limit, as the minimum period between general elections is not fixed.
- Some countries operate under a system of *fixed elections*.

See also *term-limits*.

flexible constitution: said to be a feature of an *uncodified constitution*. See also *entrenchment*.

floating voter: an individual who does not identify strongly with a particular political party and is therefore more likely to be influenced by *short-term factors* (see *recency model*), such as the election *campaign*. See also *identifier*.

- *Partisan dealignment* resulted in a rise in the number of floating or independent voters. Though many voters do identify with a particular party, far fewer now identify strongly than was the case in the 1950s and 1960s.
- The rise of floating voters has resulted in greater electoral volatility.
- Floating voters are of particular importance in marginal constituencies, where their votes are more likely to determine the eventual outcome of an election.

focus group: a representative sample of *voters* selected by a *political party* and asked to provide feedback on some aspect of that party's performance.

- Political parties consult focus groups in order to 'market-test' and fine-tune their policies ahead of an election.
- *New Labour* used focus groups extensively under the guidance of its chief *pollster* Phillip Gould. Such activities were coordinated by its communications centre at *Millbank Tower*, London.

Foley, Michael: see *spatial leadership* and *presidential prime minister*

Foot, Michael (1913–): former *left-wing* Labour MP and leader of the party between 1980 and 1983.

- Michael Foot is a founder member of the *Campaign for Nuclear Disarmament (CND)*.
- Well respected for his intellect, he was out of place in an age of increasingly image-centred campaigns.
- He resigned as leader following Labour's landslide defeat in the 1983 *general election*. The party's *manifesto* in that year was famously dubbed 'the longest suicide note in history'.

foreign secretary: the *cabinet*-level minister responsible for the work of the Foreign and Commonwealth Office. Some argue that the role of the foreign secretary has been undermined by the rise of *prime ministerial power* in the field of foreign affairs. See also *presidential prime minister*.

franchise: the right to vote as established by statute.

- The vast majority of adult UK *citizens* have the franchise. Exceptions include current members of the *House of Lords*, those convicted of election-related offences, or those detained in secure mental health facilities or prison.
- The franchise was extended significantly with the Representation of the People Act (1969), which reduced the voting age from 21 to 18.

free market: a market that operates entirely free from government regulation. A truly free market would preclude the existence of state-owned monopolies such as the Post Office. See also *neo-liberalism* and *classical liberalism*.

free trade: the principle that trade between individuals and nations should be free from government regulation and customs duties.

- This position was supported by most *Whigs* in the nineteenth century but opposed by those *Tory Party* protectionists who wanted to limit foreign imports.
- The principle is adopted in large part in modern free-trade areas such as the *EU*, the *European Free Trade Association (EFTA)* and also under the North American Free Trade Agreement (NAFTA) between Canada, the USA and Mexico.

freedom of information: the right to access information held by the government and a feature of *open government*. See *Freedom of Information Act (2000)*.

Freedom of Information Act (2000): the *Act of Parliament* that established the right of *citizens* to request non-sensitive information held by the government.

- The Act fulfilled one of *New Labour's* 1997 *manifesto* commitments.
- Despite being passed in 2000, the Act did not come into effect until January 2005.

- It did not live up to the expectations of groups such as **Charter 88** and the **Scottish Parliament** strengthened the provisions of the Act applying north of the border.
- The Information Commissioner has the task of adjudicating in the case of disputes arising under the Act.

freedom of speech: the freedom to express one's view without legal impediment or state censorship.
- The freedom of speech generally taken to refer to written forms of speech (i.e. freedom of the press) as well as the spoken word.
- It is protected under Article 10 of the **Human Rights Act (1998)**, which guarantees freedom of expression and is also protected under the First Amendment to the US Constitution (1791).

> **TIP:** In reality, the freedom of speech is limited in law by statutes restricting libel, the incitement of racial hatred and the glorification of terrorist acts.

Fresh Future: a document outlining a programme of internal **Conservative Party** reform, proposed by the then leader **William Hague** and confirmed in a **ballot** of party members.
- The document resulted in the creation of four new bodies within the party: the **Policy Forum**, the Board, the National Convention and the National Convention Executive.
- It amounted to a written constitution for the party.

Friends of the Earth: an international network of environmental **pressure groups** founded in the USA in 1969 by David Bower, a former member of the Sierra Club – the pre-eminent US environmental pressure group. The UK branch of the organisation is known as Friends of the Earth (EWNI), i.e. England, Wales and Northern Ireland.

front benches: referring literally to the front rows of benches in the **Commons** and the **Lords**, though more commonly to the teams of **government** and **opposition** spokesmen and women who occupy them, i.e. the frontbenchers. See also **backbenchers**, **cabinet** and **shadow cabinet**.

frontbencher/frontbench MP: see **front benches**

fuel protests: a **direct action** campaign against the rising costs of fuel, which started in 2000 and ended in 2001.
- The protesters adopted a range of tactics including the blockading of fuel refineries and depots.
- They forced the Labour government to suspend the fuel price escalator, a mechanism that had seen the duty on fuel rise by 6% above the rate of inflation when last applied in 1999.

Fulton Report (1968): an official report that criticised the **civil service** as amateurish and recommended promotion on the basis of merit as opposed to seniority. See also **Ibbs Report (1988)**.

functional representation: representation on the basis of **social class** or occupation. See also **corporatism**, **National Economic Development Council (NEDC)** and **resemblance theory**. Contrast with the geographical representation provided for in the **constituency**-based elections to **Westminster**.

fusion of powers: a feature of the UK system of *government* whereby the three branches of government – the *executive*, the *legislature* and the *judiciary* – overlap with one another in terms of power and personnel.

- The UK executive is drawn from the legislature. Whereas in the USA these two institutions are formally separated under the *constitution*, UK *ministers* are required to be sitting members of the *Commons* or the *Lords*.
- Historically there has also been an overlap in respect of the judiciary, with the House of Lords – or more specifically the *Law Lords* within the chamber – serving as the highest court of appeal and the *Lord Chancellor* sitting as speaker of the Lords (legislature), a *cabinet* member (executive) and the head of the judiciary. This state of affairs was addressed under the *Constitutional Reform Act (2005)*, which saw the creation of a new UK *Supreme Court* as well as significant changes to the post of Lord Chancellor. See also *separation of powers*.

Aiming for a grade A*?

Don't forget to log on to **www.philipallan.co.uk/a-zonline** for advice.

gagging order: a court-imposed order that prevents the press from publishing material relating to a particular topic.

Galloway, George (1954–): a former *left-wing* Labour MP (Glasgow Hillhead), who was elected as the MP for Bethnal Green and Bow when standing as a *RESPECT* candidate at the 2005 general election. Galloway was a fierce opponent of the decision to go to war in Iraq, ultimately becoming vice-president of the *Stop the War Coalition*. His outspoken criticism of the then Labour leader and prime minister *Tony Blair* and suggestion that British troops fighting in Iraq should disobey orders resulted in Galloway's expulsion from the Labour Party in 2003. In 2004 he announced that he would be working with the *Socialist Alliance* to form a new political party, RESPECT.

Gang of Four: in the UK context, refers to the four former Labour cabinet ministers who left the party in 1981 to form the *Social Democratic Party (SDP)*: Bill Rodgers; Roy Jenkins; Shirley Williams; and David Owen.

- The creation of the new party was announced in the Limehouse Declaration of 25 January 1981.
- The Gang of Four had left Labour believing that it had fallen under the control of Trotskyites and other *left-wingers* following the party's defeat in the 1979 *general election*.
- They lacked confidence in the party's leader at the time, left-winger *Michael Foot*.

Gascoyne-Cecil, Robert (Marquess of Salisbury): *prime minister* (Conservative), 1885–86, 1886–92 and 1895–1902.

gender gap: the historical divide between the patterns of *party* support shown by women when voting at *elections* and those of men.

- In the 1960s and 1970s there was a clear correlation between gender and *voting behaviour*.
- Women were far more likely to vote Conservative, with men favouring the Labour Party. A gap was also apparent in 1992, with just 38% of men voting Conservative compared to the 44% of women supporting the party.
- This correlation was said to result from the fact that many men were employed full-time in manual professions that were heavily unionised – and were therefore more likely to vote for the party of the unions – whereas women were still predominantly seen as homemakers and were therefore attracted by the Conservatives policies on the family and law and order.
- In recent years the gender gap appears to have closed (see table overleaf). The decline of the *unions* and the *old working class* has weakened the traditional ties

between men and the Labour Party. The proportion of women voting Labour has also risen as a result of the party's policies (e.g. the right to flexible working), its internal organisation (e.g. **women-only shortlists**) and the greater numbers of women in full-time employment.

The closing gender gap — % voting Conservative at general elections

Election	Men	Women
1992	38	44
1997	31	32
2001	32	33
2005	34	32

General Belgrano: the Argentine battleship sunk by the British submarine *HMS Conqueror* during the **Falklands War** (1982).

- The decision to sink the battleship was controversial because it was outside and steaming away from the exclusion zone that had been established by the UK government.
- *Margaret Thatcher* was accused of misleading Parliament over precisely where the vessel had been at the time of the attack. She came under scrutiny at *Prime Minister's Questions*.

general election: an election in which all **constituencies** returning MPs to the **House of Commons** are contested.

- A general election must be called within five years of the last general election.
- By **convention**, an election is triggered by the **prime minister** asking the **monarch** to grant the **dissolution** of Parliament. This gives the prime minister the opportunity to try to time the election to the political advantage of his or her party.
- All sitting MPs cease to be MPs at the time of the dissolution and must seek re-election. This is one way in which MPs are held **accountable** to their **constituents**.
- Voters have the opportunity to vote only for their constituency MP, not the government or the prime minister. The **government** is generally drawn exclusively from the party that wins the most constituencies (seats), with the leader of that party becoming prime minister.

General Secretary of the Labour Party: the senior employee of the Labour Party who plays the lead role in organising the party **bureaucracy**, which comprises over 200 staff based in the party's London headquarters and in other offices around the country.

- The general secretary is effectively nominated by the party's **National Executive Committee (NEC)** and confirmed in a vote at the annual **party conference**.
- The general secretary co-ordinates election strategy, organises the various party committees and plans the annual conference.
- The trade unionist Ray Collins was appointed general secretary in 2008.

general voting model: an overarching model of **voting behaviour** that seeks to demonstrate the links that exist between some of those features emphasised under other voting models. Advanced by William Miller in 1990.

Example

While the *social class* of individual voters might predispose them to support a particular party (see *partisan alignment*), the context unique to a particular election or the salient issues in the campaign (see *salience*) might serve to moderate their behaviour, making them more likely to vote against their natural party.

gerrymandering: the redrawing of constituency boundaries for political advantage. The term resulted from a conjunction of the surname of the one-time governor of the US state of Massachusetts, Elbridge Gerry, and the word 'salamander' – a reference to the shape of one of the electoral districts he had created. Gerrymandering is rare in the UK because parliamentary boundaries are set by the independent *Boundary Commissions*.

Example

In 1986 the Leader of Westminster City Council, Dame Shirley Porter, was fined £27m for her part in the 'homes for votes' scandal, whereby the Conservative-led council had illegally forced predominantly Labour-supporting residents out of council-owned accommodation, allegedly in an attempt to skew the profile of the electoral district.

GLA: see *Greater London Authority*

Gladstone, William Ewart: *prime minister* (Liberal), 1868–74, 1880–85, 1886 and 1892–94.

glass ceiling: an invisible barrier that is said to make it harder for women and members of ethnic minorities to progress in certain walks of life.

globalisation: a form of global integration whereby the social, political and economic barriers between nations are removed and people, goods, services and capital can move freely. It is often associated with the rise of multinational corporations and with the rise of the mass media, i.e. the 'global village'.

Glorious Revolution (1689): referring to *Parliament*'s decision to overthrow and replace King James II (a Catholic) with the Protestant William of Orange (thereafter William II) and his wife and first cousin Mary II (James II's daughter). William and Mary ruled as joint monarchs until Mary's death in 1694.

golden age of Parliament: an age in which Parliament acted as an effective and independent *legislature* comprising individual members unfettered by the need to observe the party *whip*.
- It lasted from the *Great Reform Act (1832)* through to the 1867 Reform Act, which doubled the number of adult men holding the *franchise* from around 1 million to around 2 million and resulted in the rise of modern *political parties*.
- In this period, the relationship between the *executive* and the *legislature* was balanced.

Goldsmith, James (1933–97): founder of the *Referendum Party*.

Good Friday Agreement (1998): the multi-party peace settlement concerning Northern Ireland, which ultimately saw the establishment of the *Northern Ireland Assembly* and other devolved institutions at *Stormont*. It was the culmination of the process begun with the Downing Street Declaration of 15 December 1993, when the then prime minister, *John Major*, and the Irish Taoiseach Albert Reynolds, had established the principles upon which a negotiated peace could be agreed between all groups in Northern Ireland.

governance: the act, manner or style of governing, e.g. good governance.

Governance of Britain Green Paper (2007): a *consultation* document that addressed certain aspects of *constitutional reform* and led to the publication of the *Constitutional Renewal Bill (2008)*. The Green Paper had four stated aims: to invigorate the UK *democracy*; to clarify the role of *government*, both central and local; to rebalance power between *Parliament* and the government; to give Parliament more ability to hold the government *accountable*; and to work with the general public to arrive at a stronger sense of what it means to be British.

government: in common parlance, the institutions that comprise the *state*; most commonly referred to as the *executive*, the *legislature* and the *judiciary*. In the UK it is used to refer primarily to just the *executive* branch of government, including: the *prime minister*; the *cabinet* and other *ministers*; and the various government *departments*.

government bill: a law proposed by the government, the passage of which through *Parliament* is almost guaranteed because of the *government majority* and *party discipline* in the *House of Commons*. The government routinely controls the *legislative process* as a result of its working majority in the Commons. As a result, the vast majority of bills that make it on to the timetable are government bills. See also *Private Members' Bills*.

government department: see *department*

government majority: the number of *Commons* seats that the governing party holds over and above the total number of seats held by all other parties combined.

Example

The Labour Party was returned to government with a majority of 179 seats at the 1997 *general election*; the largest majority ever held by a Labour government. In total the party won 418 seats in 1997, having secured 43% of the *popular vote*.

'government of all the talents': Gordon Brown's stated desire in 2007 to assemble a ministerial team of exceptional individuals, from both within and beyond the *Parliamentary Labour Party*. Brown's attempts to entice leading Liberal Democrats such as Paddy Ashdown into the *cabinet* provoked considerable controversy, both on the Labour backbenches and amongst the LibDem leadership. His efforts to appoint those from outside Parliament into the legislature and straight into government positions received a mixed press – not least his plan to elevate GMTV breakfast presenter Fiona Philips to the Lords to appoint her to a position in the Department of Health.

Grant, Wyn: a UK political scientist best known for his work on the classification of *pressure groups*. See *insider/outsider typology*.

grassroots: referring to political activity organised by local *activists* as opposed to that orchestrated by the national parties. See also *bottom-up* and *top-down*.

Great Reform Act (1832): the first (hence 'Great') major *statute* affecting UK *elections*. It tackled corrupt practices and extended the *franchise*.

- The Act was formally entitled the Representation of the People Act (1832).
- It dealt with the problem of **rotten boroughs** and **pocket boroughs**.
- It increased the number of adult men eligible to vote by over 50%, to around 650,000.

Greater London Assembly: the 25-member assembly created as part of the **Greater London Authority**.
- The Assembly scrutinises the work of the London Mayor, including oversight of the Mayor's budget. It can conduct investigations into matters concerning Londoners and publish reports.
- Elections to the Assembly are conducted under the **additional member system (AMS)**. The 2008 elections proved controversial because the **British National Party (BNP)** secured over 5.3% of the vote, passing the 5% **threshold** required for it to win a seat under the **party list** element of the system. The BNP candidate Richard Barnbrook – who had also stood as the party's candidate in the London Mayoral election (finishing fifth) – was duly elected to the Assembly.

Greater London Authority: referring to the tier of regional government established in the capital under the Greater London Authority Act (1999) and first elected in May 2000. It comprises the **Mayor of London** and the **Greater London Assembly**.

> **TIP:** Often seen as part of **New Labour**'s **devolution** programme, though not devolution in the strictest sense of the word because the powers granted to the Authority were not previously exercised by central government.

Greater London Council: the forerunner of the **Greater London Authority**. Created in 1965, it was abolished by **Margaret Thatcher**'s Conservative administration in 1986. **Ken Livingstone**, later the first **Mayor of London**, served as leader of the Greater London Council from 1981 until its abolition.

Green: see **ecologism**

Green Paper: a discussion paper marking the start of a period of consultation on a legislative proposal. Firm proposals, in the form of a **White Paper**, generally follow on from such consultation.

Green Party: referring to the UK ecologist party, which stood in elections around the UK between 1985 and 1990. It is now technically three separate parties: the Green Party of England and Wales; the Green Party in Northern Ireland; and the Scottish Green Party.
- Prior to 1985 the party had been known as the Ecology Party.
- Green **candidates** have generally performed poorly in elections to **Westminster** but have achieved some success in **local elections** and in elections to the **European Parliament**.
- The Green Party of England and Wales returned two MEPs in the 2009 UK elections to the European Parliament. This success can be attributed in part to the **closed list system** used in such elections since 1999.

Greenpeace: a worldwide environmental **pressure group** established in 1971.
- Greenpeace campaigns on issues including whaling, nuclear power and global warming.
- The organisation employs a range of strategies including **lobbying** and **direct action**. See also **Brent Spar**.

Grenville, George: *prime minister* (Whig), 1763–65.

Grenville, William Wyndham (Lord Grenville): *prime minister* (Whig), 1806–07.

Grey, Charles (Earl Grey): *prime minister* (Whig), 1830–34.

gridlock: a state of stalemate between the *executive* and *legislative* branches of government whereby neither is able to achieve its main goals.

- Gridlock is more commonly associated with the formal *separation of powers* present under the US system of government and the divided government that can follow on from that separation.
- It is less of an issue in the UK because of the presence of a *fusion of powers*, which facilitates executive dominance.

See also *elective dictatorship*

Guildford Four: the three men and one woman convicted in October 1975 of the *IRA*'s bomb attack on two pubs in Guildford a year earlier.

- The attacks had left five dead.
- The Guildford Four were released on appeal in 1989 after it emerged that the police had tampered with written evidence.
- The case is often given as an example of a *miscarriage of justice*.

guillotine: a device by which the *government* can cut short parliamentary *debate* and force a vote on a legislative proposal or amendment.

- Guillotines are commonly used to end or prevent a *filibuster*. A guillotine may also be used where there is simply insufficient time, either on the floor of Parliament or in *standing committee*, to discuss things at length. The guillotine allows the government to manage the passage of legislation.
- Also referred to as a cloture (or closure) motion, particularly in the USA.

A–Z Online

Log on to A–Z Online to search the database of terms, print revision lists and much more. Go to **www.philipallan.co.uk/a-zonline** to get started.

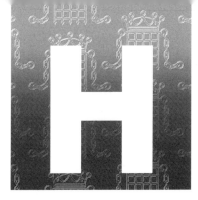

habeas corpus: a legal *writ* by which an individual can apply to be released from an unlawful detention. It is generally taken to refer to the principle that citizens should be free from arbitrary arrest and imprisonment. The right was first codified in UK *statute* in the *Habeas Corpus Act (1679)*.

Habeas Corpus Act (1679): a parliamentary *statute* under which the monarch could be forced to bring to trial or release those he had unlawfully detained.

Hague, William (1961–): Conservative MP for Richmond and one-time leader of the *Conservative Party* (1997–2001).

- Hague famously addressed the Conservative Party annual *party conference* in 1977.
- He succeeded *John Major* as the leader of the Conservative Party in the wake of the 1997 *general election* and resigned that post following the party's defeat in the 2001 general election.
- Hague was respected as an orator and proved particularly effective at the dispatch box during *Prime Minister's Questions*.
- He initiated a programme of internal reform within the party, which included a new system for electing party leaders and greater consultation within the party over policy. See *Fresh Future*.

Hailsham, Lord: see *elective dictatorship*

Hamilton, Neil (1949–): one of the MPs at the centre of the *cash for questions* scandal.

Hamilton-Gordon, George (Earl of Aberdeen): *prime minister* (Tory), 1852–55.

H'Angus the Monkey: see *Drummond, Stuart (1973–)*

Hankey, Maurice (1877–1963): appointed Secretary to the *war cabinet* when *David Lloyd George* replaced *Herbert Asquith* as prime minister in 1916. Hankey is credited with establishing the foundations of the modern cabinet system. Hankey's reputation for efficiency and organisation meant that he was retained as the first true *cabinet secretary* when full *cabinet* was restored in 1919.

> **TIP:** Hankey was responsible for a number of key developments in the structure and organisation of the cabinet system: the office of cabinet secretary was created alongside a new cabinet secretariat; a system of *cabinet committees* was established; and formal minutes of cabinet meetings were kept and circulated, allowing a record to be kept of all that was discussed and – more importantly perhaps – agreed in cabinet.

Hansard: the written record of all that is done in Parliament. Published daily and weekly in written form and also available online.

- Hansard is produced verbatim, i.e. word-for-word.
- It records all that is said during parliamentary *debates* and within parliamentary committees.
- *Written questions* tabled by MPs are also published in full along with the answers provided by the *minister* in question.

head of government: the leading figure in the *executive* branch, i.e. the chief executive.

Example

In the UK the *prime minister* performs the role of head of government with the monarch retaining the role of *head of state*. In the USA, the president takes on both roles.

> **TIP:** The role of head of government or chief executive should not be confused with that of head of state.

head of state: a national figurehead, generally less involved in the day-to-day running of the country than the head of government. In the UK, the *monarch* performs the role of head of state. The UK operates under a *constitutional monarchy*, which means that the head of state plays a largely ceremonial function; what *Walter Bagehot* called a 'dignified' as opposed to an 'efficient' role.

> **TIP:** In many countries the role of head of state is performed by an elected president, with a prime minister acting as head of government. In the USA the roles of head of government and head of state essentially come together in the office of president, though some see the speaker of the House of Representatives as a kind of prime minister.

Heath, Edward: *prime minister* (Conservative), 1970–74.

hegemonic theory: see *media theory*

Her Majesty's Government: see *government*

Her Majesty's Opposition: see *opposition*

hereditary peer: historically, a member of the *House of Lords* who sat in the chamber by virtue of a title that had been passed down the family through the male line.

- The *House of Lords Act (1999)* looked to remove the right of all hereditary peers (around 750 in total) to sit and vote in the chamber. However, under the *Cranborne Compromise*, 92 were allowed to remain in a transitional chamber, though their titles would not pass on down the family line at the time of their death.
- The majority of hereditary peers took the Conservative whip, meaning that the party had an inbuilt majority in the second chamber. See *backwoodsmen*.

> **TIP:** It is only the right to sit and vote in the House of Lords that has been removed; the hereditary titles themselves have not been removed.

Heseltine, Michael (1933–): a former Conservative cabinet minister of the 1980s and 1990s best known for precipitating the resignation of *Margaret Thatcher* as party leader and prime minister.

- Heseltine had resigned from cabinet in 1985 over the *Westland Affair*.
- He challenged Thatcher for the leadership of the Conservative Party in 1990.
- Thatcher beat Heseltine in the first ballot but not by the margin then required under party rules. She stood down ahead of the second ballot, leaving the way clear for *John Major* to enter the race and defeat Heseltine.

Heywood, Jeremy (1962–): a key advisor to *Gordon Brown*, who held the *civil service* post of *permanent secretary* at Number 10, a position second only to the Cabinet Secretary in terms of civil service rank. Heywood had previously headed the Policy Directorate under *Tony Blair*. See *Policy Unit*.

Home Office: the government *department* traditionally charged with maintaining law and order, managing the justice system and regulating immigration and border control. A restructuring of government departments in May 2007 saw the Home Office's responsibilities for criminal law and sentencing – including prisons and probation – transferred to the new Ministry of Justice.

home rule: see *devolution*

home secretary: the cabinet rank minister who heads the *Home Office*, often seen as one of the 'big three' *cabinet* posts aside from the office of *prime minister*. The others are foreign secretary and *chancellor of the exchequer*.

homogeneity: see *political culture*

honours: the titles and medals bestowed for service, achievement and deeds of bravery and awarded twice-yearly by the *monarch*. Honours can also be used to refer to the more *ad hoc* elevation of individuals to the *House of Lords*. See also *cash for peerages*.

House of Commons: a fully elected chamber of parliament, the UK's *bicameral legislature*, located in the *Palace of Westminster*.

- The UK operates under a system of asymmetrical bicameralism, where the Commons has significantly more power than the *House of Lords*. See *Parliament Act (1911)*, *Parliament Act (1949)* and *Salisbury Doctrine*.
- The Commons has three core functions: to represent, whereby *MPs* make the views of their *constituents* heard; to legislate; and to *scrutinise* the *executive*.

House of Lords: the unelected second chamber of Parliament, the UK's *bicameral legislature*.

- Evenly split between hereditary peers and life peers prior to the House of Lords Act (1999), it now consists largely of *life peers*, together with the 92 remaining *hereditary peers* and the 26 bishops of the Church of England (Lords Spiritual).
- The House of Lords shares its core functions with the *House of Commons* (see above), though its unelected status means that it performs its representative function in a more general sense.
- The Lords' limited power means that it is more of a *revising chamber* than a co-equal legislative chamber with the Commons. See *Parliament Act (1911)*, *Parliament Act (1949)* and *Salisbury Doctrine*.

House of Lords Act (1999): see *Lords Reform (1997–2010)* and *House of Lords*.

Howard, Michael (1941–): former Conservative cabinet minister in the 1980s and 1990s. Leader of the Conservative Party (2003–05).

- Howard took over as leader of the party following the forced resignation of *Iain Duncan Smith*.
- Howard led the party into the 2005 general election and resigned subsequently, ultimately being replaced in the post by David Cameron.
- Closely associated with the politics of *Margaret Thatcher*, his selection as leader was controversial in some quarters.
- His former Conservative cabinet colleague Ann Widdecombe famously said that there was 'something of the night about him'.

Howe, Geoffrey (1926–): a long-serving Conservative *cabinet minister* whose acrimonious resignation on 1 November 1990 was said to have marked the beginning of the end for *Margaret Thatcher*'s premiership. Though the leading Labour minister Dennis Healey had once described being attacked by Howe as 'like being savaged by a dead sheep', Howe's Commons resignation speech of 13 November 1990 was widely regarded as one of the finest in modern memory.

Human Embryology and Fertilisation Act (1990): a piece of *statute law* that served to license and regulate fertility treatment as well as permit pioneering experimental work with human embryos. The Act also lowered the upper time limit for abortions from 28 to 24 weeks, while permitting unlimited abortion in the case of serious foetal abnormalities. See also *Abortion Act (1967)*.

human nature: the concept of an innate set of human characteristics and forms of behaviour that are common to all normal people.

> **TIP:** Some theorists take a very positive view of human nature, arguing that individuals can live in harmony without the structures, laws and sanctions imposed by the *state*. Those who take a more pessimistic view of human nature believe that all people are flawed and that the state therefore plays a vital role in ensuring a harmonious existence for all.

human rights: see *rights*

Human Rights Act (1998): a parliamentary statue that incorporated the *European Convention on Human Rights (1950)* into UK law.

- Although the Act was passed in 1998 it did not come into effect until October 2000.
- It meant that UK citizens could exercise their rights under the ECHR through UK courts rather than having to go directly to the *European Court of Human Rights* in Strasbourg.
- It was criticism of the way in which the Act had been applied that led to calls for a proper English or British *Bill of Rights*.

Example

In the case of *A and others v. Secretary of State for the Home Department (2004),* the *House of Lords* ruled that the indefinite detention of terrorists without trial at Belmarsh Prison, as provided for under the *Anti-terrorism, Crime and Security Act (2001)*, was incompatible with Section 4 of the *Human Rights Act (1988)*.

> **TIP:** It is important to remember that the Act, like the ECHR, is not part of *European law*. As a result, UK courts can issue only a *declaration of incompatibility* where the government appears to have violated rights protected under the Act; they cannot strike down Acts of Parliament or force the government to back down.

hung parliament: where no single party commands an *overall majority* of seats in the *House of Commons* or a local *council*.

- A hung parliament can result directly from a *general election* or from a series of *by-election* defeats where the *government*'s majority was small at the outset.
- A hung parliament results in one of three outcomes: the formation of a *coalition government*; the decision to press ahead with a *minority government*; or a further election to give voters the chance to resolve the impasse.
- Hung parliaments are rare in the UK, the last example being the hung parliament that resulted from the general election in February 1974. Such outcomes are more likely under *proportional electoral systems* or *hybrid electoral systems*.

Example

Elections to the *Scottish Parliament* under the *additional member system (AMS)* in 1999 and 2004 resulted in a hung parliament. In both cases the Labour Party opted to go into coalition with the Liberal Democrats. The 2007 elections in Scotland also resulted in a hung parliament, though on that occasion the largest party (the SNP) ultimately established a minority government.

Hunter, Anji (1955–): former prime minister *Tony Blair*'s Director of Government Relations and a key figure in his inner circle. Hunter was, according to Blair's biographer Anthony Seldon, the 'fixer' within Blair's core team of loyal advisors. See *sofa government*.

hustings: an event where candidates stand on a platform and address *voters* ahead of an *election*. The term originally referred to the wooden platform upon which *candidates* in the nineteenth century would stand to address the crowds. More recently, Conservative leader *David Cameron* trialled public hustings as one way of enhancing broadening *participation* in the selection of parliamentary candidates.

Hutton Inquiry (2003–04): a report into the death of the government advisor David Kelly. See *weapons of mass destruction*.

hybrid electoral system: a mixed voting system that commonly awards a proportion of the seats available under a *majoritarian electoral system* while dividing the remainder on a *proportional* basis or as a *top-up*. See *additional member system (AMS)* and *AV plus*.

hyper-pluralism: see *pluralism*

Ian Greer Associates: the political consultancy firm involved in the **cash for questions** scandal. See also **lobbying**.

Ibbs Report (1988): a government report recommending structural changes to the **civil service**. The document, officially called *Improving Management in Government: The Next Steps*, was published by the then head of the Downing Street Efficiency Unit, Sir Robert Ibbs. It led to the **Next Steps Programme**. See also **agencification**.

identification (party): a long-term attachment to a particular **political party**. See also **partisan alignment**.

TIP: *Partisan dealignment* has resulted in increased *electoral volatility*. The number of strong party identifiers has fallen as the number of independent or *floating voters* has risen. See also *short-term factors*.

identifier: one who identifies with (i.e. has a particular attachment to) a particular **political party**.

ideological outsiders: an **outsider group** that does not seek a close relationship with **government**. See also **insider/outsider typology**.
- Groups such as Amnesty International must avoid becoming too close to any single national government if they are to preserve their reputation for **impartiality**.
- Other pressure groups, such as those campaigning against **globalisation**, may well see government as part of the problem as opposed to part of the solution.

ideological party: a party founded on ideological lines.
- The former Communist Party of Great Britain and the Socialist Workers Party could both be seen as ideological parties, as could the **Green Party**.
- The **Labour Party** was originally founded as a **socialist** party, though some argue that is has become a **catch-all party** since the mid-1990s. See **New Labour** and **Clause IV**.

ideological voting model: a model under which individuals support the party that best reflects their own ideological outlook.
- The model is based on the work of Heath et al. and their study *How Britain Votes* (1985).
- It is similar to the **issue voting model**, but it stresses the importance of the voter's underlying ideological outlook when assessing the merits and demerits of the various parties.
- The model was contradicted by polling data that showed that **Neil Kinnock**'s **Labour Party** was ahead of the **Conservatives** on most of the issues that voters said mattered to them in 1992, yet still lost the **general election**.

ideologue: an individual driven by a clear and coherent ideological outlook. *Margaret Thatcher*, her mentor Sir Keith Joseph and her acolyte John Redwood were said by some to be ideologues because of the dogmatic way in which they sought to advance the *New Right* agenda. Most modern politicians take a more pragmatic approach.

ideology: a coherent set of beliefs or values that guide one's actions. See also *ideological voting model*.

- Many mainstream UK *political parties* once subscribed to an ideology. The *Labour Party*, for example, was established on *socialist* lines.
- The way in which the main UK parties have moved towards the centre of the political spectrum in order to garner votes has led some to suggest that we have witnessed the end of ideology.

> **TIP:** Although the Labour Party was founded on socialist lines, it could be said to have moved away from this ideological position since the 1990s. See *New Labour* and *Clause IV*.

impartiality: a traditional principle of the UK *civil service* and a necessary characteristic of the judiciary's application of the *rule of law*.

impeachment: a legal process by which office holders are brought to trial with a view to removing them from post.

- In the UK the *House of Commons* holds the power of impeachment with the *House of Lords* conducting the subsequent trial.
- In 2006, General Sir Michael Rose called for the then prime minister, *Tony Blair*, to be impeached over his decision to go to war in Iraq.
- The impeachment process has not been used for over 200 years and is regarded as obsolete by many; not least because the Lord Chancellor, who is supposed to preside over the trial in the Lords, is no longer a member of that chamber.

imperialism: refers to the existence of, or the desire to establish, an empire. It is often used pejoratively in criticism of Western interference in less economically developed countries (LEDCs).

inalienable rights: see *natural rights*

incumbency: a measure of the success with which *incumbent* politicians secure re-election.

- High levels of incumbency are seen in both the UK *House of Commons* and the US Congress.
- Some see such high levels of incumbency as evidence of public support for what the sitting legislators have done. Others see the success of incumbents as a product of inequalities in candidate selection and the presence of large numbers of safe seats (see below).
- In the USA, high levels of incumbency are also associated with inequalities in campaign finance, with incumbents receiving around 75% of the monies provided by political action committees.

> **TIP:** In the UK, incumbency is in part a feature of the proportion of parliamentary constituencies that can be considered safe (see *safe seats*). In the 2005 general election, only 62 seats (9.6% of those contested) changed hands, compared to the result in 2001.

incumbent: the current holder of the office in question. See *incumbency*.

indefinite detention: the right to imprison terrorist suspects indefinitely without trial.
- The power was granted under the *Anti-terrorism, Crime and Security Act (2004)*.
- Suspects were famously held at Belmarsh Prison in London.
- It was ruled incompatible with the *Human Rights Act (1998)* in the case *A and others v. Secretary of State for the Home Department (2004)*. See also *control order*.

independent: an *MP*, *councillor* or other elected official who does not stand for or represent a *political party*; it also applies to *candidates* seeking election to an elected office.
- Independent *peers* are referred to as *crossbenchers*.
- Independent candidates often struggle because they lack the funding and campaign machinery available to those candidates representing the main UK *political parties*. Consequently, a vote for an independent candidate is often regarded as a *wasted vote*.
- The *speaker* of the *House of Commons* becomes an independent MP upon taking up that position.

Example

The former BBC correspondent *Martin Bell* was famously elected as MP for Tatton when standing as an independent anti-corruption candidate in 1997. Bell defeated the *incumbent* Conservative MP, *Neil Hamilton* (see *cash for questions*). *Richard Taylor*, a former hospital doctor, was first elected to represent the parliamentary constituency of Wyre Forest at the 2001 general election. He had stood under the banner 'Independent Kidderminster Hospital and Health Concern' in protest at the planned closure of a local hospital.

---

independent voter: see *floating voter*

individual ministerial responsibility: a *convention* under which *ministers* are held *accountable* to Parliament for their own personal behaviour (*personal responsibility*) and the conduct of their *departments* (*role responsibility*), requiring them to resign in the event that they fail in either sphere.

> **TIP:** Some argue that the process of *agencification* ushered in with the *Next Steps Programme* has undermined the role responsibility aspect of this convention as it is difficult to hold ministers responsible for decisions that have been taken by a quasi-autonomous *executive agency*.

inequality: see *equality of opportunity* and *equality of outcome*

inflation: a measure of the rate at which prices are rising over a given period of time and expressed as a percentage. See also *Bank of England*.

Information Commissioner: see *Freedom of Information Act (2000)*

initiative: a citizen-initiated *referendum*.
- Initiatives offer a form of *direct democracy*. They are used in many individual US states as well as a number of other countries including Switzerland, New Zealand and Italy.
- The initiative process normally starts with a *petition* of registered *voters*. In order to qualify for a public vote, such a petition would normally have to carry a predetermined number of valid signatures.

inner cabinet: a grouping of senior *cabinet* members working with the *prime minister* on an informal basis outside the regular meetings of the full cabinet. It is said to facilitate more efficient decision making than a full cabinet meeting of around 23 members. Critics argue that this less formal style of decision making undermines *cabinet government*.

insider group: a *pressure group* that consults on a regular basis with the government *department* that has oversight of the issue or interest with which the group is concerned. See also *outsider groups* and *insider/outsider typology*.
- Forms part of the insider/outsider pressure group typology developed by *Wyn Grant*.
- Insider groups can be further subdivided into *core insiders* (e.g. the NFU), *specialist insiders* (e.g. the Canine Defence League) and *peripheral insiders* (e.g. Greenpeace).
- Grant also highlights the presence of so-called 'prisoner groups'.

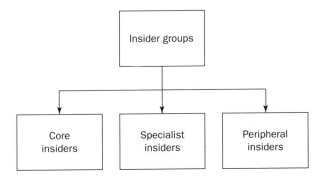

Classifying insider groups

insider/outsider typology: a means of classifying *pressure groups* according to the status afforded to them by the *government* of the day.
- The typology was developed by the political scientist *Wyn Grant*.
- Groups that work closely with government *departments* are referred to as *insider groups*. Those who are not consulted on a regular basis are known as *outsider groups*.

Institute for Public Policy Research: a left-of-centre *think-tank* established in 1988, said to have been a key influence on *New Labour* in the field of social policy.

Institute of Economic Affairs: a right-of-centre *think-tank* established in 1955 that favours a free-market *neo-liberal* approach to economic policy. See also *Margaret Thatcher* and *Thatcherism*.

instrumental voting: where voters make rational decisions based upon the relative merits of each party's positions, policies, candidate and leader.
- It is the key characteristic of the *rational choice model* of *voting behaviour*.
- It is often contrasted with *expressive voting*, which sees the casting of a ballot as an emotional, as opposed to an entirely rational, act.

integration: a unifying process within the *EU* that has seen member states cooperating more closely in areas of social and foreign policy as well as in the economic policies on which the *European Economic Community (EEC)* was originally founded.
- Integration has seen the strengthening of the EU and its institutions.
- The *Treaty of Maastricht* represented a key step in European integration because it developed the idea of European citizenship and established a roadmap towards a single European currency (the *euro*). See also *Amsterdam, Treaty of (1997)*, *Nice, Treaty of (2001)* and *Lisbon, Treaty of (2007)*.
- *Eurosceptics*, including many of those on the right of the *Conservative Party*, oppose further integration because they see it as a threat to *parliamentary sovereignty*. Integration is also said to undermine the UK government's ability to act in the national interest.

interest group: see *pressure group* and *sectional group*

intergovernmentalism: a mode of cooperation within the *EU* that sees member states free to act according to their own national interests. It is said to characterise the operation of the *Council of Ministers*. Contrast with supranationalism.

internal market: a mechanism by which the supposed benefits of a *free market* have been established within a single organisation. Designed to promote greater efficiency, it is achieved by dividing the various departments within an organisation into semi-independent units and then creating a series of business–client relationships between them.

internal party democracy: the extent to which *power* is divided within a *political party*; specifically the power afforded to individual *party members*.

Example

The three criteria commonly used to assess the extent to which a given party is internally democratic are: the way in which it formulates policy; the way in which it selects candidates for parliamentary elections; and the mechanisms by which the party leader is (s)elected and can be removed.

TIP: Though most MPs are also individual members of political parties in the Commons, it is important not to confuse talk of internal party democracy with an assessment of the power of backbench MPs.

internal pressure group democracy: the extent to which *pressure groups* that seek to exert influence over political institutions that are democratically **accountable** should themselves be organised along democratic lines.

- High levels of internal pressure group democracy would see rank-and-file members involved in electing group leaders as well as having a role in determining the group's objectives.
- Most UK pressure groups are not internally democratic.

Example

Greenpeace is often criticised for its lack of internal democracy. According to *Wyn Grant* (2002), Greenpeace is a hierarchical organisation that allows little democratic control over the direction of campaigns:

- it has a strictly bureaucratic, if not authoritarian, internal structure
- a small group of people has control over the organisation, both at the international level and within national chapters, e.g. it has 'supporters' as opposed to 'members'
- local action groups, which exist in some countries, are totally dependent on the central body
- rank-and-file supporters are excluded from all decisions

International Monetary Fund (IMF): an international organisation that has oversight of the global financial system.

- Established in 1944.
- Provides guidance and financial assistance to its members.
- Offers loans to less economically developed countries (LEDCs).
- Criticised as a result of the conditions routinely attached to the aid it offers such LEDCs.

internationalism: an approach that advocates a greater degree of cooperation between individual *states*.

IRA: see *Irish Republican Army (IRA)*

Iraq War (2003): a military operation designed to overthrow the then leader of Iraq, Saddam Hussein, thereby removing the threat posed by the *weapons of mass destruction* he was said to have stockpiled. The decision of the then prime minister, *Tony Blair*, to go to war in Iraq led to the immediate resignation of the Leader of the Commons, *Robin Cook*.

Irish Republican Army (IRA): a self-styled republican 'army of liberation' that waged a war against British forces deployed in Northern Ireland.

- The IRA hoped to force the British Army out of the province and unite the island of Ireland under a single government.
- *Sinn Fein* was traditionally said to be the 'political wing' of the IRA. Leading Sinn Fein members, including Martin McGuinness, were self-confessed former members of the IRA.
- The IRA's decision to give up the armed struggle and decommission its arms resulted in Sinn Fein becoming involved in mainstream politics in the province.

See *Good Friday Agreement (1998)*.

issue network: see *policy network*

issue of writs: a written command issued in the name of the *monarch*. Writs are commonly issued when calling a *general election* or *by-election*.

issue voting model: a theoretical model under which voters make their choices on the basis of a rational assessment of the issues of the day and the way in which parties seek address them.

- The model favours the importance of *short-term factors* over the influence of *primacy* factors such as *social class*. See also *class dealignment* and *partisan dealignment*.
- It is a key element of the *rational choice model*.

> **TIP:** As in the case of the *ideological voting model*, the issue voting model is undermined by the fact that voters do not always give their support to the party they associate with those policies they claim to favour; a mismatch particularly apparent in the 1992 *general election*.

A–Z Online

Log on to A–Z Online to search the database of terms, print revision lists and much more. Go to **www.philipallan.co.uk/a-zonline** to get started.

Jenkins Commission: the body established by **New Labour** in 1997 to consider proposals for a change in the **electoral system** used in elections to **Westminster**.
- The commission was chaired by Lord (Roy) Jenkins of Hillhead, a **Liberal Democrat** peer and supporter of **proportional representation** who had been a Labour **minister** in the 1970s before leaving in 1980 to form the **Social Democratic Party (SDP)**. See **Gang of Four**.
- The commission assessed alternative systems against their ability to deliver proportionality, stable government, better **voter choice**, and a good MP–constituent link.
- It led to the publication of the **Jenkins Report (1998)**.

Jenkins Report (1998): the report of the **Jenkins Commission** which recommended the introduction of **AV plus** (also called AV top-up) for use in elections to **Westminster**.

Jenkins, Roy (1920–2003): former Labour **cabinet minister** of the 1960s and 1970s, president of the **European Commission** (1977–81) and member of the **Gang of Four** who established the **Social Democratic Party (SDP)** in 1981. See also **Jenkins Commission** and **Jenkins Report (1998)**.

Jenkinson, Robert Banks (Earl of Liverpool): *prime minister* (Tory), 1812–27.

Johnson, Boris (1964–): one-time editor of the *Spectator* and Conservative MP for Henley (2001–08), elected **Mayor of London** in 2008.

joined-up government: the view that **government** should work in a holistic way rather than become bogged down as a result of interdepartmental rivalries.
- A more holistic approach offered the prospect of better policy as well as efficiency savings – because departments would endeavour to make their policies fit into the overall government programme as opposed to operating on a more parochial basis.
- It was championed by **New Labour** ahead of the 1997 **general election**.

Joint Cabinet Committee on Constitutional Reform: a **cabinet committee** on **constitutional reform** attended by some Liberal Democrat MPs as well as those of the governing Labour Party.
- The committee was one of the main fruits of the more cooperative approach taken by the then LibDem leader **Paddy Ashdown** towards the Labour Party in the run-up to – and the immediate aftermath of – the 1997 **general election**.
- The Liberal Democrats withdrew from these arrangements in September 2001.
See also **Constitutional Council**.

judge: an official who presides over a court of law, either alone or as part of a panel. See also **judiciary** and **senior judiciary**.

judge-made law: see **common law**

judicial activism: where *judges* provoke intense public interest or controversy by using their powers of *judicial review* to the fullest extent. The term is commonly associated with the US Supreme Court of Earl Warren (1953–69) and is more commonly used in the UK as a result of the expansion in *European law* and also the passage of the *Human Rights Act (1998)*.

Judicial Appointments Commission: a 15-member, non-departmental public body (NDPB) that selects judges in England and Wales and was established in 2006 under the authority of the *Constitutional Reform Act (2005)*.

- In the past, most senior judicial appointments were made as a result of a practice referred to as *secret soundings*.
- The involvement of the *Lord Chancellor* and the *prime minister* in this process raised concerns regarding the *separation of powers*.
- The Lord Chancellor still formally appoints judges once the commission has selected them, though even this power would be taken away from the Lord Chancellor under the *Constitutional Renewal Bill (2008)*.
- Members of the UK *Supreme Court* are appointed under a different system.

judicial independence: the ability of the *judiciary* to dispense justice without political control or interference. Judicial independence is an essential feature of *liberal democracies*. See also *separation of powers*, *judicial neutrality* and *Judicial Appointments Commission*.

Example

The independence of the UK judiciary is said to be protected by five interlocking features:

- judges' *security of tenure*
- guaranteed salaries, provided for under the *Consolidated Fund*
- the notion of *contempt of court*
- an increasingly independent appointments system
- the training and experience of senior judges, i.e. the pride they have in their role

judicial neutrality: the ability of judges to dispense justice fairly and consistently irrespective of any personal or political bias they may have. It is an essential requirement of the *rule of law*. See also *judicial review*.

judicial reform: see *Constitutional Reform Act (2005)* and *Supreme Court*

judicial restraint: where senior *judges* avoid inserting themselves into areas of political controversy, preferring instead to follow established *precedent*; a legal principle referred to as *stare decisis*, from the Latin. Contrast with *judicial activism*.

judicial review: a process by which *judges* review the actions of public officials or public bodies in order to determine whether or not they have acted in a manner that is lawful.

- The doctrine of *parliamentary sovereignty* and supremacy of *statute law* meant that judicial review in the UK was generally less significant than in the USA, where the US Supreme Court can strike down pieces of regular *legislation* where they are judged to have violated the provisions of the US *constitution*.
- In the UK, judicial review traditionally involved determining whether a public official had operated within the law as opposed to questioning the basis of the law itself. See *ultra vires*.

- The passing of the **Human Rights Act (1998)** (see **declaration of incompatibility**) and the power given to UK courts in respect of EU legislation (see **Factortame case**) has seen a change in the nature and scope of judicial review in the UK.

> **Example**
>
> In the case of **A and others v. Secretary of State for the Home Department (2004)**, the **House of Lords** ruled that the indefinite detention of terrorists without trial at Belmarsh Prison, as provided for under the **Anti-terrorism, Crime and Security Act (2004)**, was incompatible with Section 4 of the Human Rights Act (1998).

judiciary: a collective term referring to those institutions concerned with administering **justice**, interpreting the law and adjudicating in the case of disputes arising therefrom.
- The main element of the UK judiciary, the system of courts, is organised in a hierarchical fashion.
- **Magistrates' courts** sit at the bottom of the pyramid, with senior courts such as the High Court and the **Court of Appeal** above, and the UK **Supreme Court** at the apex. Prior to the opening of the UK Supreme Court in October 2009, the judicial committee of the **House of Lords** acted as the highest court of appeal.

See also **criminal law** and **civil law**.

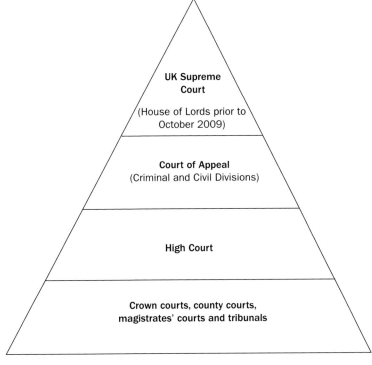

UK Supreme Court

(House of Lords prior to October 2009)

Court of Appeal
(Criminal and Civil Divisions)

High Court

Crown courts, county courts, magistrates' courts and tribunals

Hierarchy of the courts in the UK

junior minister: a departmental ministerial post immediately below *cabinet* rank.

- There are two ranks of junior minister: *ministers of state* and *parliamentary under-secretaries*.
- The number and responsibilities of junior ministers have increased since the 1960s.

Example

In July 2009, the *Home Office* was headed by Alan Johnson MP, a cabinet-rank minister. There were also five junior ministers working in the department: two ministers of state (David Hanson MP and Phil Woolas MP); and three parliamentary under-secretaries (Alan Campbell MP, Meg Hillier MP and Lord West of Spithead).

jury: a panel of *citizens*, normally 12 in England and Wales, selected to hear evidence presented and to deliver a verdict in most criminal court cases. The vast majority of cases under *civil law* and less serious cases under *criminal law* are heard without a jury. See also *magistrates' courts* and *Diplock courts*.

TIP: Though long established as a key feature of the *rule of law* in the UK, the right to trial by jury has proved controversial: first, because of the financial costs incurred; second, because of the complexity of some serious fraud cases; and third, due to the risk of jury intimidation.

justice: a legal concept based on the principles of fairness and equity, applying to all that is right and proper. See also *natural justice*.

Aiming for a grade A*?

Don't forget to log on to **www.philipallan.co.uk/a-zonline** for advice.

Kennedy, Charles (1959–): the Liberal Democrat MP for Ross, Skye and Lochaber from 2005. Also the MP representing that constituency in its previous incarnations between 1983 and 2005: Ross, Cromarty and Skye (1983–97); and Ross, Skye and Inverness West (1997–2005).

- Kennedy was one-time leader of the **Liberal Democratic Party** (1999–2006), his tenure ended in resignation following allegations that he had a drink problem; a claim he had publicly denied.
- He is credited with strengthening the party's position in the 2001 and 2005 **general elections**, having taken over from **Paddy Ashdown**.

Keynes, John Maynard (1883–1946): an economist who championed the benefits of limited state intervention as a means of providing a stimulus at the more difficult points in the economic cycle.

- Keynes's ideas are commonly referred to as Keynesianism or Keynesian economics; an approach often summed up in the phrase 'mixed economy'.
- The rise of **neo-liberalism** in the 1970s marked a downturn in support for Keynesianism, though the global economic crisis in 2008–09 saw renewed calls for the kind of state intervention Keynes favoured.

Keynesianism: see **Keynes, John Maynard (1883–1946)**

King, Oona: Labour MP for Bethnal Green and Bow (1997–2005), defeated by **George Galloway** in the 2005 **general election**.

Kinnock, Neil (1942–): former leader of the **Labour Party** (1983–92), MP for Bedwellty (1970–83) and later Islwyn (1983–95). He served as a UK-appointed European **commissioner** between 1994 and 2004.

- Originally on the **left wing** of the party, Kinnock ultimately moved to the centre. He was an early moderniser, starting the process of internal party reform that was completed by his successors **John Smith** and **Tony Blair**.
- Kinnock took on and defeated some of the more hardline left-wing elements within the party (see **Militant Tendency**).
- He stood down as party leader following the party's defeat in the 1992 general election.

kitchen cabinet: where **prime ministers** choose to hold meetings with smaller groups of ministers outside the formal weekly **cabinet** meetings. These may also involve individuals who are not members of the cabinet proper, e.g. meetings with **special advisors**. See also **bilateral meetings**, **presidential prime minister**.

Example

Some see Tony Blair's reliance on an inner circle of individuals such as *Peter Mandelson*, *Alastair Campbell*, *Jonathan Powell*, and *Anji Hunter* as constituting a kitchen cabinet, through most of these individuals were not in fact cabinet ministers.

TIP: The phrase is often used pejoratively by those in the government and the media who regret the decline of cabinet government.

Kyoto Protocol (1997): an international agreement aimed at limiting the release of carbon dioxide and other greenhouse gases into the atmosphere.

- The protocol was agreed in Kyoto, Japan, in 1997 but came into force only in 2005.
- It is often referred to as the Kyoto Agreement or the Kyoto Treaty.
- Although the USA was the largest emitter of carbon dioxide at the time of the agreement, the protocol was not ratified by the US Senate and is therefore not considered binding by the US government.

Do you need revision help and advice?

Go to pages 180–196 for a range of revision appendices that include plenty of exam advice and tips.

Labour Party: a *political party* formed by the *trade unions* and various *socialist* societies at the start of the twentieth century.
- The party was established along socialist lines to represent the *working class*.
- It first entered government with *Ramsay MacDonald*'s *minority administration* in 1924. It secured its first *overall majority* in the 1945 general election under the leadership of *Clement Attlee*. See also *New Labour*.

Labour Reform Group: established in 1996, a party committee of over 100 Labour *backbenchers* that lobbies the party's leadership.

Lamb, William (Viscount Melbourne): *prime minister* (Whig), 1834 and 1835–41.

laissez-faire economics: a form of *free market* economics favouring minimal government intervention in the economy and the provision of public services. 'Laissez-faire' comes from the French for 'let it be'. See also *Thatcherism* and *neo-liberalism*.

lame duck: an *incumbent* politician who has lost *authority* as a result of his or her imminent departure from office. Traditionally referring to a US president who has been defeated in the November election yet remains in office until his or her successor is sworn into office the following January, it is now often applied to US presidents in the later stages of their second term in office who are constitutionally barred from seeking a third.

> **TIP:** The absence of *fixed terms* and *term-limits* in the UK means that the term is used less frequently. However, Tony Blair's decision to pre-announce that he would not be leading New Labour into a fourth consecutive general election led to his being referred to as a lame duck in 2006 and 2007.

landslide effect: the tendency for *majoritarian electoral systems* such as *first-past-the-post* to over-reward the party returned to government at a *general election*. It is also referred to as the 'winner's bonus'.

Example

Labour's *landslide victory* at the 1997 general election (where the party won 63.4% of the available seats in the House of Commons) was secured on the basis of just 43.2% of the national *popular vote*.

landslide victory: an overwhelming election victory for a particular candidate or a political party.

law: commonly referring to a piece of *legislation* (i.e. *statute law*), though it might also refer to *common law*.

Law, Andrew Bonar: *prime minister* (Conservative), 1922–23.

Law Lords: the most senior judges in the UK. They sat as *life peers* (Lords of Appeal in Ordinary) in the *House of Lords* prior to the opening of the UK *Supreme Court* in October 2009. Those appointed to sit on the Supreme Court are no longer elevated to the Lords. See also *Constitutional Reform Act (2005)*.

Law, Peter (1948–2006): an *independent* MP elected to represent the Welsh constituency of Blaenau Gwent at the 2005 general election.

- Law had been a Labour member of the *Welsh Assembly* but was prevented from being selected as the official Labour parliamentary candidate for Blaenau Gwent following the imposition of an *women-only shortlist* in the constituency.
- Law stood as an *independent* in protest at that decision and won with a 58.2% share of the vote.

leader of the House: the *cabinet* members, one for the *House of Commons* and one for the *House of Lords*, charged with the task of organising business in their chamber and managing the government's legislative programme.

Example

Gordon Brown appointed Harriet Harman as Leader of the Commons and Lady Ashton as Leader of the Lords in his first cabinet in June 2007.

leader of the opposition: the leader of the *political party* that controls the second highest number of seats in the *House of Commons*. The leader of the opposition plays a key role at *Prime Minister's Questions* and is paid an additional salary by taxpayers, alongside that which he or she earns as an MP. In 2009, this amounted to an additional £73,617 on top of the MPs' salary of £64,766.

left: see *left wing*

left wing: the end of the political spectrum closely associated with *socialism* and the principle of wealth redistribution. Those on the left tend to see the needs of society as being more important than those of the individual. Contrast with *right wing*.

legislation: commonly referring to one or more *Acts of Parliament*. See also *statute law*.

> **TIP:** It is also possible to create legislation by the means of an Order in Council.

legislative process: the stages by which a *bill* becomes an *Act of Parliament*. Most major bills begin their life in the *House of Commons*. They then pass through the *House of Lords* before receiving the *royal assent*.

Example

The legislative process in outline:

1 House of Commons: *first reading*; *second reading*; *committee stage*; *report stage*; and *third reading*
2 House of Lords: first reading; second reading; committee stage; report stage; and third reading
3 Royal assent

TIP: In the UK the legislative process is dominated by the *executive* as a result of its majority in the *Commons*. See *elective dictatorship*.

legislature: the government branch concerned with creating legislation. The UK's legislature, **Westminster**, is a **bicameral** body comprising the **House of Commons** and the **House of Lords**. See also **legislative process**.

TIP: Most national legislatures also perform a role in *representation* and *scrutiny* of the *executive*.

legitimacy: the legal right or **authority** to exercise **power**.

Example

A government claims legitimacy as a result of the **mandate** it secures at a general election.

legitimisation: a process effecting **legitimacy**. Legitimisation might be achieved by the holding of an **election** or **referendum**. See also **mandate**.

Example

The decision to establish a **Scottish Parliament** was legitimised through a referendum held in September 1997.

levy: see *political levy*

levy plus: a *Labour Party* rule under which those members of **affiliated** organisations that pay a fee in addition to the **political levy** can participate when their **Constituency Labour Party** votes to selects its parliamentary **candidate**. It was introduced in 1993 alongside **one member, one vote (OMOV)**.

Liaison Committee: a non-departmental **select committee** comprising the chairs of each of the departmental select committees.
- It oversees the work of select committees, e.g. in 2000 the committee produced *Shifting the Balance*, a report into the relationship between select committees and the **executive**.
- **Tony Blair** agreed to be questioned by the committee every six months, a practice that continued under prime minister **Gordon Brown**.

Example

In the February 2006 session the then prime minister, Tony Blair, was quizzed on issues as varied as the UK's presidencies of the G8 and the EU, the government's reform agenda as regards healthcare and schools, relations with Iran, and the likely fall-out from elections in Palestine.

liberal: see *liberalism*

liberal conservatism: see *New Tories* and *Red Toryism*

liberal democracy: a style of *democracy* incorporating free and fair *elections* with a belief in the importance of certain key *rights* and responsibilities.
- Liberal democracies generally feature a wide *franchise*.
- They guarantee the *freedom of speech* and allow the people to assemble and protest for the *redress of grievances*.

Liberal Democrats: a political party created in 1988 with the merger of the *Social Democratic Party (SDP)* and the *Liberal Party*.
- The *third party* in British politics, it is regarded as a centrist party, i.e. neither on the *left wing* nor the *right wing*.
- The party has consistently supported *constitutional reform* and *electoral reform*.

Liberal Party: the *third party* in British politics between the *general election* of 1923 and the party's merger with the *Social Democratic Party (SDP)* to form the *Liberal Democrats* in 1988.
- The Liberal Party had emerged from the Whig party in the nineteenth century.
- The last Liberal Party *majority government* was established by *Herbert Asquith* in 1908, though Liberal *David Lloyd George* later served in the post following the party's split in 1916.

liberalisation: the process of becoming more liberal. Traditionally seen as moving towards a less heavily regulated economy (see *free market, laissez-faire economics, classical liberalism* and *neo-liberalism*), it now more commonly refers to a process by which a greater emphasis is placed upon individual *rights* and responsibilities in social policy.

liberalism: a political *ideology* associated with notions of personal *liberty*, toleration and limited government. See *classical liberalism, progressive liberalism* and *neo-liberalism*.

libertarianism: an *ideology* that stresses the importance of focusing on the freedom and needs of the individual as opposed to those of the broader society.
- Libertarians believe that societies function most effectively for the benefit of all where individuals are free to pursue their own interests and therefore favour a small, unobtrusive state.
- Libertarianism shares some features in common with both *anarchism* and the *neo-liberal* strand of conservatism.

liberty: a synonym for freedom, though generally taken to refer to political freedom, i.e. freedom from an oppressive state.

Liberty: a pressure group, founded by lawyers, that campaigns to protect *civil liberties*.

Lib-Lab Pact: a working arrangement between the Labour government and the 13 Liberal MPs in the *House of Commons* that helped to maintain the Labour government in office between 1974 and 1979.

life peer: a member of the *House of Lords* appointed for the duration of his or her life. Contrast with *hereditary peer*.
- Life peers can be divided broadly into two types: those appointed under the *Life Peerages Act (1958)* and those appointed under the Appellate Jurisdiction Act (1876) as *Law Lords*, prior to the establishment of the UK *Supreme Court*.
- The *monarch* has traditionally appointed life peers on the advice of the *prime minister*. See also *patronage* and *cash for peerages*.
- An Appointments Commission scrutinises the list of proposed names before they are passed on for approval.

Life Peerages Act (1958): an *Act of Parliament* providing for the appointment of *life peers*. See also *hereditary peer*.
- Prior to the Act most members of the House were hereditary peers.
- The Act also saw women appointed to the chamber for the first time.
- Very few hereditary peers have been created since the Act came into force.

light green: see *ecologism*

Limehouse Declaration: the announcement of 25 January 1981 that launched the *Social Democratic Party (SDP)*. See also *Gang of Four*.

limited government: the principle that government should legislate only for what is absolutely necessary in order to provide for the common welfare of its *citizens*.
- This is a key characteristic of the system of government established under the US *constitution*.
- It is closely associated with the *classical liberalism* of the nineteenth century and those who championed *neo-liberalism* in the 1970s and 1980s. See also *New Right*.
- Compare with 'small government' and Margaret Thatcher's commitment to '*rolling back the frontiers of the state*'.

Lisbon, Treaty of (2007): an *EU* reform treaty aimed at breaking the deadlock that followed the rejection of the draft EU constitution.
- The original draft constitution (2004) was designed to bring together a number of other EU laws and treaties into a single *codified* document. It also aimed to address issues arising from EU enlargement and *integration*.
- The ratification of the 400-page constitution was put on hold following *referendum* defeats in France and the Netherlands in June 2005.
- The treaty that replaced it was agreed at a summit held under the German presidency of the EU in Lisbon in June 2007; hence it became known as the Lisbon Treaty.
- The UK bill ratifying the treaty received its *royal assent* on 20 June 2008.

Livingstone, Ken (1945–): former Labour leader of the *Greater London Council* (GLC), Labour MP and two-term *Mayor of London* (2000–08). Livingstone's left-wing agenda during his time as leader of the GLC led to his being dubbed 'Red Ken' in the *tabloid* press.

Lloyd George, David: *prime minister* (Liberal), 1916–22.

loans for peerages scandal: see *cash for peerages*

lobby (noun): the areas around the two parliamentary chambers within the *Palace of Westminster* where MPs congregate to discuss issues before and after debates. See also *lobby system* and *division*.

lobby (verb): to seek to influence the decision-making process. See *lobbying* and *lobbying firm*.

lobby correspondent: a journalist operating in the *lobby system*.

lobby fodder: referring to the view that MPs simply vote according to the instructions given to them by their party *whips*. MPs vote in the *Commons* by passing through a voting lobby. See *division*.

lobby group: a synonym for *pressure group*.

lobby system: collectively referring to the 150 or so *lobby correspondents* who are privy to regular briefings by government representatives. Critics of the lobby system argue that it allows the government to *spin* the news and it gets in the way of proper scrutiny by the *media* based upon investigative journalism. See also *Campbell, Alastair (1957–)*.

lobbying: the act of trying to persuade those with political *power* to use it in support of one's own cause or interest. Generally, it refers to attempts to influence the behaviour of government *ministers*, legislators or senior *civil servants*.

lobbying firm: a professional organisation that arranges and manages contact between the interested parties in a particular area of policy (often *pressure groups*) and those in a position to make policy in that area (i.e. *ministers*, *civil servants* and *MPs*).

- Lobbying firms commonly employ those who have experience in or around government (see *revolving-door syndrome*).
- The relationship between lobbying firms and MPs has been more closely regulated following the *Nolan Report (1995)*.

Example

The lobbying firm Ian Greer Associates was implicated in the **cash for questions** scandal.

lobbyist: an individual engaged in *lobbying* – normally on a professional (i.e. paid) basis – on behalf of another individual or group.

local council: an elected *local government* assembly. See also *borough council*, *district council*, *county council* and *unitary authority*.

local democracy: the scope and quality of *political participation* at the local level; participation by the people in government at a local level usually through *local elections*. The health of local democracy is often assessed in terms of the opportunities for participation offered at the local level or by measuring electoral *turnout*.

TIP: Some argue that local democracy could be further enhanced by the wider use of *referendums*.

Example: local democracy in Edinburgh

2005 Edinburgh City Council Referendum:

'Should the city council introduce a congestion charge for traffic entering the city centre?'

Yes: 24%

No: 76%

Turnout: 62%

local election: an election to a *local council*.
- Such elections may coincide with a *general election* though they also take place in the intervening years.
- *Turnout* is often far lower at those local elections that do not coincide with general elections. *Voting behaviour* at local elections is also characterised by higher levels of *protest voting*.

local government: a generic term used to describe the tier of government comprising elected *local councils* and their associated bureaucracies. Local government is responsible for delivering a range of public services including education, police and fire services, and refuse collection and disposal. See also *quangos*, *regional development agencies* and *regional assemblies*.

London Assembly: see *Greater London Assembly*

long-term factors: long-standing influences on *voting behaviour* that endure from election to election. Contrast with *short-term factors*.
- Such enduring influences on voting behaviour are said to contribute to greater electoral stability and less *volatility*.
- Long-term factors include *social class*, race, the *gender gap* and geographical region.
- Such factors were said to have declined in importance after the 1970s.

Lord Chancellor: a now largely ceremonial title first held by Thomas Wolsey and more recently taken by the *secretary of state* at the Ministry of Justice.
- The Lord Chancellor was once the senior judge in the land, taking a key role in senior judicial appointments.
- The Lord Chancellor also traditionally sat as speaker of the *House of Lords*. See also *Judicial Appointments Commission*.

> **TIP:** The post of Lord Chancellor was once said to illustrate the lack of a *separation of powers* in the UK system (see also *fusion of powers*). This was because the incumbent was a member of all three branches of government. The *Constitutional Reform Act (2005)* addressed this situation.

Lord Chief Justice: the most senior judge, who has traditionally headed both the Queen's Bench division of the High Court and the criminal division of the *Court of Appeal*. See also *Supreme Court*.

Lords: see *House of Lords*

lords of appeal in ordinary: see *Law Lords*

Lords Reform (1997–2010): referring to the programme of reform for the Upper Chamber promised in **New Labour**'s 1997 general election **manifesto**, and progress in delivering it.

- Prior to the passage of the **House of Lords Act (1999)**, the Chamber included 759 **hereditary peers** amongst its 1330 members.
- Labour's 1997 general election manifesto promised both to remove the rights of hereditary peers to sit and vote in the House of Lords and to move towards a more democratic and more representative second chamber.
- The **House of Lords Act (1999)** sought to deliver on the first of these promises, though under the **Weatherill Amendment**, 92 were allowed to stay on in a transitional House prior to further reform.
- Following the report of the **Wakeham Commission** (2000), Labour's 2001 White Paper proposed a second chamber consisting of 600 members, 20% of whom would be directly elected, the remainder being appointed under the auspices – though not control – of an Independent Appointments Commission.
- The Commons was ultimately presented with eight models, ranging from a fully elected chamber to its total abolition. On 4 February, the Commons rejected all eight proposals.
- In its 2005 general election manifesto, Labour promised that a 'predominantly elected' second chamber would replace the Lords. This pledge eventually found form in the 2007 **White Paper** on Lords Reform (see below).
- Reform again stalled in the wake of votes in the Commons and the Lords in March 2007.

Example: White Paper on Lords Reform (2007)
- The House of Commons to retain its primacy over legislation.
- An upper chamber split 50:50 between elected and appointed members serving a single, fixed term, far longer than that enjoyed by those in the Commons (perhaps 12 years).
- Elections to be held under a partially open regional list system and staggered in three cohorts.
- Appointments to be made by a new, independent Statutory Appointments Commission, with 20% of those chosen being non-political appointees.
- A chamber where no single party would be allowed to enjoy an overall majority.

Lords Spiritual: the 26 senior clergy in the Church of England who hold the right to sit in the **House of Lords** during their tenure. They include the archbishops of Canterbury and York and the 24 most senior bishops.

See also **Lords Temporal**.

Lords Temporal: those members of the **House of Lords** who are not **Lords Spiritual**.

loyalist: one who supports the idea of Northern Ireland remaining part of the UK.

Maastricht, Treaty of (1992): the treaty that transformed the *European Community* into the *European Union (EU)*.

- The treaty was seen as a key step in the process of European *integration*.
- It put in place plans for a single currency (see *European Economic and Monetary Union (EMU)*).
- It enhanced the role of the *European Parliament* and extended the use of *qualified majority voting* in the *Council of Ministers*.
- It introduced the notion of European citizenship.

MacDonald, James Ramsay: *prime minister* (Labour), 1924 and 1929–35.

Macmillan, Harold: *prime minister* (Conservative), 1957–63.

magistrates' courts: the lowest tier in the UK courts system; responsible for hearing most minor cases. Magistrates' courts sit without a jury. A panel of three magistrates rules in such cases.

> **TIP:** Although magistrates' courts try only the most minor cases, all defendants are brought before magistrates in order to be formally indicted for trial elsewhere.

Magna Carta (1215): an agreement between King John and his barons under which he agreed to rule according to the *common law*. Under Magna Carta (from the Latin meaning 'Great Charter'), John agreed that he would not arbitrarily impose taxation or imprisonment. Magna Carta is seen as one of the earliest written sources of the UK's *uncodified constitution*.

Major, John (1943–): *prime minister* (Conservative), 1990–97.

- The Conservative MP for Huntingdonshire (1979–83) and Huntingdon (1983–2001), he was leader of the *Conservative Party* (1990–97).
- Major enjoyed rapid promotion under *Margaret Thatcher* (see example overleaf).
- Seen as Thatcher's natural successor, Major in fact adopted a more consultative, collegiate style. See *cabinet government*.
- He led his party to victory in the 1992 general election but saw his popularity fall following *Black Wednesday*.
- Faced opposition from within his own party over the *Treaty of Maastricht*, he subsequently saw off a leadership challenge from *Eurosceptic* John Redwood in 1995.
- He resigned the leadership of the Conservative Party following defeat in the 1997 general election.

Example: John Major's 10 steps to Number 10

1979	Became an MP
1981	Parliamentary private secretary, serving in the Home Office
1983	Assistant whip
1984	Treasury whip
1985	Under-secretary of state for social security
1986	Minister of state for social security
1987	Chief secretary to the Treasury
1989 (July)	Foreign secretary
1989 (October)	Chancellor of the exchequer
1990 (November)	Prime minister

majoritarian democracy: a system under which decision-making power is held collectively by the citizens and all decisions taken must have majority backing. It is generally taken as a synonym for *direct democracy*. Contrast with the form of indirect or *representative democracy* practised in the UK.

majoritarian electoral system: an *electoral system* under which a winning *candidate* must attract a majority of the votes cast in a *constituency*. See also *hybrid electoral system* and *proportional electoral system*.

- It is generally taken to include those systems where a candidate is required to achieve absolute majority (i.e. more than half) of the votes cast, e.g. *alternative vote system (AV)* and *supplementary vote (SV)*.
- The term is also applied to those systems that require only that a candidate secures a *simple majority*, i.e. *first-past-the-post*.

majority: the winning margin within a given *constituency*, expressed either as a percentage or as a number of votes. It also refers to the number of seats that the governing party holds over the total number of seats held by all other parties combined in the *House of Commons*.

Example

At the 2005 *general election*, the Labour party secured 355 seats, a majority of 65 over all other parties combined.

majority government: where a single *political party* is able to form a government from within its own ranks having won more seats in the *House of Commons* than all other parties combined. See also *coalition government* and *minority government*.

maladministration: where a public body is guilty of failing to discharge its duties to the public as set out in law. See also *ultra vires*.

mandarins: an English term originally applied to bureaucrats in imperial China, though now commonly applied to those in the *senior civil service*.

mandate: the right of the governing party to pursue the policies it sets out in its general election *manifesto*. The doctrine of the mandate gives the governing party the *authority* to pursue its stated policies but it does not require them to do so or prevent them from drafting proposals not included in their manifestos.

Example

In its 1997 general election manifesto, **New Labour** promised both to remove the rights of **hereditary peers** to sit and vote in the **House of Lords** and to move towards a more democratic and more representative second chamber. It largely delivered the first of these pledges in the **House of Lords Act (1999)**. See **Lords Reform (1997–2010)**.

mandatory reselection: see *reselection*

Mandelson, Peter (1953–): former Labour MP, European *commissioner* and later *life peer*.
- Mandelson was regarded as a key ally of **Tony Blair** and one of the architects of the **New Labour** project.
- He served in **cabinet** under both Tony Blair and **Gordon Brown**.

manifesto: a pre-election document in which a **political party** sets out the policies it intends to carry into *law* if elected to government. See also *mandate*.

manipulative theory: see *media theory*

marginal: a parliamentary *constituency* that is held by a small *majority* following an election (contrast with *safe seat*).
- Such marginal seats are often targeted in election *campaigns* (see *target seat*) because they are seen as winnable.
- The *media* often focus on the intentions of *floating voters* in such *marginals* as these voters have the ability to swing the contest one way or the other.

Example: the parliamentary constituency of Crawley at the 2005 general election

The constituency of Crawley was the most marginal UK parliamentary constituency following the 2005 general election, with a Labour majority of just 37 votes over the Conservatives (see below).

58.2% turnout	
Conservative	16,374 (39.0%)
Labour	16,411 (39.1%)
LibDem	6,503 (15.5%)
Other	2,685 (6.4%)
A Labour majority of 37 votes (0.1%)	

Martin, Michael (1945–): a former Labour MP and *speaker* of the *House of Commons*, he was forced to resign the post of speaker in 2009 as a result of his handling of the row over *MPs' expenses*.

Marx, Karl (1818–83): nineteenth-century German socialist philosopher and author of a number of works including *The Communist Manifesto*. Marx is widely regarded as the father of *communism*, an *ideology* favouring greater equality and common ownership of the means of production.

Marxism: an *ideology* deriving from the ideas of *Karl Marx*. See also *communism*.

mass media: see *media*

mayor: commonly the title given to the head of a *borough council* or city. New Labour favoured the introduction of directly elected mayors in England. See also *Mayor of London* and *Stuart Drummond*.

Mayor of London: the directly elected *chief executive* who leads the work of the *Greater London Authority*. In May 2000, London voters elected *Ken Livingstone* as the city's first elected mayor. Livingstone was elected for a second term in 2004. He was defeated by the Conservative candidate, Boris Johnson, when seeking a third consecutive term in 2008. See also *Greater London Assembly*.

McKenzie thesis: first advanced by Robert McKenzie in 1955, this is the view that the Conservative and Labour parties are dominated by their respective party leaders, with individual party members holding little real power. See *internal party democracy* and *Michel's Iron Law of Oligarchy*.

means testing: see *universalism*

media: referring collectively to television, radio, newspapers, the internet and other forms of mass communication. The broadcast media in the UK (i.e. television and radio) are under a legal obligation not to show party political bias (see *party election broadcasts*). See also the *press* and *new media*.

media theory: referring to the various different models that have been developed to explain the part played by the media within UK politics.
- Manipulative theory holds that the mass media are controlled by an elite that uses them with the sole purpose of preserving its own position, submerging a radical agenda in meaningless trivia.
- Hegemonic theory takes the view that those who work in the media have a particular view due to their education, age and social class. They therefore operate using a particular perspective, however unconscious their bias might be.
- Pluralist theory sees the media in a more passive light, with individuals freely choosing what to read and watch, from the wide range of media available, on the basis of their own outlook and interests. The media, therefore, reflect opinion rather than shaping it, thereby reinforcing views that the reader already has.

TIP: There is considerable debate over the question of whether the media shape or simply reflect public opinion. Writers such as the American psychologist Leon Festinger in the 1950s have argued that media influence is limited by three processes: selective exposure; selective perception; and selective retention. Selective exposure is where individuals choose to expose themselves to newspapers and television programmes that reflect, rather than challenge, their outlook. Selective perception refers to the way in which individuals mentally edit the media to which they are exposed, filtering out content that does not fit in with their own ideas. Selective retention is the tendency for individuals to forget media content that challenges the views they hold while retaining material that can be used to justify their position.

Member of Parliament (MP): an individual elected to the *House of Commons* from – and in order to represent – an individual parliamentary *constituency*. An MP must use his or her judgement to balance the needs of constituents against the demands of conscience and the party whip.

Member of the European Parliament (MEP): an individual *representative* elected to serve a five-year term in the *European Parliament*.

Member of the Scottish Parliament (MSP): an individual *representative* elected to serve a five-year term in the *Scottish Parliament* in Edinburgh.

Member of the Welsh Assembly (MWA): an individual *representative* elected to serve a five-year term in the *Welsh Assembly* in Cardiff.

member states: countries that have joined the *European Union (EU)* by signing a treaty of accession incorporating the *Treaty of Rome*.
- EU member states take part in EU decision making and are bound by European laws.
- Each EU member state has the right to *veto* applications to join the Union.
- There were 27 EU member states in 2009 with other states such as Croatia and Turkey also in the process of negotiating entry.

MEP: see *Member of the European Parliament (MEP)*

metropolitan district council: an elected unit of *local government* responsible for education, city planning, housing, refuse collection, leisure and transport infrastructure within an urban area. *Councillors* are elected to serve on such councils every 4 years.

Michel's Iron Law of Oligarchy: the rule that political organisations and popular mass movements can never be truly democratic, because they will inevitably fall under the control of a small guiding elite. See *elites theory*.

middle class: the *social class* comprising the households of most professional and managerial employees. See also *class alignment* and *class voting*.

middle way: see *third way*

Middlesex Guildhall: a building in Parliament Square that houses the UK *Supreme Court*.

Militant Tendency: a left-wing (Trotskyist) *faction* in the *Labour Party*, expelled from the party in the 1980s.
- Militant was seen as a party within a party by the then Labour leader *Neil Kinnock* and other moderates within the party.
- In 1986, Labour deselected a number of sitting MPs for being part of the Militant Tendency, including Dave Nellist and Terry Fields.
- Militant played a key role in the formation of the *Anti-Poll Tax Federation*.

Millbank Tower: the London location of the *Labour Party* headquarters between 1997 and 2003.
- Part of *Tony Blair*'s remodelling of *New Labour* involved the opening of the party's campaign and media centre at Millbank.
- Millbank subsequently coordinated all party polling and *focus groups*.
- In consequence, the word 'Millbank' became synonymous with New Labour *spin* and strategy during its first term in office (1997–2001).

miners' strike (1974): a strike credited with bringing down the government of the then Conservative prime minister *Edward Heath*.

miners' strike (1984–85): a year-long stand-off between the then prime minister *Margaret Thatcher* and the leader of the National Union of Mineworkers (NUM), Arthur Scargill.

- Thatcher rejected the more cooperative, *corporatist* approach taken by earlier governments. She instead passed a raft of anti-union legislation through Parliament.
- The miners' strike was technically illegal as Scargill had failed to hold a strike ballot in accordance with legislation introduced in the early 1980s. Thatcher was therefore able to characterise the miners and those who supported them as the 'enemy within'.
- The defeat of the NUM was widely seen as a significant landmark in the decline of *trade union* power.

minister: a member of the government with specific responsibilities within a *department*. There are two main ranks: *junior minister* (*minister of state* and *parliamentary under-secretary*) in addition to those ministers of *cabinet* rank. See *secretary of state*.

Example

In July 2009, the *Home Office* was headed by Alan Johnson MP, a cabinet-rank minister. There were also five junior ministers working in the department: two ministers of state (David Hanson MP and Phil Woolas MP); and three parliamentary under-secretaries (Alan Campbell MP, Meg Hillier MP and Lord West of Spithead).

minister of state: one of the two main ranks of *junior minister*.

minister without portfolio: commonly referring to a *minister* of *cabinet* rank who does not hold a formal responsibility for a named government *department*.

Ministerial Code: the document setting out the duties and responsibilities of a government *minister*, including a section on *collective responsibility*. Prior to 1997, the code was known as *Questions of Procedure for Ministers*.

ministerial responsibility: see *individual ministerial responsibility* and *collective responsibility*

Ministers' Question Time: a regular slot at which *MPs* or *peers* can ask oral questions of government *ministers* in the *House of Commons* or *House of Lords*. Ministers take it in turns to answer questions relating to their departmental portfolios. See also *Prime Minister's Questions*.

ministry: a division of the *civil service* that operates alongside government *ministers* in a particular government *department* or *office*, e.g. the Justice Ministry.

minor party: a party that contests a range of *elections* yet has little realistic chance of entering *government* at *Westminster*.

- Minor parties can be divided into three broad categories: *regional parties* (such as the *Scottish National Party (SNP)*); *ideological parties* (such as the *British National Party (BNP)*); and *single-issue parties* (such as the *UK Independence Party (UKIP)*).
- They are often referred to as *third parties*.

minority administration: see *minority government*

minority government: a single-party government that does not hold an *overall majority* in the *House of Commons*. A minority government will find it more difficult to control the passage of legislation. It will also be more vulnerable to a *vote of (no) confidence*.

Example

The Labour government elected with a majority of four seats in October 1974 became a minority government following defeat in the Walsall North *by-election* of November 1976. The Scottish National Party also formed a minority administration – which it referred to as the 'Scottish Government' – following elections to the *Scottish Parliament* in 2007.

miscarriage of justice: where an individual or group of individuals is ultimately found to have been falsely convicted of an offence. See *Guildford Four* and *Birmingham Six*.

mixed economy: see *Keynesianism*

modern liberalism: another term for new liberalism, *progressive liberalism* and social liberalism. Contrast with *classical liberalism* and *neo-liberalism*.

monarch: in the modern context, a *head of state* who holds his or her position by virtue of the hereditary principle as opposed to a formal appointments process or popular election. See also *constitutional monarchy* and *prerogative powers*.

monarchy: a political system operating under a *monarch*. See also *constitutional monarchy*.

Monday Club: a right-wing *faction* within the *Conservative Party*.

money bill: a *bill* that the *speaker* of the *House of Commons* has categorised as being entirely concerned with money, e.g. the *Budget*. It is significant in the context of the *Parliament Act (1911)*.

Montesquieu, Baron: see *separation of powers*

Morgan, Sally: a key advisor to the prime minister *Tony Blair* during *New Labour*'s first two terms in office. Morgan served first as political secretary (1997–2001) and later as director of political and government relations (2001–05). She stood down in the wake of the 2005 general election.

motion of no confidence: see *no-confidence motion*

MP: see *Member of Parliament (MP)*

MPs' expenses: various monies paid to *MPs* in addition to their annual salary.
- MPS' expenses traditionally included allowances to cover staffing costs, the costs associated with living away from one's normal place of residence, and those costs incurred communicating with constituents.
- They became the subject of great controversy between 2007 and 2009 as a result of alleged abuses of the system by sitting MPs.
- Conservative MP Derek Conway was one of many criticised for his payment of staffing allowances to family members (see example overleaf).
- MPs were criticised for abuses of both the Additional Costs allowance and the Incidental Expenses Provision. Much attention was focused on the payments to MPs in respect of their second homes. The practice of 'flipping' – changing the designation of one's second home for financial advantage – proved particularly controversial.

- The furnishing of such second homes at the taxpayers' expense also provoked controversy with the publication of the so-called 'John Lewis List' – a list of household goods that MPs were permitted to claim.
- Details of MPs' expenses, due to be published following a request under the **Freedom of Information Act (2000)**, were leaked to the *Daily Telegraph* in 2009.
- The House of Commons speaker **Michael Martin** was forced to resign in 2009 following criticism of the way in which he had handled the scandal.

MPs' salaries and allowable expenses (2008–09)

Salary	£61,820
Staffing allowance	£100,205
Incidental Expenses Provision	£22,193
IT equipment (centrally provided)	£3,000
London supplement	£2,916
Additional Costs allowance	£24,005
Communications allowance	£10,400
Total	**£224,539**

Source: House of Commons Research Paper 08/31

Example: MP Derek Conway's income and payments to family members (2007–08)

Derek Conway MP	£60,675	Basic salary
	£21,177	Office costs
	£22,060	Second home allowance
	£3,936	Car allowance
	£86,439	Staff allowance
Colette Conway (wife)	£30,000	Per annum as a parliamentary assistant
Henry Conway (son)	£32,000	Over three years as a research assistant (18 hours a week)
Freddie Conway (son)	£45,163	Over three years as a research assistant (17 hours a week)

Source: *Guardian*, 30 January 2008

TIP: The fallout from the scandal over MPs' expenses saw renewed interest in the incomes earned by MPs outside their roles in the **Commons**, e.g. in August 2009, the *Guardian* reported that the shadow foreign secretary **William Hague** earned around £1.3 million a year as an author, broadcaster and after–dinner speaker – on top of his MP's salary of £64,766.

MSP: see *Member of the Scottish Parliament (MSP)*

multilateral nuclear disarmament: where the UK government negotiates with other countries in order to agree a reduction in the numbers of nuclear warheads held by each side.

> **TIP:** Often contrasted with the policy of unilateralism proposed by the *Labour Party* in its 1983 *manifesto*. This policy would have seen the UK give up its nuclear capability on principle, irrespective of what other nations chose to do.

multi-member constituency: a geographical area represented by more than one elected official.

Example

Some electoral systems (such as the *single transferable vote (STV)* in *European elections* in Northern Ireland and the *hybrid electoral systems* for the *Scottish Parliament* and the *Welsh Assembly*) make use of multi-member constituencies to ensure a greater degree of *proportionality*. For instance, in European elections, Northern Ireland is treated as one *constituency* that elects three *MEPs*.

> **TIP:** Multi-member constituencies may be contrasted with the *single-member constituencies* represented by MPs at *Westminster*.

multi-party government: see *coalition government*

multi-party system: a political system in which more than two *political parties* exist and contest elections with a realistic prospect of achieving political power. Responsibility for forming the government either changes between parties from one election to another or is shared in a *coalition government*.

Example

Israel has experienced a succession of different multi-party coalition governments under the proportional *party list system* used to elected the Knesset.

municipal socialism: see *new urban left*

MWA: see *Member of the Welsh Assembly (MWA)*

National Assembly for Wales: see *Welsh Assembly*

National Economic Development Council (NEDC): a *corporatist* forum allowing government *ministers*, *civil servants*, employers and *trade union* representatives to meet and discuss economic *policy*. It ran from 1961 to 1993.

National Executive Committee (NEC): the administrative heart of the *Labour Party*.
- Established under Clause Eight of the party's *constitution*.
- Part elected by the *party conference*, the NEC comprises representatives from *trade unions* and other *affiliated* organisations as well as some MPs and MEPs.
- It ensures the smooth running of the party between annual conferences and plays a key role in the party's two-year policy-making cycle.
- It also has the final say on candidate selection, having the power to impose a *candidate* on a *Constituency Labour Party*.

National Farmers' Union (NFU): a *pressure group* representing the sectional interests of UK farmers. Traditionally regarded as a *core insiders* group, the NFU is said to have declined in importance in recent years. It is part of the *Eurogroup* COPA-COGECA.

National Front: an extreme right-wing *political party*.
- Founded in 1967.
- Split in the early 1980s, resulting in the formation of the *British National Party (BNP)* in 1982.
- Fielded only 13 candidates in the 2005 *general election*, compared to 303 in 1979.

national party list system: see *party list system*

National Policy Forum: an internal *Labour Party* organisation that plays a key role in the development of party policy.
- Established in 1990.
- The Forum establishes policy commissions that explore particular areas of policy. Policy proposals emanating from these commissions are agreed by the *National Executive Committee (NEC)* before being passed to the annual *party conference* for final approval.
- The *Conservative Party* also has a *Policy Forum*. See also *William Hague* and *Fresh Future*.

TIP: The creation of Labour's National Policy Forum was widely seen as part of a process by which the Labour Party leadership secured a greater degree of control over the policy-making process. Previously, the annual party conference was seen as the party's sovereign policy-making body. Now conference considers only those proposals that have already been passed from the commissions through the NEC.

nationalisation: the process by which a private business is transferred into public (i.e. state) ownership. It is a feature of *socialism*. Contrast with *privatisation*. See also *Clause IV*.

nationalism: a belief in a nation's right to independence and self-determination.

Example

The *Scottish National Party (SNP)* is a nationalist party. It campaigns for full independence for Scotland and does not contest elections outside Scotland. Extreme nationalism is often associated with *right-wing* ideologies such as *fascism*.

nationalist parties: parties that campaign for greater self-determination or independence for their nation or region within the UK.
- Nationalist parties include the *Scottish National Party (SNP)* and *Plaid Cymru* (in Wales).
- In Northern Ireland those parties that seek to break away from the UK and form a united island of Ireland are commonly referred to as republican parties, as opposed to nationalist parties, e.g. *Sinn Fein*.

TIP: Nationalist parties often tend to perform relatively well at *general elections*, when compared to other *minor parties*, because their support is concentrated geographically. This makes it far easier for them to win seats under the *first-past-the-post* system. For example, the SNP won only 1.5% of the UK vote at the 2005 general election but that equated to 17.7% of the vote and six seats in Scotland, the only part of the UK where it fielded candidates.

NATO: see *North Atlantic Treaty Organisation (NATO)*

natural justice: the application of the principles of fairness and reasonableness when applying the law.

Natural Law Party: a quasi-religious *minor party* that advocates transcendental meditation.
- The party fielded 309 candidates in the 1992 *general election* and 177 candidates in the 1997 general election, securing an average of 0.5% and 0.3% of the popular vote, respectively, in those seats contested.
- All 486 candidates lost their deposits.

natural rights: universal and inalienable rights, including the right to life, liberty and property.
- Often referred to as God-given rights, as they are said to be available to all, from birth.
- Philosophers such as John Locke believed that such natural rights rested on the concept of a natural human state that predated the establishment of political structures and developed society.
- They are echoed in the words of the American Declaration of Independence (1776). See the example overleaf.

Example: extract from the American Declaration of Independence (1776)

'We hold these truths to be self-evident, that all Men are created equal, that they are endowed by their Creator with certain unalienable Rights, that among these are Life, Liberty and the Pursuit of Happiness. That to secure these Rights, Governments are instituted among Men, deriving their just Powers from the Consent of the Governed that whenever any Form of Government becomes destructive of these Ends, it is the Rights of the People to alter or to abolish it, and to constitute new Government, laying its foundation on such principles, and organising its powers in such form, as to them shall seem most likely to effect their safety and happiness.'

NEC: see *National Executive Committee (NEC)*

NEDC: see *National Economic Development Council (NEDC)*

negative campaigning: where *candidates* or *political parties* focus on the perceived weaknesses of their opponents as opposed to articulating a positive vision of their own. See also *attack-ads*.

Example

In its 1997 'demon eyes' campaign, the *Conservative Party* questioned whether or not *Tony Blair* could be trusted.

negative rights: those rights that are not explicitly set out but exist in the absence of any law forbidding individuals from exercising them. See also *positive rights*.

Example

The UK was traditionally said to operate under a system of negative rights. This was because rights existed simply as a result of citizens' ability to exercise them free from legal impediment, as opposed to their being formally set out in a *Bill of Rights*. Some argue that the passing of measures such as the *Human Rights Act (1998)* has changed this state of affairs.

Neill Report (1998): a report that recommended limits on party funding, controls on election expenditure and new rules under which future referendums would operate.
- The report was authored by Lord Neill, who had succeeded Lord Nolan as chair of the *Committee on Standards in Public Life*. See also *cash for questions*.
- Its main recommendations were included in the 1999 *Queen's Speech* and subsequently brought into law under the *Political Parties, Elections and Referendums Act (2000)*.

neo-liberalism: a political *ideology*, closely related to *classical liberalism*, that stresses the importance of the free market, individual rights and limited government. In the UK context, neo-liberalism is closely associated with *Thatcherism*.

neutrality: the absence of *bias* – one of the traditional principles upon which the UK *civil service* was said to operate. See also *impartiality, anonymity* and *permanence*.

New Labour: characterising the party that emerged to fight the 1997 *general election* following a process of party modernisation completed by *Tony Blair*.
- Blair first used the phrase when addressing the Labour *conference* as party leader in 1994.
- Labour's modernisation programme had begun under *Neil Kinnock*, following the party's landslide defeat at the 1983 general election.
- It involved the expulsion from the party of hard-line *left-wing* elements such as the *Militant Tendency*, a less powerful role for the *trade unions*, and a rebranding process designed to make the party more appealing to *middle class* voters. Contrast with *Old Labour*. See also *Clause IV*.

new liberalism: see *progressive liberalism*

new magistracy: referring to the way in which various government functions have been transferred to *quangos* and other unelected bodies since the 1980s.

new media: referring to the internet, mobile telephones and associated technologies.
- New media are said to have an influence on political activity in the UK and beyond.
- Political weblogs (blogs) are reaching an ever-growing audience and there has also been a growth in the use of new media technologies by political parties in their *campaigns*.
- The *Westminster* government is committed to encouraging the growth of e-democracy; where citizens engage with and influence the political process online. This has been seen with the innovation of e-petitions on the Number 10 website.

New Right: a political *ideology* that stressed the importance of the individual, law and order, and free-market economics. The New Right married a *neo-liberal* economic policy with a conservative social policy.

New Tories: referring to the *Conservative Party* under the leadership of *David Cameron*.
- Cameron did not use the phrase himself publicly, though he did use the phrase 'liberal conservatives'. See also *Red Toryism*.
- Cameron was said to have re-branded the party by focusing less on the things that divided the party (e.g. Europe) and more on the issues that had the potential to broaden the party's electoral appeal (e.g. green issues).
- He also looked to change the way in which the party selected candidates for elected office, with a view to making Conservative candidates more socially representative of the communities they were seeking to represent. See *primary election* and *resemblance theory*.

> **TIP:** The phrase was used as a means of suggesting a parallel between the changes to the Conservative Party under Cameron and those made to the *Labour Party* under *Tony Blair*. See also *New Labour*.

new urban left: a political movement closely associated with the *socialist*, *Old Labour*-controlled *local councils* of the mid-1980s. It is often referred to as *municipal socialism* as a result of the way in which left-wing Labour councils looked to achieve socialist objectives at a local level during the party's 18 years out of office at *Westminster* (1979–97).

new working class: a section of the *working class* that is not heavily unionised and does not vote along class lines alone. See also *social class*, *class alignment* and *class dealignment*. Contrast with *old working class*.

- Political scientist Ivor Crewe first drew a distinction between the 'old' and 'new' working class in the 1980s.
- The new working class is more likely to be working in the service sector and in the private sector.
- The emergence of this new working class coincided with a decline in the heavily unionised primary industries (e.g. mining) and manufacturing industries. It was accompanied by a process of *embourgeoisement*.
- Crewe argued that the new working class was less likely to vote for the *Labour Party* because it no longer identified with the core values espoused by the party.

New World Order: according to a conspiracy theory, a hidden guiding elite that controls the world irrespective of what happens in the public arena. See also *elites theory* and *Bilderberg Group*.

Newton Report (2001): a report that considered ways of improving government *accountability*. The report was the product of a commission established by the Hansard Society under the chairmanship of Lord Newton of Braintree. It concluded that that there needed to be a strengthening of the system of *departmental select committees*.

Next Steps agency: see *executive agency*

Next Steps Programme: see *Ibbs Report (1988)*

NFU: see *National Farmers' Union (NFU)*

Nice, Treaty of (2001): an *EU* treaty addressing the issue of EU enlargement and the reorganisation of EU institutions that such enlargement necessitated.

- The treaty provided for an extension of the *European Parliament's co-decision* powers into new areas and a reapportioning of European Parliament seats between member states.
- It proposed a restructuring of the *European Commission* with one *commissioner* for each member state.
- The treaty also reworked the system of *qualified majority voting* used in the *Council of Ministers* to reflect the planned expansion from 15 to 25 EU member states in 2004.

9/11: shorthand for the Al Qaeda attacks on a number of US targets on 11 September, 2001.

- Al Qaeda terrorists planned to destroy the World Trade Center, the Pentagon and the White House by flying hijacked commercial airliners into their targets.
- The iconic Twin Towers of the World Trade Center were entirely destroyed with the loss of nearly 3,000 lives. The Pentagon building, housing the Defense Department, was badly damaged. Another aircraft crashed in Pennsylvania en route to its supposed target, the White House, possibly as a result of the efforts of passengers seeking to overpower the hijackers.
- The attacks were used as justification for US president George W. Bush's 'War on Terror' and the invasions of Afghanistan and Iraq that followed. They were also used to justify the Patriot Act in the USA and the UK's *Anti-terrorism, Crime and Security Act (2001)*. See also *7/7*.

1922 Committee: a *Conservative Party* committee comprising all the party's *backbenchers*. It communicates the views of the party's backbenchers to the party leadership. The committee's elected chair acts as returning officer in party leadership elections.

No Turning Back group: a *right-wing* Conservative Party faction established to promote Thatcherite policies in the 1980s.

no-confidence motion: a formal *debate* called in the *House of Commons* on the question of whether the Chamber has confidence in the government of the day.
- By *convention*, the loss of a vote of confidence results in the prime minister seeking *dissolution* of Parliament, resulting in a *general election*.
- It is most likely to be called by the *opposition* where there is a *minority government* or where the government's *majority* is wafer thin.

> **Example**
>
> *James Callaghan*'s Labour government lost a vote of confidence in 1979, resulting in a general election in which the party was defeated by *Margaret Thatcher*'s Conservatives. The Callaghan administration had been a minority government since a *by-election* loss in 1976.

> **TIP:** Governments that fear defeat in a Commons vote sometimes say that they regard it as a vote of confidence in order to get their backbenchers to toe the party line, e.g. *John Major* over the European Finance Bill (see *whipless wonders*) or *Tony Blair* over the *Iraq War (2003)*.

Nolan Committee: the alternative name for the first *Committee on Standards in Public Life*.

Nolan Report (1995): the report of the first *Committee on Standards in Public Life* under Lord Nolan.
- The report came in the wake of the *cash for questions* scandal.
- It recommended the banning of paid advocacy work by MPs (see *lobbying firm*), the establishment of a new *Register of Members' Interests* and the creation of a new post of *parliamentary commissioner for standards*.

non-departmental public body: an alternative name for *quango*.

non-departmental select committees: a parliamentary committee whose scrutiny of government activity is not limited to a single departmental area. Such committees may be established on either a permanent or an *ad hoc* basis. The *Public Accounts Committee* falls into the former category while the *Committee on Standards in Public Life* is an example of the latter. See also *departmental select committees*.

non-money bill: a legislative proposal not defined as a *money bill*. See also *Parliament Act (1911)* and *Parliament Act (1949)*.

non-partisan: the absence of political *bias*. Commons *select committees* are expected to operate in a non-partisan manner, as is the *speaker* of the *House of Commons*.

non-voter: one who holds the franchise but chooses not to vote. See *abstention*, *apathy* and *turnout*.

North Atlantic Treaty Organisation (NATO): a military alliance of Western democratic states, founded in 1949.

- NATO was formed at the start of the Cold War in order to address the perceived threat posed by communist states such as the USSR.
- In 1955 the communist Warsaw Pact was formed in opposition to NATO.

North East referendum (2004): a *referendum* held in the North East region on the question of whether or not to establish an elected *regional assembly* to serve the area. The referendum saw voters reject the plans for a North East Assembly by 78% : 22% on a 48% *turnout*. The *landslide victory* for the 'No' campaign effectively signalled the mothballing of New Labour's plans for elected English regional assemblies outside London.

North, Frederick (Lord North): *prime minister* (Tory), 1770–82.

Northcote-Trevelyan Report (1854): a report on *civil service* reform addressing abuses of patronage, and nepotism within the *bureaucracy*. It advocated a move towards a politically neutral civil service, appointed on meritocratic lines through examinations.

Northern Ireland Assembly: the elected *legislature* created in the *Good Friday Agreement (1998)* to meet at Stormont Castle in Belfast and exercise devolved administrative powers in areas such as agriculture, education and the environment (see *devolution*).

Northern Ireland Executive: the *executive* branch of the devolved government established in Northern Ireland as a result of the *Good Friday Agreement (1998)*.

- The agreement provided for an executive of 12 members, headed by a First Minister.
- The executive was suspended between 2002 and 2007 as a result of an upsurge in paramilitary violence.
- The *Northern Ireland Assembly* elections that took place in 2007, following the restoration of devolved government, resulted in the then *Democratic Unionist Party (DUP)* leader, the *Revd Ian Paisley*, taking on the role of First Minister with *Sinn Fein*'s Martin McGuinness as Deputy First Minister. At that time the two parties held 9 of the 12 ministerial seats on the executive.

North–South divide: the socio-economic divide between the more prosperous South and the poorer Northern regions, Scotland and Wales.

- The phrase entered common usage in the 1980s, when the decline in heavy industry and manufacturing in the North contrasted sharply with the rise of the service and financial sectors in the South.
- By 1994 the average income per head of those in the North was only 89% of the UK average, while unemployment was 2.2% higher.
- There were also marked differences in health and life expectancy between those living in the North and those in the South.

TIP: Because this North–South divide reflected long standing socio-economic cleavages, it was also reflected in *voting behaviour*. Labour was strong in the North, Scotland and Wales, whereas the Conservatives fared better in the south-east (the home counties). Even though the North–South divide was said to have weakened towards the end of the twentieth century, voting behaviour in the 2005 general election still reflected these traditional party strongholds (see below).

Example: an illustration of the North–South divide at the 2005 general election

North East region (Cleveland, Durham, Northumberland and Tyne & Wear)

	Conservative	Labour	LibDem	Other	Total
% vote	19.5%	52.9%	23.3%	4.3%	100%
Seats	1	28	1	0	30

Eastern region (Bedfordshire, Cambridgeshire, Essex, Hertfordshire, Norfolk and Suffolk)

	Conservative	Labour	LibDem	Other	Total
% vote	43.3%	29.8%	21.8%	5.0%	100
Seats	40	13	3	0	56

Source: adapted from House of Commons Research Paper 05/33.

No2ID: a *political cause group* that opposes the proposed introduction of biometric national identity (ID) cards in the UK.

Number 10: the *Prime Minister's Office* at 10 *Downing Street*, London.

Are you studying other subjects?

The *A–Z Handbooks (digital editions)* are available in 14 different subjects. Browse the range and order other handbooks at **www.philipallan.co.uk/a-zonline**.

occupational class: see *social class*

office: a *ministry* within the *civil service* that develops and administers a specific aspect of government policy. Offices are headed by a *cabinet*-rank minister.

> **Example**
>
> In July 2009 the *Home Office* was headed by Alan Johnson MP, a leading cabinet member. There were also five other *ministers* working in the department below cabinet rank: two ministers of state (David Hanson MP and Phil Woolas MP); and three parliamentary under-secretaries (Alan Campbell MP, Meg Hillier MP and Lord West of Spithead).

> **TIP:** Note that other ministries within the civil service are referred to simply as ministries or government departments.

official committees: committees of *civil servants* who support the work of *cabinet committees*. Official committees prepare the ground for discussions by *ministers* in *cabinet committees* and more informal ministerial groupings.

official opposition: the *political party* with the second largest number of MPs in the *House of Commons* and officially referred to as Her Majesty's Loyal Opposition. The official opposition's *front bench* team makes up the *shadow cabinet*, which is led by the *leader of the opposition*. See also *Opposition Days*.

> **TIP:** It is common to refer to all parties in the Commons who are not in government as opposition parties.

Old Labour: characterising the *Labour Party* prior to the modernisation programme begun by *Neil Kinnock* in 1983 and completed by *Tony Blair*. It refers to the party's historic commitment to *socialism* (see *Clause IV*) and its links with socialist societies, *trade unions* and the *old working class*. Contrast with *New Labour*.

old working class: those employed in heavily unionised primary (e.g. mining) and manufacturing industries, who were traditionally seen as the Labour Party's core support. Contrast with *new working class*. See also *Old Labour* and *New Labour*.

ombudsman: literally a 'people's friend' who has the task of investigating accusations of *maladministration* made by members of the public against government bodies.

- The term 'ombudsman' is commonly used when referring to the parliamentary commissioner for administration, a post created in 1967 to investigate accusations of maladministration by government **departments**.
- Ombudsmen have little real **power**, though they have the ability to embarrass and shame government bodies.
- Ombudsmen also operate in areas such as healthcare.

Example

In 2001 the then Health Service Ombudsman, Michael Buckley, found in favour of a woman who had complained about the way in which an NHS hospital trust had treated her following a miscarriage. Buckley criticised the hospital's 'insensitive disposal of the foetus'.

OMOV: see *one member, one vote (OMOV)*

one-line whip: an indication that the party **whip** would expect that party's MPs to attend the Commons and vote in a particular way in a **division**. See also **two-line whip** and **three-line whip**.

one member, one vote (OMOV): the practice under which the ordinary members of **political parties** and other political organisations are given an equal say in the procedures of that organisation.

- Most commonly used with reference to the Labour Party modernisation programme that led to the decline of the union **block vote** from 1993.
- The **Liberal Democrats** have long been committed to the principle of OMOV and the Conservative leader **William Hague** also introduced an element of OMOV to the process by which the party selects its leaders.

one-nation conservatism: a form of **paternalist conservatism** that promotes inclusiveness, closely associated with the nineteenth-century Conservative prime minister **Benjamin Disraeli**. See also **wets**. Contrast with the **New Right** and **Thatcherism**.

one-nation Tories: those who subscribe to **one-nation conservatism**.

open government: the principle that the **media** and the broader public should have free access to information held by government **departments** and **agencies**. See **freedom of information** and **Freedom of Information Act (2000)**.

open list: a characteristic of some **party list systems** whereby voters can express a preference for particular candidates within their chosen party's list. Contrast with **closed list system**.

opinion poll: a survey of **public opinion** based upon a representative sample of between 1,000 and 2,000 voters. See also **focus groups**.

- Opinion polls are used to provide data on popular voting intentions, the relative popularity of party leaders and party policy.
- They are most visible at elections times when the major polling companies such as MORI and NOP question the voting intentions of large sample groups.
- **Exit polls** are normally more accurate than the ordinary polls conducted during the election **campaign** because they use larger samples and ask people how they have

voted, rather than surveying voting intentions. For example, in 2005, the BBC's exit poll came within two seats of predicting Labour's actual parliamentary majority.

- Even with good sampling pollsters normally allow a margin of error of plus or minus 3%.

Example

At the 1992 *general election* the average final poll error was 8.9%. This was said to be the result of four related factors:

- Respondents were not registered: in 1992 it appeared that some of those being asked the questions (the respondents) had not registered to vote; possibly in an effort to avoid the *poll tax*.
- Respondents were lying: it has been suggested that people were too embarrassed to admit publicly that they were going to vote Conservative.
- Respondents were unrepresentative of the broader electorate: sampling errors and samples that were too small meant that some surveys were skewed from the start.
- Many respondents were 'floating': there was clearly a late swing to the Conservatives. Was this perhaps due to a large number of floating voters?

TIP: In some countries (France for example) opinion polls are banned in the days leading up to elections for fear that they might influence voting intentions. Some believe that voters are more likely to vote for parties that are doing well in the polls (the so-called *bandwagon effect*). Others argue that there is a *boomerang effect*, where people vote for parties that are doing badly in the polls because they see them as the underdogs or, more likely, don't turn out to vote when the polls show their party well ahead. Opinion poll findings can also result in an increase in *tactical voting*. Michael Portillo believed that his loss in Enfield in 1997 resulted, in part, from tactical voting based upon poll findings.

---

opposition: those parties that hold seats in the *House of Commons* but are not in *government*. See also *official opposition* and *Opposition Days*.

Opposition Days: the 20 days in each *parliamentary session* where *opposition* parties are able to determine the topic of debate.

- Established under *House of Commons* Standing Order SO14 (2).
- Seventeen days are at the disposal of the leader of the *official opposition* with the remaining three allocated to the second largest *opposition* party.

opt-out: see *European Economic and Monetary Union (EMU)* and *Social Chapter*

order: see *Order in Council*

Order in Council: a government directive that is issued through the *Privy Council*.

- Orders in Council carry the force of *law*. They therefore offer a way of implementing legal changes quickly in an emergency without the need to go through *Parliament*.
- They are commonly used when Parliament is not in session.
- Orders in Council represent a further written source of the *constitution*, alongside regular *statute law*.

Osmotherley Rules: rules governing those questions that parliamentary committees may and may not ask of *civil servants*.

- The rules are named after the *civil servant* Edward Osmotherley.
- They are designed to protect the traditional *civil service* principles of *neutrality*, *anonymity* and *permanence* – but are widely seen as a barrier to proper *scrutiny*.
- They prevent committees from asking 'questions in the field of political controversy'.

Oughton Report (1993): a report recommending wider recruitment and better training within the UK *civil service*, drafted by Sir John Oughton, the head of the *Cabinet Office* Efficiency Unit.

outsider group: a type of *pressure group* that is not involved in regular consultation with government, and part of the *insider/outsider typology* developed by *Wyn Grant*.
See also *potential insiders*, *outsiders by necessity* and *ideological outsiders*.

outsiders by necessity: a *pressure group* (a sub-category in the *insider/outsider typology*) that is forced to operate as an *outsider* as a result of its being unable to establish close contacts with *government*. Groups that are newly established and/or very small often fall into this category because they are seen to lack *legitimacy*. Groups that engage in *direct action* are similarly unlikely to gain access to government, e.g. *Fathers 4 Justice*.

overall majority: more than half of the *votes* cast in a given *constituency* or a number of seats in the *House of Commons* that a party must secure in order to hold more seats than all other parties combined. See also *majority*, *majority government*, *minority government* and *hung parliament*.

oversight: see *scrutiny*

A–Z Online

Log on to A–Z Online to search the database of terms, print revision lists and much more. Go to **www.philipallan.co.uk/a-zonline** to get started.

pairing: an arrangement by which *MPs* from *government* and *opposition* parties are matched by their respective party *whips* so as not to affect the outcome of *divisions* in their absence. See *two-line whip*.

Paisley, Revd Ian (1926–): a long-serving former leader of the *Democratic Unionist Party (DUP)* and First Minister in the *Northern Ireland Executive* (2007–08). Paisley's decision to enter government with *Sinn Fein* in 2007 was seen as a major landmark in the peace process.

Palace of Westminster: the building that houses the debating chambers of the *House of Commons* and *House of Lords* along with a number of committee rooms.

paramilitaries: the illegal private armies operating in Northern Ireland during the Troubles. The paramilitaries were broadly divided into Catholic groups such as the *Irish Republican Army (IRA)* and Protestant groups such as the *Ulster Volunteer Force (UVF)*.

parish council: the smallest unit of *local government* in most parts of England.

Parliament: the UK *legislature*.
- Parliament is located in the *Palace of Westminster*.
- It comprises the *House of Commons*, the *House of Lords* and – strictly speaking – the *monarch*.
- It can also refer to the *Scottish Parliament*, the *European Parliament* or to the period between one *general election* and the next.

Parliament Act (1911): a piece of *statute law* that enforced the supremacy of the *House of Commons* over the *House of Lords*.
- The Act replaced the Lords' power to *veto* legislation with the right to delay *non-money bills* by up to two *parliamentary sessions*.
- Under the Act those bills defined as *money bills* by the Commons *speaker* pass into law one month after they have been passed by the Commons, with or without Lords' approval.
- The Lords retained the power to veto any attempt by the Commons to extend the life of a *Parliament* beyond the five-year limit.

Parliament Act (1949): reduced the Lords' power to delay *non-money bills* from two *parliamentary sessions* to one. See *Parliament Act (1911)*.

parliamentary candidate: an individual seeking election to the *House of Commons* in a particular parliamentary *constituency*.
- A parliamentary candidate must be a *citizen* of the UK, the Republic of Ireland or another Commonwealth country.

- The minimum age for candidates was reduced from 21 years to 18 in 2006.
- A candidate's nomination papers must carry the signatures of ten *registered voters*.
- Candidates must put down a *deposit* of £500, which is forfeited in the event that they fail to secure 5% of the vote in their chosen constituency.

parliamentary commissioner for administration: see *ombudsman*

parliamentary commissioner for standards: the individual responsible for scrutinising MPs' conduct and interests. See also *Register of Members' Interests* and *MPs' expenses*.

- This post was created as a result of the *Nolan Report (1995)*.
- The commissioner conducts investigations into the conduct of MPs who are alleged to have acted improperly.
- The commissioner works hand-in-hand with the *Select Committee on Standards and Privileges*.

parliamentary debate: an ordered exchange of views on the floor of either chamber of *Parliament* concerning an individual *bill* or motion. See also *Opposition Days* and *adjournment debate*. The term commonly refers to the often heated parliamentary exchanges that take place at the *second reading* and *third reading* stages in the passage of legislation.

parliamentary democracy: see *parliamentary government*

parliamentary government: where the government or chief *executive* is drawn from a sovereign *legislature* and relies upon its support in order to remain in office. See also *parliamentary sovereignty*. Contrast with *presidential government*.

> **TIP:** The notion of a parliamentary government under a *constitutional monarchy* is said to be one of the key principles of the UK *constitution*.

Parliamentary Labour Party: the body comprising all *Labour Party* MPs.
- It elects a chairperson who liaises between the party's MPs and the party leader.
- It elects the party's *shadow cabinet* when in *opposition*. It also has a hand in electing the party leader, holding one third of the vote in the *electoral college* with the party's *MEPs*.

parliamentary lobby: see *lobby system*

parliamentary private secretary: an *MP* who assists a *minister* in his or her work.
- Ministers appoint their own parliamentary private secretary with the approval of the *prime minister*.
- Often dismissed simply as 'bag-carriers', the post is often the first rung on the ladder to high office.

Example

John Major became a parliamentary private secretary in 1981, two years after being elected to *Parliament* for the first time.

> **TIP:** Whereas it was once only senior ministers who appointed a parliamentary private secretary, many *junior ministers* now also do so. This has increased the *payroll vote*.

parliamentary questions: oral questions put to government *ministers* by backbenchers at *Ministers' Question Time* or *Prime Minister's Questions*. Such questions are usually employed in order to raise the profile of a particular issue or embarrass the government in some way. Contrast with **written questions**.

parliamentary reform: collectively referring to proposals to enhance the composition, procedures and effectiveness of the **House of Commons** and the **House of Lords**.
- Often taken simply as a synonym for **Lords Reform (1997–2010)**.
- Could also refer to innovations such as the introduction of **departmental select committees** in the Commons in 1979 or to more recent changes to procedure, e.g. changes to **Prime Minister's Questions**.
- Recent years have also witnessed more far-reaching proposals for reform of the Commons, e.g. the Conservative Party has suggested a reduction in the number of MPs who sit in Parliament as well as the introduction of **English votes for English laws**.

parliamentary secretary: a government rank immediately below the two main ranks of **junior ministers**. See **minister of state**.

parliamentary session: the parliamentary 'year' during which a **bill** must pass its various legislative stages if it is to become **law**. See also **Parliament Act (1911)** and **Parliament Act (1949)**. It begins with the **Queen's Speech** in November and ends within the year with what is known as a prorogation.

parliamentary sovereignty: the central constitutional **doctrine** that holds that **Parliament** is the supreme law-making body within the UK system of government.
- Parliamentary sovereignty is closely linked to the primacy of **statute law**.
- Rooted in **common law**, the doctrine of parliamentary sovereignty is based upon three interlocking principles: first, that only Parliament can make UK law; second, that Parliament can make or unmake any UK law; and third, that no Parliament can bind its successors.

> **TIP:** Some argue that parliamentary sovereignty has been undermined by the rise of the UK executive (see **elective dictatorship**), UK membership of the **EU**, and the process of **devolution** begun by **New Labour** in 1997.

parliamentary under-secretary: one of the two main ranks of **junior minister**. See also **minister of state**.

participation: see **political participation**

participatory democracy: a democracy characterised by high levels of popular participation in political activity.

partisan: having political **bias**. Contrast with **non-partisan**. See also **adversarial politics** and **bipartisan**.

Example

The influence of **whips** within Commons **standing committees** means that such bodies tend to operate on a partisan basis.

partisan alignment: an individual's long-standing psychological attachment to a particular **political party**.
- Partisan alignment is also known as 'party identification'. See also **partisanship**.
- It is linked to the concept of **socialisation**.

- It was a key influence on **voting behaviour** in the 1950s and 1960s, i.e. prior to the advent of **partisan dealignment**.

> **TIP:** It is important to be able to differentiate between partisan alignment and *class alignment*. Though the two concepts are linked, they are not analogous.

partisan dealignment: an apparent decline in the number of people who strongly identify with a particular **political party**.
- Partisan dealignment is a process that has been accompanied by the rise of **short-term** factors in **voting behaviour.**
- It is often associated with an increase in the number of **floating voters** and the greater prevalence of **protest voting.**

partisanship: holding a political **bias** and a synonym for **partisan alignment.**

party: see *political party*

party activist: a *grassroots* party member who participates actively in party activities such as fundraising and **canvassing.** Those sufficiently motivated to become activists are often more ideologically extreme than the rank-and-file membership of a party.

party alignment: see *partisan alignment*

party chairman: a key *Conservative Party* official responsible both for the day-to-day organisation of the party and national election **campaigns.** The party chair is responsible for the operation of Conservative **Central Office.**

> **TIP:** The *Labour Party* also has a party chair, though this individual plays a less significant role as a result of the existence of the *National Executive Committee (NEC).*

party conference: commonly referring to the annual national meetings held by all three main **political parties** each autumn. Conferences play a key role in helping parties to gain greater media exposure for their policies. They also give parties the opportunity to make a public show of unity.
- The **Labour Party** conference was traditionally seen as the sovereign policy-making body within the party before the creation of the **National Policy Forum** and the adoption of a two-year policy cycle. See also **block vote.**
- The **Liberal Democrats** are organised along **federal** lines with national conferences held in Scotland and in Wales – as well as the main annual conference attended by delegates from across Britain. The Liberal Democrats annual conference retains significant policy-making powers.
- The **Conservative Party** conference was traditionally regarded as and remains an opportunity for the party to garner positive media exposure, with the key policy decisions being made elsewhere.

party dealignment: see *partisan dealignment*

party discipline: see *whip* and *deselection*

party election broadcast: a party political advertisement put out on television or radio during the course of an election.
- Parties are prohibited from buying airtime in order to run political advertisements under the Broadcasting Act. This contrasts with the situation in the USA where candidates often buy up large quantities of airtime in order to run **attack-ads.**

113

- UK parties are therefore awarded free broadcast slots by virtue of the number of candidates they field in a given election and their representation in the outgoing **Parliament**.
- The three main parties normally get four or five slots but smaller parties can also qualify for party election broadcast slots where they field sufficient numbers of candidates.

Example

The **Natural Law Party** qualified for a slot when fielding 177 candidates at the 1997 **general election**. The **Referendum Party** also qualified to run an advertisement by fielding 547 candidates at the same election.

> **TIP:** Such advertisements aired outside an election *campaign* are referred to as party political broadcasts.

party funding: see *Political Parties, Elections and Referendums Act (2000)*

party identifier: see *identifier*

party list system: a *proportional electoral system* under which voters cast a **ballot** in favour of their preferred party, as opposed to the individual **candidate** who will represent them in a **legislature**. See also **European elections** and **threshold**.

- Seats are divided between parties in broad proportion to the **popular vote**, from lists drawn up by each party in advance of the election, i.e. if a party wins ten seats then the first ten names on that party's list will be duly elected.
- Under a **closed list system**, voters have no say over the order in which candidates appear on each party's list. Under an **open list** system, voters are able to express a preference for a candidate within their chosen party's list, with the order of the list then being determined by the number of preferences won by each candidate.
- In a **national party list system**, all the seats in the **legislature** are apportioned in relation to the national popular vote. Under a **regional list system** the seats available are divided into regions and apportioned in proportion to the popular vote within each region.
- National list systems offer greater **proportionality** than regional list systems. Regional list systems enhance **representation** because voters are electing those who will represent their own region.
- **Hybrid electoral systems** award a proportion of the available seats in a legislature on the basis of a party list system, with the remainder being allocated under a majoritarian system, e.g. 20 of the 60 seats in the **Welsh Assembly** are awarded under a party list system.

party member: an individual who has joined a **political party**, normally by paying a membership fee or subscription.

- Party members generally have some say in the way in which their chosen party operates.
- They may have an input into the formulation of party **policy** or have a say in selecting the party's **parliamentary candidate** in their constituency, or the party leader.
- The most active grassroots members are commonly referred to as **party activists**.

See **internal party democracy**.

party political broadcast: see *party election broadcast*

party system: a measure of competition between *political parties* in a given country.
- The UK has traditionally been seen as a *two-party system*, though some argue that it has in fact become a *multi-party system*.
- Other types of party system include the *single-party system* and the *dominant-party system*.

party voter: an individual who votes consistently for a single *political party*. See *identifier* and *partisan alignment*.

party whip: see *whip*

passage of legislation: see *legislative process*

paternalism: where power and authority are held centrally but the state acts benevolently, caring for the most needy. Paternalism was said to be a key characteristic of traditional *one-nation conservatism*.

patronage: power over political appointments; the power to 'hire and fire'. Patronage is formally held by the *monarch* but exercised in practice by the *prime minister*.
- The prime minister's powers of patronage include the appointment of *cabinet* members and other government *ministers*, members of the *House of Lords*, the heads of nationalised industries and chairs of *royal commissions* and bishops in the Church of England.
- The prime minister's powers of patronage are not subject to formal confirmation as is the case of appointments made by the US president.

payroll vote: the support of the 100 or so *MPs* whose support in *Commons* votes can be relied upon because they hold paid ministerial positions in the *government* of the day.
- The payroll vote covers *cabinet*-rank ministers and the two ranks of *junior ministers*.
- It could also extend to the unpaid *parliamentary private secretaries*, as their desire to further their career in government will normally guarantee their loyalty on the floor of the House.

peak group: an umbrella group speaking on behalf of a number of *pressure groups* that share a common interest or interests.

Example

The *Trades Union Congress (TUC)* is a peak group speaking on behalf of a large number of individual *trade unions*. In a similar vein, the *Confederation of British Industry (CBI)* represents a range of UK businesses and employers. The Make Poverty History campaign and the *Stop the War Coalition* could also be seen as peak groups.

Peel, Sir Robert: *prime minister* (Tory), 1834–35 and 1841–46.

peer: a member of the *House of Lords*. See *life peer* and *hereditary peer*.

Peerages Act (1963): an *Act of Parliament* that allowed peers to disclaim (i.e. give up) their titles. See also *Tony Benn*. The Act also allowed a number of women to enter the *House of Lords* as hereditary peeresses, where the absence of a male sibling would previously have left the seat vacant upon the death of their father.

Perceval, Spencer: *prime minister* (Tory), 1809–12.

peripheral insiders: an *insider pressure group* whose area of expertise or interest is so narrow that government would consult its members fairly infrequently; a sub-category in the *insider/outsider typology*.

Pelham, Henry: *prime minister* (Whig), 1743–54.

Pelham-Holles, Thomas (Duke of Newcastle): *prime minister* (Whig), 1754–56 and 1757–62.

Performance and Innovation Unit: a *Cabinet Office* body designed to ensure the better delivery of government policies that straddle two or more *departments*. It was established in 1998 as a body designed to help deliver *New Labour*'s promise of *joined-up government*. See also *Social Exclusion Unit*.

permanence: the view that *civil servants* should not come and go with governments but remain to serve whichever party is returned to office. The view is also held that civil servants should not be held accountable and sacked for failures within government *departments*. Permanence is one of the three traditional principles upon which the *civil service* was said to operate, the others being *neutrality* (*impartiality*) and *anonymity*. See *ministerial responsibility*.

permanent secretary: the top-ranking *civil servant* in charge of an individual government *department*, appointed at the discretion of the *prime minister* and reporting directly to the *cabinet minister* holding that departmental portfolio.

personal bill: a type of *private bill* that often affects only one or two individuals. Personal bills are generally passed in order to grant individuals a dispensation from existing law, e.g. the right to marry someone whom they might legally be barred from marrying.

personal responsibility: a strand of the constitutional *convention* of *individual ministerial responsibility* that requires ministers to resign when their personal conduct falls below that expected of a government minister.

Example

Ron Davies resigned as Secretary of State for Wales in 1998 following what he referred to as a 'moment of madness' on Clapham Common. His comment referred to his being mugged by a man he had first met on the common, a well-known meeting place for gay men. Davies subsequently announced that he was bisexual.

petition: a collection of signatures demanding government action on a particular issue. Under the premierships of *Tony Blair* and *Gordon Brown* the government trialled the use of so-called e-petitions on the *Number 10* website.

Petty, William (Earl of Shelburne): *prime minister* (Whig), 1782–83.

Pitt, William 'The Elder' (Earl of Chatham): *prime minister* (Whig), 1766–68.

Pitt, William 'The Younger': *prime minister* (Tory), 1783–1801 and 1804–06.

Plaid Cymru: a Welsh *nationalist party* committed to protecting the Welsh language and culture.

- The party has achieved some success in elections to *Westminster* and to the *Welsh Assembly*. In the 2005 general election the party fielded 40 candidates in Wales, winning 3 seats. In the 2007 Welsh Assembly Elections the party won 15 of the 60 seats available.

- Plaid Cymru entered into a **coalition government** with the Labour Party in Wales following the 2007 Welsh Assembly Elections.

Plane Stupid: an **attitude cause group** that had campaigned against the further expansion of air travel on environmental grounds. It was formed in 2005 by Richard George, Graham Thompson and Joss Garman and is a group employing high-profile direct action.

> **Example**
>
> On 27 February 2008, Tamsin Omond, a Plane Stupid activist, took to the roof of the **Palace of Westminster** in order to launch paper aeroplanes made from documents condemning the government's plans for a third runway at Heathrow. She also unfurled two massive banners; one demanding 'No third runway', the other labelling Parliament as 'British Airports Authority HQ'.

PLP: see **Parliamentary Labour Party**

pluralism: see **pluralist democracy**

pluralist democracy: a system of government that encourages **participation** and allows for free and fair competition between competing interests. Such a democracy is characterised by the presence of three features: a diverse range of competing interests; numerous **access points**; and the inability of any single group to exclude any other from the political process.

> **TIP:** It is commonly argued that the UK is a pluralist democracy. Others, however, maintain that the UK system of government is in fact dominated by elites: that members of a particular social class, those of a particular educational background, or those who move in particular social circles (virtuous circles) dominate the higher levels of government, industry and the media. See **elites theory**.

pluralist theory: referring collectively to the principles upon which a **pluralist democracy** is said to operate. Closely associated with the work of writers such as Robert A. Dahl and their opposition to the ideas put forward by C. Wright Mills in his seminal work, The Power Elite (1956). See also **elites theory**.

plurality: a majority. See **simple plurality**.

pocket boroughs: parliamentary boroughs where the number of eligible voters was so small as to allow them to be individually 'bought-off' or coerced in the days before the **secret ballot**.

policy: a proposed or actual strategy addressing a particular issue or area of government provision.

- The policies a party intends to pursue are set out in its election **manifesto**.
- The government's policies in a particular area are referred to collectively as a 'programme'.

policy communities: see **policy network**

Policy Directorate: see **Policy Unit**

Policy Forum: a *Conservative Party* body allowing individual *party members*, *MPs* and experts to advise the party leader on matters of *policy*. See also Labour's *National Policy Forum*.

- The Forum was established in 1998 under *William Hague*'s *Fresh Future* initiative.
- It is only an advisory body; it lacks the power to make party policy itself.
  It operates on the basis of regional conferences that table proposals for discussion at the annual *party conference*.

policy network: the politicians, *civil servants*, policy specialists, *pressure groups* and other interested parties that work together in formulating *policy* in a particular field.

- The pressure groups specialist R. Baggot and others offer more precision by dividing the term into two subcategories: policy communities and issue networks.
- Policy communities are said to be more focused and more stable than issue networks, as they involve fewer parties and generally operate on a more formal and permanent basis.

Policy Unit: the body in the *Prime Minister's Office* that has traditionally provided the *prime minister* with advice on *policy*. Established in 1974, it is staffed by political appointees serving as temporary *civil servants*, as well as permanent civil servants brought in from various government departments.

Example

After the 2001 general election, the Policy Unit and the prime minister's *Private Office* were merged to form the Policy Directorate, which was headed by *Jeremy Heywood*.

political adviser: see *advisor*

political cause groups: *pressure groups* that campaign in pursuit of a cause that is essentially political in nature, e.g. *Charter 88* (now part of Unlock Democracy). A subcategory in the *sectional/cause group typology*.

political culture: the opinions, attitudes and values that shape political behaviour. A nation's political culture consists of the collectively held attitudes of *citizens* towards the political system and their place in it.

Example

In the 1950s and 1960s, UK political culture was said to be based on three principles.

- **homogeneity:** the view that people within a country share certain key values, a sense of togetherness that transcends that which divides them. Developments such as the expansion of immigration since the 1960s, the rise of Scottish and Welsh nationalism, and the decline of the Church of England have created a situation in which the UK is often said to be characterised more by multiculturalism than by homogeneity.
- **consensus:** where UK citizens accept the basic 'rules of the game'. These rules include the need for toleration and for pragmatism; for peaceful negotiation and compromise. The *postwar consensus* ended with the rise of politicians such as *Margaret Thatcher* in the 1970s. In recent years this decline in consensus has also been reflected in the proliferation of single-issue campaigns, the rise of *direct action*, and increased support for *nationalist parties*.
- **deference:** that people defer to an elite that is seen as 'born to rule'. A natural willingness to accept an ingrained class-based inequality; a hierarchy. The power

of the ruling elite was often perpetuated by the veil of secrecy and mystery that surrounded it. In recent times, the development of a modern, less deferential media has done much to demystify such individuals and institutions. Unthinking deference to such elite figures has, as a result, declined significantly.

political levy: the sum paid to the *Labour Party* by an *affiliated* organisation, such as *trade unions*, in order to enrol its members as affiliated party members. Payment of a political levy grants voting rights to affiliated organisations and their members at the annual *party conference*. This has raised concerns about affiliated organisations, particularly trade unions, being able to 'buy votes'. See also *levy plus* and *block vote*.

political networks: see *policy networks*

political office: see *Political Unit*

political participation: the ways in which individuals involve themselves in political processes.
- Political participation is often measured simply in terms of electoral *turnout*.
- Other forms of political participation include membership of or involvement in *political parties*, *pressure groups* and protest movements.
- Some choose to participate by seeking election to public office. Others may *campaign* or carry out *canvassing* on behalf of others.

> **TIP:** In March 2006, the *Power Inquiry* published 'Power to the People', its report into the state of political participation in the UK. It concluded that declining electoral *turnout* reflected a process of disengagement caused, in part, by a lack of confidence in democratic institutions and a sense that the main political parties were too similar.

Political Parties, Elections and Referendums Act (2000): a piece of *statute law* that regulated campaign finance and changed the basis on which future UK *referendums* would be held.
- The Act followed on from some of the recommendations made in the *Neill Report (1998)*.
- It imposed overall limits on party spending in general election campaigns (£30,000 per constituency) as well as requiring that the national parties had publicly to declare all donations over £5,000.
- The Act also introduced limited state funding of parties under the Policy Development Fund.
- In addition, the wording of the questions posed in future referendums and the funding of the 'yes' and 'no' campaigns were to be regulated.

> **TIP:** The Act sought to make parties less reliant on wealthy individual backers, challenging the perception that politics was 'for sale'. However, despite these changes, Labour, Conservatives, and the Liberal Democrats still declared £9m, £8m and £4m in donations respectively in 2005. Indeed, some of these 'donations' had been given in the form of long-term interest-free or low interest loans as a way of circumventing the Act's regulations on donations. See also *cash for peerages*.

political party: a group of like-minded individuals who organise themselves in order to select **candidates**, secure election to political office and, ultimately, pursue their chosen policies by entering **government**.

- The main UK political parties were traditionally said to operate along ideological lines, though this has been less apparent in an age of **catch-all parties**.
- Political parties seeking to field candidates in UK elections must first register with the Electoral Commission.

> **TIP:** Some *pressure groups* and *single-issue parties* field candidates as a way of raising their profile or the profile of their cause, even where they have little realistic chance of being elected. Such groups generally have no desire to form a government. In a similar vein, the *nationalist parties* operating in Scotland and Wales have no desire to field candidates outside their home nation (i.e. in other parts of the UK) because they seek greater political autonomy for their own nations.

political recruitment: the means by which individuals are selected and equipped for life in public office. **Political parties** play a key role in filtering and selecting **candidates** for elected office. The **House of Commons** is said to play a key role in political recruitment to ministerial office. See also **primary election**.

Political Unit: the body in the **Prime Minister's Office** responsible for liaising between the **prime minister** and the broader party. It is staffed by individuals employed and paid by the party as opposed to regular **civil servants**, whose salaries are funded through taxation. It was previously called the Political Office.

politician: an individual seeking election to or serving in a political office. See **incumbent**.

politicisation: the process by which issues or individuals normally regarded as being beyond the party-political fray are drawn into it.

- Politicisation of the *judiciary* is said to result from appointments being made on political grounds as opposed to being simply meritocratic.
- The way in which the UK judiciary was drawn into areas of political controversy in the wake of the **Human Rights Act (1998)** was also seen by some as evidence of politicisation.
- **Margaret Thatcher** was accused of politicising the **civil service** by appointing sympathetic individuals to senior posts in the service.
- The rise of **special advisors** (or **spin doctors**) under **New Labour** was also said to have politicised the civil service.

politics: a process of conflict resolution whereby **power** and resources are divided between individuals, between individuals and the **state** and between the different institutions that comprise the state.

> **TIP:** Within any society conflict will arise as a result of:
> - scarcity of resources – where certain goods are in short supply, conflict will result over the distribution of the available resources
> - ideological differences – individuals might take a radically different view of the way in which society should be organised

- differences in approach – individuals may share an ideology but have a different approach in achieving their common goals
- divisions of labour and power – individuals might be unhappy about their own position within society; conflict might result from their desire to challenge the status quo

poll: referring to an election ('going to the polls') or the results recorded in an election. See also *opinion poll*.

poll tax: a system of local taxation introduced in place of the *rates* in 1989 (in Scotland) and 1990 (England and Wales).

- Officially known as the Community Charge, the tax was dubbed the 'poll tax' because all those over the age of 18 (i.e. those who were eligible to vote at the polls) were required to contribute.
- It was argued that adults would be more likely to participate in local elections (and thereby hold their local *councils* accountable) if those voting were all required to help pay for council services through taxation.
- The tax provoked widespread opposition (see *Anti-Poll Tax Federation*).
- *Margaret Thatcher*'s ongoing support for the poll tax was one of the factors that precipitated her departure from office in November 1990.
- The *council tax* replaced the poll tax in 1993.

polling card: a card sent to a *registered voter* ahead of an *election*.

- The polling card tells voters when the election is taking place and also gives them the location of their *polling station*.
- Electors present their polling card at the polling station and have their names checked off against the *electoral register* before being given a *ballot paper*.

polling day: *election* day.

polling station: one of a number of venues where *votes* can be cast at an *election*.

- Polling stations are generally set up in schools or church halls, though they have also operated from supermarkets and other public areas in recent years as part of an effort to improve turnout.
- Voters are generally expected to attend the polling station printed on their *polling card*.

pollster: an individual who compiles and analyses *opinion polls*.

Example

New Labour's polling activities at its media centre in *Millbank Tower* in London were co-ordinated by its chief pollster Phillip Gould.

pooled sovereignty: describing the style of collective decision making practised within the *EU*. A form of power-sharing that stops short of *federalism* because individual *member states* ultimately retain their national *sovereignty*.

popular vote: the total number of *votes* cast across a nation or region.

positive rights: those rights explicitly assigned to *citizens* and commonly *entrenched* as a part of the overall constitutional settlement. See also *negative rights*.

postal voting: where voters cast their ballots by post as opposed to attending a *polling station* on the day of the election. Recent elections have seen UK governments encouraging the wider use of postal voting as a way of improving voter *turnout*.

postmodern election campaign: characterising an election *campaign* where the national parties use *opinion polls*, *focus groups* and paid political consultants to capture target seats. See also *pollster*.

Example

The Conservative Party employed the Australian consultant Lynton Crosby to run its 2005 *general election campaign*. Crosby targeted *floating voters* in *marginal* target seats by focusing on issues such as immigration.

postwar consensus: characterising the broad agreement between the **Labour Party** and **Conservative Party** over domestic and foreign *policy* that emerged after the Second World War.

- The consensus saw the parties cooperating over the creation of the **welfare state** and the adoption of a Keynesian economic policy (see **Keynesianism**).
- The postwar consensus began to break down in the 1970s and was said to have ended with the more ideological, **adversarial politics** that accompanied **Thatcherism**.

> **TIP:** Some argue that the rise of New Labour and, more recently, David Cameron's New Tories, has heralded the emergence of a new consensus.

potential insiders: an *outsider group* that might ultimately achieve insider status and a subcategory within the *insider/outsider typology*. Such groups are often small and lacking in experience. Governments may choose not to grant them insider status because they regard them as lacking legitimacy.

Powell, Jonathan (1956–): *Tony Blair*'s *chief of staff*.

power: the ability to do something or make something happen.

- Power can be sub-divided into four different forms: absolute power; persuasive power; legitimate power; and coercive power.
- Absolute power is the unlimited ability to do as one wishes. In reality, this form of power exists only in theoretical terms, as even the ultimate threat (i.e. death) will not force every individual to comply with one's instructions.
- Persuasive power is the ability to make things happen because others are persuaded of the merits of a given course of action.
- Legitimate power is the ability to make things happen because others accept an individual's right to make decisions.
- Coercive power is the ability to make things happen because others are pressured into complying by means of laws and penalties.
- In a *democracy*, governments generally exercise legitimate power, though there will also be elements of persuasive and coercive power at play.

> **TIP:** It is important to be able to distinguish between power and *authority* – which may involve the legitimate use of power.

Power Inquiry: an inquiry into the state of political participation in the UK initiated by the Joseph Rowntree Trust.

- The inquiry resulted in the publication of the Power Report – *Power to the People. The report of Power: an independent inquiry into Britain's democracy.*
- The report's main conclusion was that the popular disillusionment with democratic institutions and the main political parties demanded immediate attention.

Example: recommendations of the Power Report:
- A rebalancing of power away from the executive and unaccountable bodies towards Parliament and local government
- The introduction of greater responsiveness and choice into the electoral and party systems
- Allowing citizens a much more direct and focused say over political decisions and policies

Power Report: see *Power Inquiry*

PPER (2002): see *Political Parties, Elections and Referendums Act (2002)*

PPS: see *parliamentary private secretary*

PR: see *proportional representation*

precedent: a legal principle established under *common law* that guides the courts when determining the outcome of subsequent cases. See *judicial restraint* and *stare decisis*.

pre-modern election campaign: a style of *campaign* with local *canvassing*, local public meetings and the use of low-budget *media* such as posters and pamphlets. Typical of campaigns before the 1980s

prerogative powers: constitutional powers resting with the *monarch* but exercised in practice by the *prime minister.*

Example

The prerogative powers include the power to dissolve *Parliament* (i.e. call a *general election*) as well as the power of *patronage*.

President of the European Commission: the head of the *European Commission*, nominated by the *European Council* and confirmed in post by the *European Parliament*.

President of the Supreme Court: the formal title held by the most senior of the 12 justices serving on the UK *Supreme Court*.
- The second most senior justice holds the position of Deputy President.
- Under the terms of the *Constitutional Reform Act (2005)*, both the President and Deputy President sit on the five-member *ad hoc* selection commission that nominates new members of the court when vacancies arise.

presidential: a style of leadership associated with a president, particularly the president of the USA.

presidential government: a system of government under which a president acts as chief executive or *head of government*. See also *parliamentary government*.

Example

In the USA the president is a directly elected *head of government*, with the US *legislature* (Congress) being elected independently. See also *separation of powers*.

presidential prime minister: the view that the prime minister has become a presidential figure, both in power and in style.
- This concept was developed by writers such as Michael Foley with his work on *spatial leadership*.
- Both *Margaret Thatcher* and *Tony Blair* were criticised for adopting a presidential style because of their powerful positions, their aloofness, their dismissive attitudes towards *Parliament* and their lack of consultation with *cabinet* (see *bilateral meetings* and *sofa government*).
- The concept of a presidential prime minister also reflected the increasing concentration of power around the premier within the *core executive*.

> **TIP:** There is some debate, however, over how far comparisons with the USA can be taken, as they underestimate the limitations imposed by both the influence of *political parties* in the UK and the power of some *cabinet ministers*.

presidentialism: referring either to a system of *presidential government* or to the emergence of a *presidential prime minister*.

press: part of the *media* comprising *broadsheet* and *tabloid* newspapers. The UK press is privately owned. It is therefore free to criticise government and take an active part in election *campaigns*. See also *media theory*.

> **TIP:** The importance of the UK press is reflected in *New Labour*'s efforts to court the press baron Rupert Murdoch ahead of the 1997 *general election*. Murdoch's publications, most notably the *Sun* newspaper, were said to have contributed to the party's defeat at the hands of *John Major*'s Conservatives in the 1992 general election. The paper famously ran with the headline, 'It's the Sun Wot Won It' on the morning after that election.

Press Office: the body in the *Prime Minister's Office* that handles *media* relations for the *prime minister*.
- The Press Office is staffed by *civil servants* and political appointees and operating under the guidance of the *press secretary*.
- It has gained a higher profile in recent years as a result of the role played by *press secretaries* such as Bernard Ingham (under *Margaret Thatcher*) and *Alastair Campbell* (under *Tony Blair*). See also *Director of Communications and Strategy* and *spin doctor*.

press secretary: a government official responsible for looking after relations with the *media*. The term generally refers to the press secretary to the *prime minister*, who heads the Number 10 *Press Office*. See also *Director of Communications and Strategy* and *spin doctor*.

Example

Bernard Ingham brought increased influence to the role as *Margaret Thatcher*'s press secretary. Alastair Campbell, *Tony Blair*'s press secretary between 1997 and 2001, was renowned for his central role in government decision making.

pressure group: a group of individuals who share a sectional interest (see *sectional group*) or cause (see *cause group*) and come together in order to put pressure on policymakers at *Westminster* and elsewhere. Pressure groups are a key feature of a *pluralist democracy*. See also *sectional/cause group typology* and *insider/outsider typology*.

Prevention of Terrorism Act (2005): the piece of *statute law* under which *control orders* were introduced. See also *Anti-terrorism, Crime and Security Act (2001)*.

primacy model: a simple voting model that holds that *long-term factors* such as *social class* are more important than *short-term factors* in determining *voting behaviour*. Supporters of this view tend to see stability in *voting behaviour* as opposed to *volatility*. Contrast with *recency model*.

primary election: an election held in order to select a party's candidate(s) for the election proper.
- Primaries are used in most US states, both in the selection of each party's presidential candidate and in the selection of congressional candidates.
- Primaries enhance public *participation* in the process of candidate selection.
- In open primaries, all *registered voters* are allowed to have their say on who they think should represent the party. In a closed primary, only the registered supporters of a party are given a say.

Example

Primaries are not a feature of the UK system as candidates are normally selected by the *constituency* party. However, the *Conservative Party* has experimented with primaries as a way of engaging with the broader public. In 2009, the party held an open primary in order to choose the *candidate* who would represent it in the parliamentary constituency of Totnes at the *general election*. The danger of such open primaries is that they allow the supporters of other parties to raid the primary and vote for a candidate whom they feel they will be able to defeat more easily.

primary legislative powers: the power to initiative and pass *legislation* alone without having to seek approval from some higher sovereign authority. See also *Scottish Parliament*. Contrast with secondary legislative powers (see *Welsh Assembly*).

prime minister: the *head of government* (i.e. chief executive) under the UK system.
- Formally appointed not as prime minister but as *First Lord of the Treasury*.
- Appointed by the monarch as a result of being leader of the single largest party in the *House of Commons* following a *general election*.
- The central figure in the UK *cabinet*. See also *primus inter pares*, *cabinet government*, *prime ministerial government* and *presidential prime minister*.

prime ministerial government: a model of relations within the *core executive* that sees the *prime minister* as a dominant figure. See also *presidential prime minister*. It is closely associated with the ideas of Richard Crossman, a Labour *cabinet minister* in the late 1960s and author of *Diaries of a Cabinet Minister*. Contrast with *cabinet government*.

prime ministerial power: the *power* exercised by the UK *head of government*.

- The power of the modern prime minister can be said to be divided into five broad areas: powers of *patronage*; powers over *cabinet*, government and *civil service*; powers over *Parliament* as party leader; powers over *agenda-setting* and policy making; and powers on the world stage.
- Prime ministerial power is said to have grown in recent years, with *incumbents* increasingly relying upon *bilateral meetings* and smaller ministerial groupings as opposed to making decisions in meetings of the full cabinet. See also *prime ministerial government* and *presidential government*.

> **TIP:** The extent to which incumbent prime ministers can exercise power to their fullest extent will depend upon their own abilities, the abilities of those around them and the prevailing political context, which will include the size of their Commons majority as well as what *Harold Macmillan* referred to as 'Events, dear boy. Events'. *Herbert Asquith* famously asserted that 'the office of the Prime Minister is what its holder chooses and is able to make of it'.

prime minister's department: a body that does not formally exist but has been proposed as a means of affording the *prime minister* better *policy* advice and administrative support.

> **TIP:** Some argue that the extent to which the *Prime Minister's Office* and *Cabinet Office* have grown and been made more directly *accountable* to the prime minister since 1997 has created a de facto prime minister's department. This view is made more plausible by the extent to which such bodies have been physically relocated in and around *Downing Street* since 2001.

Prime Minister's Office: describing a collection of bodies supporting the work of the *prime minister*. It is located in *Number 10*, though it is not a room in the sense of the US president's Oval Office. Populated by a blend of appointees, career *civil servants* and *special advisors*, the Prime Minister's Office has expanded in recent years to employ well over 150 staff. It traditionally comprises bodies such as the *Private Office*, the *Press Office*, the *Political Unit* and the *Policy Unit*. See also *prime minister's department*.

> **TIP:** The Prime Minister's Office was reorganised by Tony Blair in the wake of the 2001 general election:
> - The *Private Office* was merged with the *Policy Unit* to form the *Policy Directorate*.
> - The prime minister's *press secretary*, *Alastair Campbell*, was given a new title: *Director of Communications*. Two civil service deputies took over the management of press briefings.
> - The post of prime minister's *principal private secretary* was abolished and replaced by a policy advisor.
> - Three new bodies, the Delivery Unit, the Office of Public Services Reform and the Forward Strategy Unit were created.

Prime Minister's Questions: a half-hourly slot in the *House of Commons* every Wednesday when MPs may ask the *prime minister* oral questions.

- First introduced under prime minister *Harold Macmillan* in 1961.
- Originally consisted of two 15-minute sessions on Tuesday and Thursday afternoons. Changed to a single 30-minute Wednesday slot in 1997, under *Tony Blair*.

> **TIP:** Though widely criticised, Prime Minister's Questions is a high-profile example of the way in which the *legislature* exercises *scrutiny* over the *executive*. The decision to switch from two slots to a single longer slot in 1997 was supposed to allow for more detailed questioning. However, it is still largely seen as an opportunity for *opposition* parties to try to embarrass the premier with the use of *supplementary questions*, while the prime minister's own *backbenchers* routinely ask questions that allow the premier to reel off scripted responses trumpeting the government's many achievements.

Primrose, Archibald (Earl of Rosebery): *prime minister* (Liberal), 1894–95.

primus inter pare: Latin for 'first among equals'; the view that the *prime minister* is simply one member of a *cabinet* that operates as a collective decision-making body. See *cabinet government*.

principal private secretary: the high-ranking career *civil servant* who traditionally ran the prime minister's *Private Office* at Number 10.

- Traditionally, the principal private secretary acted as a gatekeeper to the prime minister, controlling access to the premier.
- Each *cabinet minister* is served by a principal private secretary within his or her own *department*.

> **TIP:** The role of principal private secretary declined with the emergence of the post of prime minister's *chief of staff*. In 2001, Tony Blair replaced the post of principal private secretary with a policy advisor. See *Prime Minister's Office*.

private bill: a legislative proposal that applies only to a particular company, public body or section of the population. See also *personal bill* and *public bill*.

private finance initiative (PFI): see *public–private partnership*

Private Members' Bill: a legislative proposal proposed by a backbench MP. Such bills can be initiated in one of three ways: through the private members' ballot (see *ballot bill*); under the *Ten Minute Rule*; or through *Standing Order 58*.

> **TIP:** A lack of parliamentary time means that most Private Members' Bills do not make it into *law*. Those that succeed generally do so because the government has provided the additional time required for the various debates and divisions to be concluded.

Private Office: the body that manages the *prime minister's* official engagements and helps to control the flow of information both to and from the premier. It is a constituent part of the *Prime Minister's Office*, staffed mainly by career civil servants and headed by the *prime minister's principal private secretary*.

privatisation: the sale of state-owned, nationalised industries into private ownership. A policy closely associated with *Margaret Thatcher*'s stated desire to 'roll back the frontiers of the state' in the 1980s, but also continued under the premierships of *John Major* and *Tony Blair*.

Privy Council: a *bipartisan* grouping of senior politicians, both past and present.
- Originally established as a group of advisors to the *monarch*.
- Members are appointed for life by the monarch, on the advice of the *prime minister*.
- The Council can make laws when Parliament is not sitting by means of an *Order in Council*.

> **TIP:** The Privy Council's judicial committee traditionally had the role of resolving disputes between *Westminster* and the devolved governments in Northern Ireland, Scotland and Wales. In October 2009, this role was transferred to the new UK Supreme Court under the terms of the *Constitutional Reform Act (2005)*. However, the Council's judicial committee will retain its role as the final court of appeal in cases originating in some Commonwealth countries.

professional politician: a politician whose income comes solely from his or her work as an *MP*.
- Professional politicians are often referred to as 'career politicians'.
- In an age before MPs received salaries, it was common for members of the *Commons* who did not have independent means to have paid jobs outside *Parliament* in order to support themselves. Indeed, many regarded their work in Parliament as an act of 'public service' as opposed to a 'job'.
- Though some MPs still hold down jobs, take directorships or have other financial interests outside Parliament, many now see political service and their own advancement at *Westminster* as a career in itself.

> **TIP:** Critics argue that such professional politicians can lose touch with the real world of work. Career politicians who are *backbenchers* are said to be less willing to defy the party *whip* for fear of missing out on a future promotion to ministerial office. Career politicians already serving as government ministers are said to be reluctant to resign their posts under the *role responsibility* strand of *individual ministerial responsibility* because they have no other income to fall back on. Some take the opposite view, arguing that MPs should be focusing on their roles in Parliament and the needs of their constituents, rather than pursuing outside interests.

programme: see *policy*

progressive liberalism: also known a 'new liberalism', a more compassionate form of liberalism that saw the need for some regulation of the market as well as the provision of basic welfare. It was originally advanced by writers such as T. H. Green and L. T. Hobhouse. It later developed into the mixed economy supported by *John Maynard Keynes* and William Beveridge. Contrast with *classical liberalism*.

Pro-life Alliance: an anti-abortion pressure group and single issue political party that fielded candidates in the 1997 and 2001 *general elections*.

- In 1997, the party fielded 53 candidates and secured 18,545 votes nationwide. In 2001, it fielded 27 candidates and garnered a total of 9,453 votes. The party did not field candidates in the 2005 general election.
- The party successfully took legal action against the BBC's decision to prevent the broadcast of the party's 2001 party political broadcast, which had included images of aborted foetuses. Such images could have been broadcast had the party fielded candidates in 2005.
- The group also took legal action in a number of cases relating to embryology, euthanasia and abortion.

promotional group: see *cause group*

proportional electoral system: see *proportional representation*

proportionality: where the percentage share of the *popular vote* won by each party is in broad proportion to the percentage of the available seats that each party wins in a *legislature*. It is an electoral outcome achieved under a system of proportional representation.

proportional representation: describing any *electoral system* that seeks to apportion seats in a *legislature* in broad proportion to the percentage of the *popular vote* won by each *political party*.

- It is a feature of proportional systems such as the *party list system* and *single transferable vote (STV)*. *Hybrid electoral systems* such as the *additional member system (AMS)* used in elections to the *Scottish Parliament* also offer a degree of proportional representation as a result of the *top-up* mechanism employed.
- *Majoritarian electoral systems* such as *first-past-the-post* and *supplementary vote (SV)* do not offer proportional representation, e.g. at the 2005 *general election* the *Labour Party* secured 35.2% of the popular vote but won 55.0% (355) of the seats contested. The *Liberal Democrats*, in contrast, won only 9.6% of the seats (62) even though they secured 22.1% of the popular vote.

prospective voting model: a model of *voting behaviour* that holds that voters make their choices on the basis of how well they think each party would perform in the future, if elected. See also *retrospective voting model*.

protest voting: where *voters* cast a *ballot* in favour of a *candidate* or party they would not normally support in order to send a message either to their 'natural' party, or to the *government* of the day. Protest voting is often more prevalent at elections where the outcome is less crucial to the voter, e.g. in local elections or elections to the *European Parliament*. See *voting context model*.

Example: UKIP performance at general elections and European elections (1997–2009)

Support for the *UK Independence Party (UKIP)* at *European elections* is commonly seen as evidence of protest voting, as the party rarely performs as well at the *general elections* that occur between such contests. See the table overleaf.

UKIP election performance

Type of election	Year	Popular vote (%)	Seats won (total)
General election	1997	1.10%	0
European election	1999	6.96%	3
General election	2001	2.10%	0
European election	2004	16.10%	12
General election	2005	2.80%	0
European election	2009	16.50%	13

psephology: the study of *elections* and *voting behaviour*.

Public Accounts Committee: a *non-departmental select committee* operating in the *House of Commons*.

- First established in 1861.
- Retrospectively scrutinises government expenditure in order to ensure that money has been well spent.
- Has no power to stop government spending – due to the retrospective nature of its work – but can embarrass the government and thereby force it to adopt more efficient practices.

Public Administration Committee: a *non-departmental select committee* operating in the *House of Commons* that scrutinises the way in which central government *departments* operate.

public bill: proposed *legislation* applying to the public as a whole. Public bills account for the majority of legislation passing through *Parliament*. The government sponsors most public bills, though around 10% are *Private Members' Bills*. See also *private bill*.

public inquiries: public investigations that serve either to examine the merits or demerits of a particular policy or to scrutinise the past actions of public officials such as *MPs* or government *ministers*.

- The Heathrow Terminal 5 inquiry would be an example of the former. The *Nolan Committee* would be an example of the latter.
- Public inquiries are criticised, first, because they have no ultimate power to deflect governments from their chosen course of action and, second, because most inquiries are headed up by establishment figures: the 'great and the good'. These individuals rarely criticise government in their final reports.
- The cost of such inquiries also prompts criticism. The Heathrow Terminal 5 inquiry (1995–99) cost taxpayers £80 million.

public opinion: collectively held attitudes and beliefs as revealed periodically in the findings of *opinion polls*.

public–private partnership: describing the collaboration between the public and private sectors in the delivery of government services and a feature of *New Labour*'s *third way*.

QMV: see *qualified majority voting (QMV)*

qualified majority voting (QMV): a system of weighted voting employed in the *EU*'s *Council of Ministers*.

- Under QMV, each EU *member state* is given a number of votes in broad proportion to its population. A predetermined number of voters is then required in order for a measure to pass.
- QMV was introduced under the *Single European Act (1986)* but extended into a greater number of policy areas under subsequent EU treaties. See *Maastricht, Treaty of (1992)*; *Amsterdam, Treaty of (1997)*; *Nice Treaty of (2001)*; *Lisbon, Treaty of (2007)*.

> **TIP:** QMV was introduced into most areas of decision making because EU enlargement made voting on the basis of unanimity unworkable. Most decisions are now taken under QMV, although existing member states still retain a national *veto* over the accession of new states.

quango: an acronym for quasi autonomous non-governmental organisation.

- Quasi (or semi) autonomous (independent) because they tend to work with a degree of independence, and non-governmental because their members are not normally drawn from the ranks of elected politicians or the *civil service*.
- The number of quangos has increased massively since the end of the 1970s. Some estimate that there are now over 7,000 such bodies.

Example

Different types of quango:
- **Advisory quangos:** specialist bodies established to advise and guide government, e.g. the Spongiform Encephalopathy Advisory Committee (SEAC), which advised the government on 'mad-cow disease' (BSE).
- **Regulatory quangos:** bodies that apply and sometimes formulate regulations governing particular areas of activity, e.g. the Office for Standards in Education (OFSTED) that organises the inspection of state schools.
- **Administrative quangos:** organisations that administer an area of policy on behalf of the government, e.g. the Qualifications and Curriculum Authority (QCA) that managed various aspects of educational assessment.
- **Spending quangos:** bodies that are set up to distribute funds on the behalf of government, e.g. the various National Lottery Boards that allocate the money raised for good causes.

quangocracy: government by *quangos* as opposed to by directly **accountable** elected institutions.

quangocrat: an unelected bureaucrat working within a *quango*.

quasi-federalism: describing the way in which the UK appears to have moved closer to *federalism* as a result of the process of *devolution* initiated by **New Labour** from 1997. The term is particularly apt in respect of the *primary legislative power* given to the *Scottish Parliament*.

quasi-government: where a public sector body is run by unelected and unaccountable government appointees as opposed to elected politicians or the regular *civil service*. See also *quangos* and *regional development agencies*.

quasi-legislative power: the ability of senior courts to establish legal precedents that appear to have the effect of 'changing' as opposed to simply 'applying' the law. See also *judicial review*.

Queen's Speech: the speech setting out the government's legislative programme for the year ahead, delivered in the **House of Lords** at the **State Opening of Parliament**. It marks the start of the *parliamentary session* in November. Although drafted by the government, it is delivered by the *monarch*.

Question Time: see *Prime Minister's Questions* and *Ministers' Question Time*

Questions of Procedure for Ministers: see *Ministerial Code*

quota the number of votes a *candidate* must secure in order to be elected to one of the seats being contested under a *single transferable vote (STV)* electoral system. Known as the Droop Formula, the quota varies from election to election.

$$THE\ DROOP\ FORMULA: \left(\frac{\text{total valid votes cast}}{\text{seats in constituency}} + 1\right) + 1$$

rates: a property-based system of local taxation that was replaced by the Community Charge. See *poll tax*.

rational choice model: an explanation of *voting behaviour* that sees *voters* as rational individuals choosing between *political parties* on the basis of their *policies*, leaders and prior performance in office. Such rational choices can be made on a *retrospective voting model* or *prospective voting model* basis. See also *issue voting model* and *supermarket voting model*.

realignment: the emergence of new long-term bonds between specific groups of voters and individual political parties.

> **TIP:** Some saw the emergence of *working-class Tories* in the 1980s and increasing numbers of middle-class Labour voters in the 1990s (see *champagne socialist*) as evidence of a realignment in British politics. Others argued that such developments were temporary and should therefore be seen as further evidence of the process of *dealignment* that had taken place from the 1970s.

rebellion (backbench): where *MPs* vote against the instructions issued by their party *whips*. Rebellions in the *House of Commons* rarely lead to a government defeat but they do reflect unhappiness on the part of the *backbenchers*.

> **Example**
> According to Philip Cowley, there were 6,520 individual votes cast against the Labour Party *whip* during *New Labour's* first decade in office (1997–2007): 139 Labour MPs rebelled against the decision to go to war in Iraq, 72 rebelled on the introduction of top-up fees and 65 opposed the introduction of foundation hospitals.

recall election: a procedure that allows *registered voters* to petition for a public vote by which an elected official can be removed from office before the end of his or her term.
- In most cases recalls are permitted only where there is evidence of corruption, negligence or, in some cases, incompetence.
- Around one in three US states offer this power to voters, though in practice recalls are often difficult to execute. Recall petitions normally have to secure the support of a predetermined number of *votes* before they can qualify for a *ballot*.
- Recalls have not traditionally been available to voters in the UK, though the scandal over *MPs' expenses* in 2009 led to calls for the introduction of such a system.

Example

In the US state of California a recall of a state-wide official such as the Governor would require a number of signatures equal to at least 12% of the total votes cast in the last election for the office in question. Those organising the 2003 recall of California Governor Gray Davis claimed that the Democrat had 'mismanaged state finances', 'threatened public safety by cutting services' and been 'slacking-off' in his job, having allegedly 'gone two years without calling a cabinet meeting'. Davis lost the recall vote (55.3% to 44.7%) and was replaced by Arnold Schwarzenegger, who was subsequently elected with 48.7% of the vote in a field of 135 candidates.

TIP: Though the recall process can make politicians more *accountable* to voters, it also undermines the principle of *representative democracy*, e.g. when the 'Recall Gray Davies' campaign launched in February 2003, the Governor was only weeks into his second term having been convincingly re-elected the previous November. There was even evidence that the campaign had been organised and funded by disgruntled Republicans.

recency model: a simple theory that holds that *short-term factors* such as the *campaign*, events and the images of the party leaders are now more important than *long-term factors* in determining *voting behaviour*.
- Advocates of this model argue that voting patterns are increasingly volatile because processes such as *embourgeoisement* have resulted in *dealignment*.
- As many as 10 million *voters* are now said to make up their minds in the month leading up to a *general election*. Contrast with *primacy model*.

Red Ken: see *Livingstone, Ken (1945–)*

Red Toryism: a brand of *paternalist conservatism* that harks back to the era of *one-nation conservatism*. It seeks to address social problems such as civil *disengagement* and the breakdown of communities. It is closely associated with the ideas of Philip Blond and his *think-tank* ResPublica. See also *Centre for Social Justice*.

redress of grievances: any means by which a *citizen* might seek to overturn improper treatment at the hands of a publicly funded body. Citizens might seek redress of grievances via their *MP* or through *court* action. The *ombudsman* and *tribunals* also provide another avenue through which wrongs can be righted. See also *maladministration*.

referendum: a vote on a single issue put to a public ballot by the government of the day. See also *initiative*, *recall election* and *threshold*.
- Referendums are a device offering a degree of *direct democracy*.
- They are generally framed in the form of a simple 'yes/no' question.
- Rarely used in the UK, they are employed more widely in countries such as Switzerland.
- UK-wide referendums have been promised before the UK adopts the *euro* or changes the *electoral system* used in elections to *Westminster*.

TIP: Those who oppose the wider use of referendums in the UK argue that such devices undermine our system of *representative democracy*.

Referendums called by the Westminster Parliament (1973–2009)

Date	Who voted	Question (paraphrased)	% Yes	% No	% Turnout
1973 (March)	N. Ireland	Should Northern Ireland stay in the UK?	98.9	1.1	58.1
1975 (June)	UK	Should UK stay in the EEC?	67.2	32.8	63.2
1979 (March)	Scotland	Should there be a Scottish Parliament?	51.6	48.4	63.8
1979 (March)	Wales	Should there be a Welsh Parliament?	20.3	79.7	58.3
1997 (Sept.)	Scotland	Should there be a Scottish Parliament?	74.3	25.7	60.4
		With tax-varying powers?	63.5	36.5	
1997 (Sept.)	Wales	Should there be a Welsh Assembly?	50.3	49.7	50.1
1998 (May)	London	A London Mayor and London Assembly?	72.0	28.0	34.0
1998 (May)	N. Ireland	Approval for the Good Friday Agreement.	71.1	28.9	81.0
2004 (Nov.)	North East	A Regional Assembly for the North East?	22.0	78.0	48.0

Referendum Party: a *single-issue party* that advocated a *referendum* on the future of the UK's relationship with the *European Union*.
- Founded by the late Sir James Goldsmith ahead of the 1997 *general election*.
- The party fielded 547 *candidates* at the 1997 general election, averaging 3.1% of the *popular vote* in those *constituencies* where it ran, and 42 of the party's candidates won enough votes to retain their *deposits*.
- The party did not win any seats but almost certainly resulted in the defeat of a number of *Conservative Party* candidates by appealing to Conservative *Eurosceptics*.

regional assemblies: nine regional English bodies charged with the task of keeping the nine *regional development agencies* in touch with public opinion.
- New Labour's 2002 *White Paper*, 'Your Region Your Choice', envisaged nine directly elected assemblies.
- The 'no' vote in the 2004 *referendum* on an elected assembly for the North East saw plans for elected regional assemblies shelved.
- Of the nine assemblies, only one, the 25-member *London Assembly*, is directly elected, the other eight consisting of members appointed by elected local councils and regional stakeholders.

TIP: It was hoped that the creation of an additional tier of directly elected regional assemblies in England would go some way towards addressing the *West Lothian*

regional development agencies: nine regional bodies established in England in order to stimulate business and encourage regional economic development.
- Established under the Regional Development Agencies Act (1998).
- Expected to work alongside the nine *regional assemblies.*
- Widely seen as part of an emergent *quangocracy.*

regional government: see *regional assemblies* and *regional development agencies*

regional list system: see *party list system*

regional party: a *political party* that fields *candidates* in only one region or nation within the UK (i.e. England, Scotland, Wales or Northern Ireland). See *nationalist parties.*

regionalism: a desire to recognise regional differences through the creation of regional governments. See also *regional assemblies* and *regional development agencies.*

registered voter: a *citizen* whose name appears on the *electoral register* in a given *constituency*. Only those whose names appear on the register are entitled to *vote* at an *election.*

Register of Members' Interests: a record of monies and goods received by *MPs* in return for services provided in their capacity as MPs.
- First established in 1975 as a means of addressing perceived corruption in the *House of Commons.*
- Strengthened following the *Nolan Report (1995)*. See *cash for questions.*

reinforcement theory: the view that the media only reinforce the opinions and attitudes that individuals already hold as opposed to changing their outlook. See also *media theory.*

report stage: the stage of the *legislative process* that takes place between the *committee stage* and *third reading* in the *House of Commons* or the *House of Lords.* It involves each chamber considering those *amendments* made to a *bill* in *standing committee* and takes place on the floor of the House, often combined with the third reading.

representation: the act of speaking on behalf of someone else. See also *representative democracy*, *trustee model* and *delegate model.* It is said to be a core function of *political parties* and *pressure groups* as well as *MPs*, though the latter are also required to represent the interests of their political party.

representative: someone engaged in the act of *representation.* It generally refers to elected representatives such as *MPs.* See also *representative democracy.*

TIP: It is important to understand the difference between a representative and a delegate. See *trustee model* and *delegate model.*

representative democracy: a political system under which *citizens* elect the *representatives* who will make decisions of their behalf.
- Representative democracy is sometimes referred to as 'indirect democracy'.
- It is the basis upon which MPs in the *House of Commons* operate.

- It is often associated with the ideas of the writer and MP **Edmund Burke**, who in 1774 stated that 'Your representative owes you not his industry only but his judgement, and he betrays you if he sacrifices it to your opinion.'
- What Burke meant by this is that, under the **trustee model** of representation, our representatives are expected to use their judgement when making decisions. They are not simply delegates (see **delegate model**) and may therefore act against our wishes where they believe that to do so would be in our best interests. Contrast with **direct democracy**.

representative government: see *representative democracy*

reselection: a party procedure under which **incumbent** MPs are required to reapply to be that party's **candidate** ahead of an election.
- The **Labour Party** operated a system of mandatory reselection between 1980 and 1990.
- This policy allowed many **Constituency Labour Parties**, which were often dominated by **left-wing activists**, to remove their more **right-wing** sitting MPs as candidates.

See also **deselection**

> **TIP:** It is now the norm for incumbent MPs to be reselected to defend their seats at the *general election*, though a number of MPs were deselected and others stood down in the wake of the row over *MPs' expenses*.

resemblance theory: holds that those serving in an elected **legislature** should be typical of the communities that they serve. Thus, it is argued, they can more fully reflect their communities' collective values and beliefs.
- Neither the **Commons** nor the **Lords** reflects the socio-economic make-up of the broader UK population.
- Following the 2005 **general election**, the average age of MPs in the Commons was 50½ years; only 19% (125) were women; there were only five black MPs and four Muslim MPs.

> **TIP:** There are any number of reasons why the young, women, ethnic minorities and those from non-Christian faiths might be so underrepresented in the Commons, and not all are to do with ageism, sexism or racism, e.g. the unrepresentative profile of those putting themselves forward as candidates. A bigger question is whether or not this failure to elect a Commons that reflects the composition of the broader population is really a problem.

reshuffle: a process by which the **prime minister** moves **MPs** and **peers** in and out of government while at the same time reallocating departmental responsibilities between some or all of those already serving in ministerial positions.
- Reshuffles affect both **cabinet**-rank **ministers** and **junior ministers**.
- They may be used as a means by which the prime minister can demote or remove rivals while promoting his or her allies.
- They often occurring in the wake of cabinet resignations or ahead of Parliament's long summer recess as a way of bringing new blood into the **government**.

Example

The prime minister, **Gordon Brown**, was forced into a cabinet reshuffle on 5 June 2009, following the resignations of three high-profile cabinet ministers: the Home Secretary, Jacqui Smith; the Communities Secretary, Hazel Blears; and the Work and Pensions Minister, James Purnell.

RESPECT – The Unity Coalition: a left-wing *political party* founded in 2004.
- Commonly referred to simply as Respect.
- According to article 1 of the party's constitution, the word RESPECT in is an acronym for Respect, Equality, Socialism, Peace, Environment, Community and Trade unionism.
- Respect opposes war and campaigns on a broad *socialist* platform.
- *George Galloway* was elected as the Respect MP for the parliamentary *constituency* of Bethnal Green and Bow at the 2005 *general election*.
- In all, the party fielded 26 candidates at the 2005 general election, securing an average of 6.8% of the *popular vote* in those constituencies it contested.

responsibility: see *ministerial responsibility*, *individual ministerial responsibility* and *collective responsibility*

responsible government: a political system under which the *executive* is held accountable by the *legislature*.
- Under the UK system the executive is drawn from Parliament and relies upon the confidence of the legislature in order to remain in office. See *no-confidence motion*.
- Individual *ministers* are also answerable to Parliament through ministers' questions. See *Ministers' Question Time*.
- Responsible government is another term for *parliamentary government* and the *Westminster model*.

ResPublica: meaning 'commonwealth'. A moderate conservative *think-tank*. See *Red Toryism*.

retrospective voting model: an explanation of *voting behaviour* that regards a voter's choice of *political party* as being made according to the perceived competence of the parties based on their past performance. See also *prospective voting model*.

returning officer: an official responsible for managing electoral procedures and practices in each *constituency*. Such officials receive the *candidate* nominations, oversee the counting of *ballot papers* and announce the *election* result.

revising chamber: characterising the *House of Lords* in its role as the subordinate chamber in the UK's bicameral *legislature*. See also *Parliament Act (1911)* and *Parliament Act (1949)*, and *bicameralism*.

revolt (parliamentary): see *rebellion (backbench)*

revolving-door syndrome: characterising the way in which individuals in a *legislature* or an *executive* branch leave elected office to take up well-paid consultancy jobs with *pressure groups* or *lobbying firms*, while former consultants find themselves being offered key positions in the administration of the day. The term is more commonly applied when discussing the US system, though could also be applied to the work of lobbying firms in the UK.

right: see *right wing*

rights: the fundamental freedoms (civil or human rights) enjoyed by citizens. Many UK rights were originally established under *common law*, though many are now enshrined in *statute law*. See also *positive rights*, *negative rights*, *Bill of Rights*, *European Convention on Human Rights (1950)* and *Human Rights Act (1998)*. Similar to *civil liberties*.

right wing: referring to those *ideologies* that stress the importance of capitalism and 'small government', i.e. the right of citizens to live free from unnecessary government intervention.
- Right wing describes any position on the right of the political spectrum, from the centre-right through to extreme right-wing ideologies such as fascism. See also the *British National Party (BNP)*.
- It is closely associated with policies stressing the importance of the nation, the family and law and order.
- It is also used when referring to the right-most wing within a political party, even where the party as a whole is seen as being *left wing*.

rigid constitution: said to be a feature of a *codified constitution*. See also *entrenchment*.

roads protests: a series of high-profile *direct action* campaigns in opposition to *New Labour*'s road-building programme in the 1990s.
- Campaigners such as Daniel Hooper (who became known as 'Swampy') dug themselves into the ground and took up residence in trees, delaying a number of road-building projects, e.g. the construction of the Newbury Bypass, which passed through the environmentally sensitive Twyford Down.
- The actions of such protesters resulted in multi-million pound security bills.
- Many argue that such non-violent campaigns forced the *government* to rethink its road-building strategy.

Robinson, Frederick (Viscount Goderich): *prime minister* (Tory), 1827–28.

role responsibility: the strand of the constitutional *convention* of *individual ministerial responsibility* that requires *ministers* to resign as a matter of principle when they or their subordinates fail to discharge their departmental responsibilities to the required standard. See also *personal responsibility*.

Example

Lord Carrington resigned as *foreign secretary* in the wake of the Argentine invasion of the Falkland Islands in 1982 because he believed that his department had failed in its dealings with the Argentine government.

TIP: The convention is said to have been undermined by the apparent unwillingness of ministers to resign as required, e.g. the chancellor of the exchequer Norman Lamont was widely criticised for his handling of the economy at the time of *Black Wednesday*, yet did not resign at the time. Some have attributed this reluctance of ministers to resign to the rise of *professional politicians*. Others feel that it is unreasonable to expect ministers to step down following failures in areas of policy controlled by *executive agencies*.

rolling back the frontiers of the state: referring to *Margaret Thatcher*'s stated desire to reduce government intervention in people's lives, privatise nationalised industries and encourage free enterprise. See also *neo-liberalism*.

Rome, Treaty of (1957): the treaty that established the *European Economic Community (EEC)*. It was signed in 1957 by Belgium, France, West Germany, Italy, Luxembourg and the Netherlands, and the UK eventually signed the treaty in 1972 ahead of becoming a member of the EEC in January 1973. It established the superiority of *European law* over the domestic laws of member states. See also *European Union*.

rotten boroughs: parliamentary boroughs in the early nineteenth century that continued to return *MPs* to the *Commons* even though the area of land in question was no longer populated.

royal assent: the final stage of the *legislative process* in which a *bill* receives the *monarch*'s approval and passes into *law*.

- The monarch no longer physically signs all bills and instead issues letters patent granting the *authority* under which a bill may pass into law.
- By *convention* the royal assent is simply a formality. No monarch has refused to give approval to a bill passed by *Parliament* since Queen Anne vetoed the Scottish Militias Bill in 1707.

royal commission: a body established by the *government* with a remit to explore and report on an issue of national importance and/or concern. The recommendations of such commissions often form the basis of further consultation (see *Green Paper*) or firm proposals for *legislation* (see *White Paper*).

> **Example**
>
> See the *Wakeham Commission* (formally the Royal Commission on Reform of the House of Lords) and the *Wakeham Report (2000)*.

royal prerogative: see *prerogative powers*

Royal Society for the Protection of Birds (RSPB): an *attitude cause group* that campaigns for the protection of wild birds and their habitats. The RSPB boasts well over a million members, more than all the main UK *political parties* combined. The organisation is regarded as a *core insider* group as it is involved in consultation with government across a range of related policy areas.

RSPB: see *Royal Society for the Protection of Birds (RSPB)*

rule of law: a key principle of the UK constitution guaranteeing justice and said to be common to all *liberal democracies*. See also *judicial independence*.

> **TIP:** A. V. Dicey (1885) saw the rule of law as one of the 'twin pillars' of the constitution, the other being *parliamentary sovereignty*. According to Dicey, the rule of law has three main strands: first, that no person can be punished without trial; second, that no one is above the law and all are subject to the same justice; and third, that the general principles of the constitution (e.g. personal freedoms) result from the decisions of judges (case law or *common law*) rather than from parliamentary *statute* or executive *order*.

Russell, John (Earl Russell): *prime minister* (Liberal), 1846–51 and 1865–66.

safe seat: a parliamentary *constituency* that consistently returns *MPs* from the same *political party*.
- Safe seats can still be lost where there is a large *swing* against the party of the *incumbent* MP, though such an outcome is more likely to occur at *by-elections* as a result of low *turnout* and/or high levels of *protest voting*.
- Party leaders tend to be drawn from the ranks of those representing safe seats.

Example

John Major represented the Conservative safe seat of Huntingdon; *Tony Blair* represented the Labour safe seat of Sedgefield.

salience: relevance or pertinence – a term commonly used when discussing the *issue voting model* of *voting behaviour*. It also refers to the view that elections are won or lost on those issues that have particular salience. *Political parties* try to make sure that the issues on which they are seen as strong are the salient issues in any campaign, i.e. they seek to set the political agenda.

Example

In 2001, the then Conservative Party leader *William Hague* tried, unsuccessfully, to make the EU the salient election issue with his 'seven days to save the pound' campaign.

Salisbury Doctrine: the convention that the *House of Lords* – as an unelected chamber – should not oppose *government bills* at *second reading* where the government has established a clear electoral *mandate* to act by including a measure in its *manifesto*. It was established by Lord Salisbury, the Conservative leader in the Lords in 1945.

sample: a group of voters questioned by a polling company compiling an opinion poll; a polling organisation's group of voters selected to represent the *electorate* and consulted to produce *opinion polls*.
- A sample generally numbers between 1,000 and 2,000 voters.
- Voters are selected either randomly or, more commonly, with a view to creating a representative cross-section of the electorate in terms of race, gender, age, etc.

Scottish Executive: the devolved 'Scottish government'. It comprises a *cabinet* drawn from the largest party in the *Scottish Parliament* and led by the leader of that party, serving as *first minister*. See *devolution*.

S

Scottish National Party (SNP): a centre-left *nationalist party* contesting elections in Scotland.

- The SNP supports full independence for Scotland.
- It formed a *minority government* in Scotland after becoming the single largest party in the *Scottish Parliament* following elections in 2007.
- It also fields candidates in Scottish *constituencies* returning *MPs* to *Westminster*, winning 6 seats in 1997, 5 in 2001 and 6 in 2005.

Scottish Parliament: the devolved *legislature* in Scotland. See *devolution*.

- Established in 1999 and based in Edinburgh.
- Comprising 129 *MSPs* elected under an *additional member system (ASM)*.
- Possesses both *primary legislative powers* and *tax-varying powers*.

scrutiny: the process by which the *government* (i.e. the *executive*) is checked and held accountable by the *legislature* and other bodies.

- The government is scrutinised by *Parliament*, in particular by the *standing committees* and *select committees* that operate in the Commons and the Lords.
- The *media* are also said to play a key role in scrutinising the work of government.

SDLP: see *Social Democratic and Labour Party (SDLP)*

SDP: see *Social Democratic Party (SDP)*

SDP–Liberal Alliance: see *Social Democratic Party (SDP)*

seat: an elected position in a *legislature* that is often an alternative description for a parliamentary *constituency*. The size of a *political party's majority* or *representation* in the *House of Commons* is often expressed in terms of seats.

second chamber: referring to the *House of Lords*, the subordinate *revising chamber* in the UK's bicameral *legislature*. See also *bicameralism*.

second reading: the stage of the passage of legislation that sees *debate* and a *division* on the main principles of a *bill* in the *Commons* or the *Lords*. It takes place between the *first reading* and the *committee stage*.

secondary legislative powers: see *Welsh Assembly*

secret ballot: where individuals vote alone, in private, as opposed to taking part in the kind of public show of hands that was common in elections in the early part of the nineteenth century.

- Secret ballots were introduced in the UK under the Ballot Act (1872) as a way of stopping voters being threatened and/or bribed.
- Those voting in person at a *polling station* fill in their *ballot papers* alone in a polling booth.

> **TIP:** Those who criticise postal voting argue that it leaves voters vulnerable to coercion, whether by family members or other acquaintances.

secret soundings: the informal and secretive way in which most senior UK judges were once appointed. See also *Judicial Appointments Commission* and *Constitutional Reform Act (2005)*. They involved the Lord Chancellor consulting in secret with close associates and those already serving in the *senior judiciary*. The resulting lack of transparency led to accusations of elitism.

secretary of state: the *cabinet*-rank minister leading a government *department* or top-tier *ministry*.

Example

The Secretary for Foreign and Commonwealth Affairs (the *foreign secretary*).

sectional cause group: a *cause group* that represents a specific section of society that is distinct from its own membership, i.e. not simply a *sectional group* – a subcategory in the *sectional/cause group typology*. The National Society for the Prevention of Cruelty to Children (NSPCC) is a sectional cause group because it seeks to represent the interests of children but is not made up of children.

sectional/cause group typology: a means of classifying *pressure groups* according to their core aims.
- This typology was first developed by writers such as J. D. Stewart.
- Under this typology *sectional groups* are those that seek to advance the direct interests of their members, while *cause groups* seek to promote issues or ideas that are not of direct benefit to those in the group.
- The cause group category is often subdivided into three further categories: *attitude cause groups*; *political cause groups*; and *sectional cause groups* (see *cause groups*).

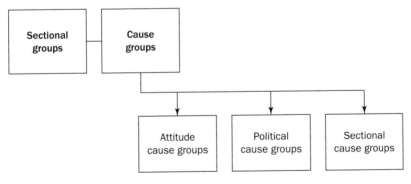

The sectional/cause group typology

> **TIP:** Critics of the sectional/cause group typology argue that it is more helpful to look at group status (see *insider/outsider typology*) than the nature of a group's aims when assessing its prospects. A further criticism of the typology is that some groups might be said to fit into more than a single category. For example, a teaching union such as the National Union of Teachers (NUT) campaigns for the sectional interests of its members (i.e. teachers) but also looks to promote reform in the field of primary and secondary education (attitude cause group?) that will bring educational benefits for school pupils (sectional cause group?).

sectional group: a *pressure group* that aims to advance the shared interests of its members as opposed to campaigning for a broader cause. See *sectional/cause group typology*.

- Sectional groups are sometimes referred to as a 'protectionist group', a 'private interest group', or simply an 'interest group'.
- They are normally 'exclusive' in the sense that individuals must meet certain requirements in order to qualify for group membership. For example, those seeking to join the British Medical Association (BMA) must either be qualified medical practitioners or be engaged in training to become such.

> **TIP:** The term is most often used when discussing the sectional/cause group typology, a model that seeks to classify pressure groups according to their aims. It is important to be aware of the advantages and disadvantages of this typology and to be able to compare it to the *insider/outsider typology* advanced by writers such as *Wyn Grant*.

security of tenure: the principle that judges should retain their positions on good behaviour until they retire. This ensures that governments cannot remove those judges who find against them in court cases. See also *judicial independence*.

select committee: a parliamentary committee established for the purpose of scrutinising the *executive* or investigating a particular area of policy or practice. See *departmental select committee* and *non-departmental select committee*.

Select Committee on European Legislation: the House of Commons *non-departmental select committee* that considers proposals for *European law* coming from the *European Commission* and *European Council*.

Select Committee on Standards and Privileges: the House of Commons *non-departmental select committee* that scrutinises the conduct of *MPs*. See also *parliamentary commissioner for standards* and *Register of Members' Interests*. It was established in the wake of the *cash for questions* scandal.

selectorate: a small group responsible for appointing an individual to a particular post. It is generally used pejoratively to imply a lack of democratic *accountability*.

senior civil service: commonly referring to the top five grades in the UK civil service, employing some 4,500 staff.

- The top four grades (around 1,000 staff) have a significant input into the policy-making process.
- Grade 1 refers to the senior civil servant in a government department: the Permanent Secretary.

senior judiciary: collectively referring to those judges serving in the UK *Supreme Court*, the *Court of Appeal* and the High Court.

separation of powers: a *doctrine* requiring that the three elements of government power – executive power, legislative power and judicial power – be held by separate branches of *government* in order to prevent tyranny.

- The **executive** branch has the role of executing policy (i.e. putting the laws into effect), the **legislature** legislates (i.e. makes the laws) and the **judiciary** has the task of enforcing and interpreting the laws.
- The term 'separation of powers' is often associated with the philosopher Charles Louis de Secondat Montesquieu, Baron de la Brède (1689–1755), more commonly known as Baron de **Montesquieu**, and his work, *The Spirit of the Laws* (1748).

> **TIP:** The Founding Fathers who met to draft the US constitution in the summer of 1787 were heavily influenced by writers such as Montesquieu. The separation of powers is, therefore, a central feature of the system of government they established. The UK, in contrast, has traditionally operated under an 'incomplete separation' of powers or a system of **fusion of powers**. This is because the UK executive is drawn from the legislature and the **Lord Chancellor** traditionally sat in the cabinet, in the *legislature* (as a member and speaker of the Lords) and as head of the judiciary. However, the **Constitutional Reform Act (2005)** enhanced the UK's separation of powers by redefining the role and powers of the Lord Chancellor as well as moving the **Law Lords** from the **House of Lords** to a new UK **Supreme Court** from October 2009.

Service First: also known as 'Charterism', the **New Labour** programme that replaced the **Citizen's Charter** in 1998, run by a **Cabinet Office** team, as had been the case with the Citizen's Charter. It aimed to guarantee certain levels of public service.

session: see **parliamentary session**

7/7: shorthand for the Al Qaeda-inspired attacks that took place in London on 7 July 2005. Those involved in these suicide attacks were British Muslims rather than foreign nationals. They targeted transport infrastructure, including the London Underground, killing 52 people.

shadow cabinet: a 'government in waiting' comprising the senior members of the **official opposition**'s **frontbench** team.
- The shadow cabinet plays a crucial role in **scrutinising** the work of the **government**.
- Each member of the shadow cabinet scrutinises the work of a **cabinet minister**.
- The activities of the shadow cabinet are supported by taxpayers through **Short money**.

Example

In 2009, the shadow chancellor of the exchequer was the Conservative frontbench MP George Osborne.

Short money: monies paid to **opposition** parties in order to help them cover their administrative costs and thereby provide proper **scrutiny** of the **government**.
- Named after Edward Short, the Leader of the **House of Commons** when the scheme was introduced in 1974.
- Available to all opposition parties that win at least two seats or receive over 150,000 votes at a **general election**.

Example

The Conservative Party was eligible for £4,715,454 in 2008–09. The Liberal Democrats qualified for £1,691,355 in the same year.

TIP: In the *House of Lords* such payments to opposition parties are known as 'Cranborne money', after Lord Cranborne, the leader of the Lords when the scheme was introduced in 1996.

shortlist: a list of potential *parliamentary candidates* drawn up by a *constituency* party prior to their final selection. See also *women-only shortlists* and *one member, one vote (OMOV)*.

short-term factors: transitory influences on *voting behaviour*. See also *recency model*. Contrast with *long-term factors*.

- Short-term factors are said to have increased in importance over *long-term factors* such as *social class* since the 1970s.
- They include the images of the party leaders, party policies and events. See also *issue voting model*.

simple majority: also known as 'simple plurality', the difference between the number of votes received by the winning *candidate* or *political party* and the candidate or party in second place. Contrast with *overall majority*.

simple plurality: see *simple majority*

TIP: The *first-past-the-post electoral system* used in elections to *Westminster* is sometimes referred to as the 'simple plurality in *single-member constituencies* system'.

single currency: see *euro*

Single European Act (1986): the piece of *European law* that established an internal market within the *European Economic Community (EEC)* (now the *EU*) allowing the free movement of people, goods and capital. See also European *integration*.

- The Act amended the *Treaty of Rome*.
- It also involved an extension of the system of *qualified majority voting* within the *Council of Ministers*.

single European currency: see *euro*.

single-issue party: a *political party* that campaigns on a single issue or across a narrow range of issues. Single-issue parties have little chance of electoral success nationally as they make no attempt to articulate a coherent programme for government in a *manifesto*. In effect, they are *pressure groups* that field candidates as a means of gaining greater publicity for their cause, while at the same time forcing those candidates representing mainstream parties to address their single issue.

Example

The *Pro-life Alliance* operated as a single-issue party at the time of the 1997 and 2001 *general elections*. Focusing on its opposition to abortion, embryology and euthanasia it fielded 53 candidates in 1997 and 37 in 2001, garnering a total of 18,545 and 9,453 votes respectively. All 90 candidates lost their deposits.

single-issue pressure group: a *pressure group* or protest movement that focuses on a single issue as opposed to a range of issues connected to a central theme or cause. Single-issue groups often disband once their objective is achieved, e.g. the *Snowdrop Campaign*.

Example

Activists from the group 'Save the Newchurch Guinea Pigs' were ultimately successful in shutting down a guinea pig farm accused of providing animals for use in vivisection. This single-issue pressure group used a variety of tactics, some of which were illegal. Most notably, members of the group exhumed the dead body of a relative of the family that owned the farm – one of a series of crimes for which some members of the group were subsequently given lengthy prison sentences.

single-member constituency: a geographical area returning a single elected representative to office. Contrast with *multi-member constituencies*.
- Single-member constituencies are often seen as a feature of *majoritarian electoral systems* such as *first-past-the-post*, *supplementary vote (SV)* and *alternative vote system*.
- *Westminster* operates on the basis of single-member constituencies with each parliamentary constituency returning a single *MP* to the *Commons*.

Example

A *by-election* in the parliamentary constituency of Glenrothes on 6 November 2008 saw a single MP, Labour's Lindsay Roy, returned to the House of Commons.

single-party government: see *majority government*

single-party system: a political system in which only one *political party* is allowed by law to contest elections and form a government.

Example

Germany became a single-party system under the Nazi Party. The USSR also operated as a single-party system under the Communist Party.

> TIP: Single-party systems are generally undemocratic and authoritarian in nature.

single transferable vote (STV): a *proportional electoral system* employing *multi-member constituencies*.
- STV is a preferential system, meaning that *voters* rank *candidates* in order of preference.
- Candidates are elected when they achieve a *quota* (also known as the Droop formula).

Example

The system is used in Northern Ireland in local elections, Assembly elections and elections to the *European Parliament*. STV has also been used in Scottish local elections since 2007.

Sinn Fein: a Catholic, republican *political party* operating primarily in Northern Ireland.
- Sinn Fein was long seen as the political wing of the *Irish Republican Army (IRA)*. The party supported the *Good Friday Agreement (1998)*.
- It took a lead role in the *Northern Ireland Executive* following the restoration of devolved government in 2007.

sleaze: a term used widely in the media to characterise inappropriate and/or disreputable behaviour by *MPs*.
- Sleaze originally referred to a series of scandals surrounding Conservative MPs in the 1990s (see also *cash for questions* and *Nolan Committee*).
- The term is now employed more widely to refer to any such behaviour. See also *MPs' expenses*.

Smith, Adam (1723–90): eighteenth-century philosopher and economist. See also *Adam Smith Institute*.

Smith, John (1938–94): the former Labour MP for Monklands East and leader of the *Labour Party* from 1992 until his sudden death following a heart attack in 1994. Smith is credited with continuing the modernisation of the Labour Party begun by his predecessor *Neil Kinnock*. Significantly, he secured the adoption of *one member, one vote (OMOV)* in 1993.

Smith Square: the London site of the *Conservative Party*'s *Central Office*.

Smith-Stanley, Edward (Earl of Derby): *prime minister* (Conservative), 1852, 1858–59 and 1866–68.

smoke-filled rooms: alluding to the idea that decisions are being made behind closed doors by an unaccountable elite. See *elites theory*.
- The term implies a lack of transparency and *legitimacy* in decision making.
- It is often used in conjunction with the phrase *fat cats*, i.e. fat cats in smoke-filled rooms.

Snowdrop Campaign: a *single-issue pressure group* that successfully campaigned for a ban on handguns following the Dunblane massacre. The massacre had seen a teacher and 16 children killed by a lone gunman at a school in Dunblane, Scotland, in March 1996. The Snowdrop Campaign was successful in mobilising most of the *tabloid* press behind its bid to see all handguns banned.

SNP: see *Scottish National Party (SNP)*

Social Chapter: a European Union protocol concerning the rights of employees.
- The Social Chapter is sometimes referred to as the 'Social Charter'.
- Originally part of the *Treaty of Maastricht*, it was reduced to the status of a protocol when the then prime minister *John Major* secured an opt-out from the Chapter. Major also secured a UK opt-out in respect of *European Economic and Monetary Union (EMU)*.
- The incoming *New Labour* government signed up to the Social Chapter in 1997 and it subsequently became part of EU treaties under the *Treaty of Amsterdam* (1997).

social class: a group of individuals who share a common socio-economic position within society.

- Those within a given social class often come from similar occupational or educational backgrounds.
- *Karl Marx* drew a simple distinction between the capitalist bourgeoisie, who accumulated their wealth through inheritance, investments and their control of business (i.e. the 'means of production') and the working classes, or proletariat, who were forced to work for the bourgeoisie in return for wages.
- In the study of UK politics a distinction is often drawn between the **working class** and the **middle class** when analysing **voting behaviour**.
- Market researchers tend to divide people up into six socio-economic classes based upon occupation, as shown in the table.

Social class by occupation

A	higher professional, managerial and administrative
B	intermediate professional, managerial and administrative
C1	supervisory, clerical and other non-manual
C2	skilled manual
D	semi-skilled and unskilled manual
E	residual, casual workers, people reliant on state benefits

> **TIP:** Social class was seen as a major influence on *voting behaviour* in the period between 1945 and the mid-1970s. In the 1960s, Peter Pulzer famously concluded that, 'class is the basis of British party politics; all else is embellishment and detail'. See *class alignment* and *class voting*.

social democracy: a political *ideology* that accepts the basic premise of capitalism while advocating a more equitable distribution of wealth. See also **socialism**.

> **TIP:** Although *Clause IV* of the *Labour Party*'s 1918 *constitution* appeared to commit it to a socialist course, it is generally seen as a social democratic party.

Social Democratic and Labour Party (SDLP): a Northern Irish, Catholic, *nationalist party* that supported the *Good Friday Agreement (1998)*.

Social Democratic Party (SDP): the *political party* established following the decision of the *Gang of Four* to leave the *Labour Party* in 1981.

- The Gang of Four – Bill Rodgers; Roy Jenkins; Shirley Williams; and David Owen – believed that the Labour Party had fallen under the control of Trotskyites and other *left-wingers* following the party's defeat in the 1979 *general election*. They lacked confidence in the party's leader at the time, left-winger *Michael Foot*.
- The four announced the launch of the Social Democratic Party in the *Limehouse Declaration* of 25 January 1981.

- The party contested the 1983 and 1987 *general elections* in alliance with the Liberal Party (the SDP–Liberal Alliance), securing 26.0% of the votes (23 seats) and 23.1% of the votes (22 seats) respectively. The party merged with the Liberal Party in 1988, forming the *Liberal Democrats*.

Social Exclusion Unit: a body in the *Cabinet Office* established in 1998 with the task of improving interdepartmental coordination in relation to the delivery of a range of social policies.

- The unit was designed to improve government provision for the most socially deprived groups within society.
- It was a feature of *New Labour*'s commitment to *joined-up government*. See also the *Performance and Innovation Unit*.

social inclusion: characterising a desire to tackle the factors that prevent certain groups within society from participating fully economically, socially and politically.

- Social inclusion was an aim closely associated with the *New Labour* government that came to power in 1997.
- It was reflected in the establishment of the *Social Exclusion Unit*; a Cabinet Office *taskforce* established in 1998.

social justice: the goal of greater *equality of outcome* as opposed to *equality of opportunity* alone. It is achieved through progressive taxation and other forms of wealth redistribution. The idea is closely associated with the *Green Party* and with other parties of the left and centre-left, including the UK *Labour Party*.

social liberalism: another term for new liberalism, modern liberalism and *progressive liberalism*. Contrast with *classical liberalism* and *neo-liberalism*.

social structures model: a *voting model* that emphasises the influence of social cleavages such as *social class*, ethnicity, occupation and gender on electoral outcomes. See also *socialisation*.

- It is a belief that the enduring influence of such *long-term factors* would suggest that voting behaviour should be relatively stable, with relatively low levels of electoral *swing* between elections. This is because such social factors change only very slowly.
- In essence, the social structures model is another way of framing the *primacy model*.

socialisation: the process by which an individual's beliefs and values are shaped within a society. Socialisation is often seen as a function of family upbringing and education.

socialism: a political *ideology* advocating greater equality and the redistribution of wealth. See also *social democracy*.

- Socialists are suspicious of *capitalism*. They favour greater government intervention, both in economic policy and in social policy.
- In the nineteenth century socialism was often seen as similar to *communism*.
- In the UK, socialism was closely associated with the *Labour Party*, from the party's creation at the start of the twentieth century through to the emergence of *New Labour* under *Tony Blair* in the 1990s. See also *Clause IV*.

Socialist Alliance: a *left-wing* electoral coalition between the *Militant Tendency* and the *Socialist Workers Party* that fielded 98 *candidates* at the 2001 *general election*. Socialist

Alliance candidates averaged 1.7% of the *popular vote* in those *constituencies* where they ran. All but two of the party's candidates lost their *deposits*.

Socialist Labour Party: a minor left-wing *political party* founded in 1996 by the former leader of the National Union of Mineworkers, Arthur Scargill.

- It was essentially a breakaway from the *Labour Party*, prompted by *Tony Blair*'s decision to reform *Clause IV*.
- The party fielded 64 candidates at the 1997 *general election*, 114 in 2001 and 49 in 2005, averaging 1.8%, 1.4% and 1.2% respectively in those *constituencies* where they ran.

Socialist Workers Party: a minor, extreme left-wing *political party* founded by Tony Cliff, a one-time member of the *Labour Party* expelled for being a Trotskyite.

sociological model: see *social structures model*

sofa government: describing the way in which prime minister *Tony Blair* was said to have directed government through a series of informal and unminuted *bilateral meetings* conducted on the sofas at Number 10. Contrast with *cabinet government*.

Example

In a similar vein, Blair's biographer, Anthony Seldon, used the term 'denocracy'; a reference to Mr Blair's preference for making decisions following informal meetings in the 'den' at Number 10.

soundbite: a short phrase, slogan or catchphrase designed to be picked up and used by the *media*.

- Such phrases are designed to encapsulate a key point while remaining short enough to be inserted into time-sensitive news broadcasts.
- The term is often used pejoratively when accusing someone of courting the media as opposed to advancing fully developed and costed proposals.

Example

The *Labour Party*'s use of phrases such as 'education, education, education', 'joined-up government' and 'tough on crime, tough on the causes of crime' ahead of the 1997 general election.

sovereignty: the ultimate power to make decisions within a state. See *parliamentary sovereignty*.

spatial leadership: where political leaders seek to create a clear separation between themselves and the other actors and institutions within the *core executive* as a means of strengthening their own position.

- The phrase is more commonly applied to the study of US presidents but is also applied to the UK *prime minister* by Michael Foley in his 1993 book, *The Rise of the British Presidency*. See *presidential prime minister*.

- Foley argued that successive prime ministers had become increasingly willing both publicly to criticise government institutions and personally to intervene in the broader public interest where government policy was seen to be failing.
- This, Foley argued, helped prime ministers both to separate themselves from and elevate themselves above other players at the heart of government.
- The ability of prime ministers to dissociate themselves from the government in this way allows **incumbents** to exercise their **prerogative powers** to the full, while at the same time avoiding full responsibility for anything that may go wrong.

Example

Foley cited the example of **John Major**, whose **Citizen's Charter** required public bodies to meet clearly defined targets in respect of service. **Tony Blair**'s pursuit of his 'reform agenda', in the face of wide-ranging opposition within the executive branch and beyond, might also be seen in this context – as might his personal intervention at the time of the foot and mouth outbreak in 2001.

> **TIP:** Inextricably linked to this notion of spatial leadership is the desire of recent prime ministers to portray themselves as political outsiders. This 'cult of the outsider' is a further key element of Foley's thesis.

spatial voting model: a model that holds that the parties most likely to attract voters are those that adopt the median point on the political spectrum, thereby avoiding alienating too many potential supporters. It is a variant of the **issue voting model**. See also **valence voting model**.

> **TIP:** The main problem with this model is that it assumes that parties can appeal to voters simply by not offending them. In an age when parties are less ideologically based than they were in 1983, for example, there will be little to choose between them; they will both be targeting 'middle England'.

speaker: the **non-partisan** chair and presiding officer in the **House of Commons**.
- The speaker is an **MP** elected to the post by fellow MPs.
- Speakers give up their party affiliation once appointed and stand in future elections not as a **candidate** for a party but as the speaker seeking re-election, unopposed by the major parties.
- The speaker chairs **debates** and ensures order in the chamber.
- He or she is supported by a number of deputies.

Example

The Conservative MP John Bercow was chosen as speaker in 2009 when the sitting speaker, Michael Martin, was forced to resign following criticism of his handling of the scandal over **MPs' expenses**.

special advisor: a political appointee employed by and answerable directly to a government minister or the prime minister.
- They are often seen as being similar to **spin doctors**.
- It is common to draw a distinction between such special advisors and career **civil servants**.
- An increase in the number of advisors under **Thatcher** and **Blair** led to accusations of **politicisation** in the **civil service**.

Example

Chancellor of the exchequer Nigel Lawson cited Margaret Thatcher's over-reliance on her economics advisor Sir Alan Walters as the reason for his resignation from cabinet in 1989.

special relationship: the close, mutually beneficial relationship said to exist between the USA and the UK.
- The special relationship is said to have developed as a result of the two nations working together at the time of the Second World War and during the Cold War years that followed.
- The bond between the UK prime minister **Margaret Thatcher** and the then US president Ronald Reagan was said to exemplify the special relationship between the two nations.

> **TIP:** Some argue that the relationship has grown increasingly asymmetrical in recent years, with the UK being very much the minor partner. Critics of *Tony Blair* argued that he was too easily controlled by George W. Bush. The cartoonist Steve Bell, of the *Guardian*, routinely portrayed Blair as a poodle.

special standing committee: a *standing committee* that is permitted to call specialist witnesses and consider a **bill** in general terms before it conducts its **scrutiny** of the proposal clause by clause.

specialist insiders: an *insider group* with which the government consults across only a narrow range of policies, e.g. the Canine Defence League. A subcategory under the *insider/outsider typology*.

spin: a pejorative term applied to any effort to garner more favourable media coverage. All political parties attempt to influence the way news items are reported: for instance, through the use of press releases. **New Labour** has been accused of having an obsession with spin rather than with the substance of its **policies**. See **spin doctor**.

spin doctor: a pejorative term applied to those employed by politicians to manage the way in which the **media** report their activities. It is generally applied to those working in bodies such as the **Press Office** but also to those individuals employed on a consultancy basis by **political parties**. The former are commonly paid for by taxpayers because they are employed as **civil servants**. See also **spin**.

Example

The highest profile example of a spin doctor is **Alastair Campbell**, prime minister Tony Blair's **press secretary** (1997–2001) and **Director of Communications and Strategy** (from 2001). Transport Secretary Stephen Byers' spin doctor Jo Moore provoked controversy on **9/11** when she circulated an e-mail suggesting that it was a 'good day to bury bad news'.

> **TIP:** The rise of such spin doctors after **New Labour**'s election to office in 1997 proved controversial because they appeared to be serving a party-political function, even though they were in many cases paid for by the taxpayer.

spoilt ballots: *ballot papers* that cannot be counted in favour of any **candidate** because they have not been completed in accordance with the instructions issued.

- Voters sometimes spoil their ballot papers deliberately as an act of protest against the limited choice of candidates available, against some aspect of the election process itself or against the institution being elected.
- Spoilt ballots may also result from poorly set out or confusing ballot papers. This was the case in the Scottish Parliament elections of 2007, where there were around 150,000 spoilt ballots.

stable government: generally another term for *majority government*.

- Stable government is seen as one of the key benefits of the *first-past-the-post* electoral system employed in elections to *Westminster*.
- It can be contrasted with the instability that often characterises the multi-party **coalition governments** common in countries such as Israel – though more stable two-party coalitions in Germany and elsewhere have delivered stable government.
- It is one of the four criteria identified by the **Jenkins Commission** when assessing the relative merits of various **electoral systems**.

> **TIP:** Whereas some see stable, single-party majority government as a 'good thing', others regard it as potentially dangerous. See also *elective dictatorship*.

Standards and Privileges Committee: see *Select Committee on Standards and Privileges*

Standards in Public Life: see *Committee on Standards in Public Life*

standing committee: a committee of the *House of Commons* or the *House of Lords* charged with the task of scrutinising proposed *legislation*.

- Such committees consist of around 20 members of the House of Commons or House of Lords and are established on an *ad hoc* basis.
- The party composition within each committee reflects that in the legislative chamber from which it is drawn. Individual committee members are chosen by the **Committee of Selection** in consultation with *party whips*.
- The *government* can use a *guillotine* as a means of cutting debate short within committee and returning the bill to the floor of the house.

Standing Order 58: the *House of Commons* rule that allows a *backbencher* to introduce a *Private Members' Bill* as long as the *speaker* is given one day's notice.

standing orders: rules governing *House of Commons* procedure.

stare decicis: see *judicial restraint*

state: referring collectively to all the governmental institutions that operate within a country and exert *power* over its *citizens*.

State Opening of Parliament: a ceremonial occasion at which the *monarch* begins a *parliamentary session*. It usually takes place in November. See also *Queen's Speech*.

status quo: the established order of things; the way things are.

statute: see *statute law*

statute law: *legislation* passed by *Westminster*.
- Such measures are often said to be on the 'statute books', with individual pieces of legislation referred to as *Acts of Parliament*.
- In the absence of a *codified constitution*, statute law is the highest source of UK law and a key source of the UK *constitution*.
- The high status of statute law is closely linked to the constitutional principle of *parliamentary sovereignty*.

Stop the War Coalition: a *single-issue pressure group* that opposed the UK government's decision to go to war in Iraq in 2003.
- The coalition was a mass protest movement as opposed to a regular membership group.
- It was an umbrella group or *peak group* that brought together a number of pre-existing pressure groups in furtherance of a single cause.
- The respected former Labour MP and one-time cabinet minister *Tony Benn* served as the group's president.

Stormont: see *Northern Ireland Assembly*

Strategic Communications Unit: the team of special *advisors* and career *civil servants* who devise and coordinate the strategy that guides the *government*'s dealings with the *media*.
- Established by New Labour in 1997.
- Operates alongside the *Press Office* within the *Prime Minister's Office*.

strong government: characterising the single-party *majority governments* common in the UK.
- Strong government is said to result from the majoritarian *first-past-the-post* system employed in elections to *Westminster*. See also *landslide effect*.
- It is widely seen as the antithesis of coalition government, though coalitions have delivered both *stable government* and strong government in countries such as Germany.

> **TIP:** Although some see strong government as desirable, others associate it with the concepts of elective dictatorship and executive dominance.

Stuart, John (Earl of Bute): *prime minister* (Tory), 1762–63.

STV: see *single transferable vote (STV)*

subnational: below the level of national government, i.e. regional or local government. See also *supranational*.

subpoena: the legal power to require an individual or individuals to attend legal proceedings and give evidence. See *departmental select committees*.

subsidiarity: the principle that decisions should be taken at the lowest tier of government possible. See also *federalism*.

- Subsidiarity is an idea closely associated with discussions around the time of the *Treaty of Maastricht* and with the then prime minister, *John Major*.
- It is an approach designed to enhance local *accountability* and *local democracy*.
- It is limited by the extent to which it is practical and economically viable to deal with certain issues at a local level.

suffrage: the right to vote. See *franchise*.

supermarket voting model: the view that voters behave as consumers, selecting the party that they will vote for on the basis of the policies offered by each party (i.e. the 'product') and the way in which those parties market themselves (i.e. the 'brand'). It is often referred to as the 'consumer voting model'. See *issue voting model*, *valence voting model* and *salience*.

supplementary question: an oral question asked by an *MP* in follow-up to a question formally tabled at *Prime Minister's Questions* or *Ministers' Question Time*.

- One supplementary question is permitted per tabled question.
- Such questions provide MPs with an opportunity to try to embarrass the *prime minister* or *minister* in question, because their content is not known in advance.

supplementary vote (SV): a *majoritarian electoral system* used in London mayoral elections and in the election of a number of other directly elected mayors around the UK.

- It is a preferential voting system operating on the basis of a *single-member constituency*.
- Voters have the opportunity to indicate a first and a second choice from the candidates on the ballot paper. Any candidate winning 50% or more of first preference votes is duly elected.
- In the event that no candidate secures an overall majority of first preference votes, all candidates bar the top two are eliminated, with their votes being transferred in accordance with their second preferences. The candidate securing the largest total of first and second preferences is then declared the victor.

Example: the 2008 election for Mayor of London

Elections for the post of *Mayor of London* take place every four years under the SV system. In the elections held on 1 May, 2008 (see the table oppsite) the *incumbent* mayor, Labour's *Ken Livingstone*, who was seeking a third successive term in office, was defeated by the Conservative Party's candidate, *Boris Johnson*. Although Johnson failed to win on the basis of first preference votes, having failed to secure the 50% share of the vote required, he won by a comfortable margin once second preference votes had been transferred.

2008 election for Mayor of London

Candidate	Party	1st pref. votes	% 2nd pref.	2nd pref. votes	% 2nd pref.	Final
Boris Johnson	Con.	1,043,761	42.5	124,977	10.49	1,168,738
Ken Livingstone	Lab.	893,877	36.4	135,089	12.34	1,028,966
Brian Paddick	LibDem	236,685	9.3			
Siân Berry	Green	77,374	3.2			
Richard Barnbrook	BNP	69,710	2.8			
Gerard Batten	UKIP	22,422	0.9			
Andy Craig	CPA	39,249	1.6			
Lindsey German	LL	16,796	0.7			
Matt O'Connor	END	10,695	0.4			
Winston McKenzie	IND	5,389	0.2			

Key: BNP (British National Party); UKIP (UK Independence Party); CPA (Christian People's Alliance); LL (Left List); END (English Democrats); and IND (Independent).

supranational: refering to cooperation between governments and their appointees at a level that ignores national interests and considerations, as featured in the *European Commission* and the *European Court of Justice*.

Supreme Court: the highest court of appeal in the UK.

- The Supreme Court was established under the *Constitutional Reform Act (2005)* and is located in Middlesex Guildhall, Parliament Square. It opened for business in October 2009.
- It consists of 12 justices appointed by an *ad hoc* selection commission convened in the event of a vacancy arising, i.e. not appointed by the *Judicial Appointments Commission*, which has the task of selecting most other senior judges.
- Under the Constitutional Reform Act, the new UK Supreme Court took on the four roles previously performed by the *Law Lords* sitting in the Appellate Committee of the House of Lords: to act as the final court of appeal in England, Wales and Northern Ireland; to hear appeals on issues of public importance surrounding arguable points of law; to hear appeals from civil cases in England, Wales, Northern Ireland and Scotland; and to hear appeals from criminal cases in England, Wales and Northern Ireland (the High Court of Justiciary will retain jurisdiction over criminal cases in Scotland).

> **TIP:** The new Supreme Court was created in response to three widely held concerns: worries over a *fusion of powers*; an opaque and widely criticised appointments system for Law Lords; and confusion over the work of the Law Lords – a particular problem being the failure to distinguish between the House of Lords' legislative and judicial functions.

Swampy: see *roads protests*.

swing: a measure of the movement of votes from one party to another between two consecutive elections.

- Expressed as a percentage.
- Calculated by adding the percentage rise in one party's share of the **popular vote** to the fall in the other party's share and then dividing the total by two.
- Commonly quoted on a constituency or national basis.
- The swing from the Conservatives to Labour in the 1997 **general election** was over 10%, the largest in any general election since 1945. The recorded swings at the 2001 and 2005 general elections were much more modest (1.80% and 3.05% respectively).

> **TIP:** Although swing is routinely calculated on a national level, the levels of swing recorded in individual constituencies can vary enormously (see **differential swing**). Larger swings are often seen at **by-elections** as a result of lower **turnout** and higher levels of **tactical voting** and **protest voting** (see example below).

Example: swings at Glasgow East

The table compares results for Glasgow East in the general election and by-election contests in 2008, showing the large swing from Labour to SNP.

Party	General election (5 May 2008)		By-election (24 July 2008)	
	Votes	%	Votes	%
Labour	18,775	60.7%	10,912	41.7%
SNP	5,268	17.0%	11.277	43.1%
Liberal Democrat	3,665	11.8%	915	3.5%
Conservative	2,135	6.9%	1,639	6.3%
Others	1,096	3.5%	1,431	5.5%
Turnout:	48.2%		42.2%	

Swing: 22.5% (Labour to SNP)

tabloid: an A3 newspaper associated more with celebrity news and human interest stories than with in-depth political coverage. Such newspapers are sometimes referred to as the 'red-tops', a phrase describing the front pages of tabloids such as the *Daily Mirror* and the *Sun*. Contrast with **broadsheet**.

tactical voting: where an individual chooses to vote for a **candidate** who is not his or her preferred candidate in order to prevent the candidate they least favour from being elected.

- Tactical voting commonly involves Liberal Democrat voters in Labour/Conservative **marginals** voting Labour, with Labour voters in Liberal Democrat/Conservative marginals voting Liberal Democrat. Tactical voting was encouraged by a number of so-called 'vote-swapping' websites in the 2001 and 2005 **general elections**. These sites matched those who promised to vote tactically in one constituency with those who would vote tactically in the opposite direction in another constituency. Though it relied entirely on trust, the system had the effect of allowing people to 'cast a vote' by proxy in a constituency where it might make a difference.
- **Broadsheets** such as the *Independent* have also produced tactical voting guides, telling voters how they might vote in their **constituency** to best achieve their desired outcome in government.

> **Example**
>
> Michael Portillo believed that his defeat in the Enfield constituency at the 1997 general election resulted from tactical voting by Liberal Democrats. See also **opinion polls**.

target seat: a **marginal** to which a **political party** devotes more **campaign** resources in the belief that it will win. The tendency to focus the national campaign on the things most likely to appeal to **floating voters** in marginal target seats is a feature of **postmodern election campaigns**.

taskforce: a **civil service** team established in order to inform government **policy** in a particular field. The creation of task forces is often seen by critics as a way of avoiding or delaying action in a particular area. **New Labour** was widely criticised for what was seen as excessive use of taskforces after 1997.

tax-varying powers: the power to vary the basic rate of income tax set by **Westminster** by plus or minus 3%.

- It was granted to the **Scottish Parliament** as a result of the second 'yes' vote in the two-part **devolution referendum** held in Scotland in September 1997.

- Scots had voted 74.3% : 25.7% in favour of establishing a Scottish Parliament and *executive* in response to the first question posed in the referendum. The second question saw them vote 63.5% : 36.5% in favour of granting the new Parliament tax-varying powers.
- The Parliament's tax-varying powers were not used in the first decade following devolution.

Taylor, Dr Richard (1934–): an *independent* MP and former doctor, first elected to represent the parliamentary constituency of Wyre Forest at the 2001 general election.

- Taylor stood under the banner 'Independent Kidderminster Hospital and Health Concern' in protest at the planned closure of a local hospital. He defeated the sitting Labour MP.
- Taylor was elected for a second term in 2005 and has served on the Health *departmental select committee*.

Temple, Henry John (Viscount Palmerston): *prime minister* (Liberal), 1855–58 and 1859–65.

Ten Minute Rule: a procedural rule of the *House of Commons* that allows a *backbencher* 10 minutes to present the case for a new *bill*. It is one of the three ways in which a backbencher can introduce a *Private Members' Bill*; the others being under *Standing Order 58* and via the Private Members' Bills ballot (see *ballot bill*).

term-limits: a legal limit on the number of terms an elected official can serve in a given office.

- Term-limits have not traditionally been a feature of the UK system, though the 2007 *White Paper* on *Lords Reform (1997–2010)* offered the possibility that members of the reworked second chamber might be appointed or elected for a single 12-year term.
- Politicians in many other countries face term-limits, e.g. the 22nd Amendment (1951) to the US constitution limits the US president to two four-year terms. Thus Barack Obama would not be able to remain in office beyond 20 January 2017.

terrorism legislation: see *counter-terrorism*

Thatcher, Margaret (1925–): *prime minister* (Conservative), 1979–90, Conservative MP for the constituency of Finchley 1959–92 and leader of the *Conservative Party* 1975–90. She was the first woman to serve as prime minister and the longest-serving prime minister of the twentieth century. She adopted a *free-market*, *neo-liberal* approach to government characterised as *Thatcherism* and challenged the traditional *one-nation Tory* approach. Thatcher:

- oversaw significant changes in British society including *privatisation* and the introduction of a raft of *legislation* restricting the activities of *trade unions*
- was premier at the time of the *Falklands War*
- declined in popularity after the 1987 *general election* and was further damaged as a result of her steadfast support for the *poll tax*
- resigned as party leader and prime minister following a leadership challenge by *Michael Heseltine*

Thatcherism: an *ideology* combining a *free-market*, *neo-liberal* economic policy with a more orthodox conservative social policy in areas such as the family and law and order. See also *New Right*.

- Thatcherism was the dominant **Conservative Party** ideology of the 1980s and 1990s, but was challenged by **David Cameron**'s **New Tory** approach.
- It was closely associated with the ideas of Sir Keith Joseph and right-wing **think-tanks** such as the **Adam Smith Institute**.

Theakston's models: the four models of ministerial–**civil servant** relationship identified by Kevin Theakston in a 1991 *Talking Politics* article entitled 'Ministers and mandarins'.

> **Example: Theakston's models**
>
> - **Formal constitutional model:** where civil servants serve **ministers**; providing information but preserving **impartiality**, **anonymity** and, therefore, **permanence**.
>
> - **Adversarial model:** ministers and civil servants engaged in a struggle for power. The **civil service** has its own agenda and seeks to obstruct government.
>
> - **Village life in the *Whitehall* community model:** ministers within the department would provide the vision and drive; the civil servants would fill in the detail based upon their knowledge and experience of what worked.
>
> - **Bureaucratic expansionism model:** civil servants serve their own interests by creating bureaucratic empires that are financially inefficient and get in the way of clear and effective government.

think-tank: an ideas-based **pressure group** that looks to influence key decision-makers in government by undertaking research and developing detailed **policy** proposals.
- Think-tanks are often ideologically driven. For example, the **Adam Smith Institute**, the **Centre for Policy Studies** and the **Institute of Economic Affairs** were closely associated with **Thatcherism**.
- Other notable think-tanks include the **Centre for Social Justice**, **Demos**, the **Fabian Society**, the **Institute for Public Policy Research** and **ResPublica**.

third party: literally the political party holding the third largest number of seats in the **House of Commons**, though often applied collectively (i.e. third parties) to all parties other than the Conservative and Labour parties. The term can also be applied to the party placed third in a given region or home nation (e.g. Scotland or Wales). See also **minor party**.

third reading: the final stage in the passage of legislation within the **House of Commons** or the **Lords**, where MPs or peers vote on a **bill** in its entirety.
- It takes place following the **committee stage** in each chamber and is routinely combined with the **report stage**.
- A bill that has passed third reading in the Commons and the Lords will pass on to the monarch for the **royal assent**.

third way: a political **ideology** said to exist between **socialism** and mainstream capitalism, closely associated with **Tony Blair** and **New Labour**, and also referred to as the 'middle way'. See example overleaf.

Example

Critics of the third way argue that it is not a true ideology at all: first, because it has no intellectual consistency; and second because it is defined in terms of what it is not, as opposed to what it is. Even Tony Blair, one of the supposed architects of the approach, struggled to define it: 'When I talk of a third way,' he said in 1998, 'I mean neither *laissez-faire*, nor state control and rigidity.'

three-line whip: an indication that the party's *chief whip* absolutely requires that party's MPs to attend the *Commons* and vote according to instructions in a *division*. See also *whip*, *one-line whip* and *two-line whip*.

- Failure to act in accordance with a three-line whip would normally result in some disciplinary measure being taken against the MPs in question by their party. See also *withdrawal of the whip*.
- Three-line whips do not normally allow non-attendance under the *pairing* arrangements.

threshold: either a predetermined level of support that must be met in order for a *referendum* result to be valid, or a minimum percentage of votes a party must secure before it wins any seats under a *party list system*.

- Thresholds are normally added to referendums as a means of enhancing the *legitimacy* of the result.
- In the case of the party list system, thresholds are generally imposed as a way of ensuring that those parties achieving very small percentages of the popular vote do not win seats in a legislature.
- The list element of the *additional member system (AMS)* used in the election of the *Greater London Assembly* operates on the basis of a 5% threshold. In 2009, the *British National Party (BNP)* broke through this threshold, winning one of the 25 seats on the Assembly.

Example

In the referendum of March 1979, Scots voted 51.6% : 48.4% in favour of a devolved Parliament. However, the terms of the vote stated that there needed to be support from 40% of the electorate for the plans to go ahead. With turnout at only 63.8%, the 'yes' camp fell short of the margin required. In September 1997, a second referendum ran on the basis of a simple majority of those voting, i.e. without the 40% threshold that had caused the 1979 proposal to fall.

top-down: characterising an organisation that exhibits low levels of internal democracy, all key decisions being taken by a controlling elite; also referring to any process that limits opportunities for *political participation*. See *internal pressure group democracy* and *internal party democracy*.

top-up: the use of seats awarded under a *party list system* to equalise the representation of those parties that have fared badly under the *majoritarian* element of an *additional member system (AMS)*.

Tories: see *Tory Party*

Tory Party: the *political party* that developed into the **Conservative Party** in the nineteenth century. The term 'Tory' is now used interchangeably with the term 'Conservative'. See *one-nation conservatism* (*one-nation Tory*).

Tory Reform Group: a moderate grouping of Conservative parliamentarians.
- Founded in 1975.
- Consists largely of *one-nation Tories*.
- Broadly pro-European, *Europhile Kenneth Clarke* served as the group's president from 1997.

trade union: an association established to protect the sectional interest of workers in a particular field. See *sectional group*.
- Trade unions campaign for better pay and conditions for their members in negotiations with employers.
- They also seek to *lobby* the *government* as a means of securing favourable *legislation* in the areas of trade and employment law.
- Trade unions worked together with *socialist* societies to establish the **Labour Party** at the start of the twentieth century. Many trade unions are still **affiliated** to the party. See also *block vote*.

Trades Union Congress (TUC): a *peak group* representing many *trade unions*.
- The TUC enjoys close formal links with the **Labour Party**. See also *block vote*.
- It is consulted by *government* (particularly Labour governments) across a wide range of policy areas.

Treasury: the government *department* responsible for managing the UK government's economic policy.
- It is headed by the *chancellor of the exchequer* and also contains another *cabinet-rank* minister, the Chief Secretary to the Treasury.
- The Treasury oversees taxation policy, and apportions and manages government spending across the various departments of state.

Treaty of Amsterdam: see *Amsterdam, Treaty of (1997)*

Treaty of Lisbon: see *Lisbon, Treaty of (2007)*

Treaty of Maastricht: see *Maastricht, Treaty of (1992)*

Treaty of Nice: see *Nice, Treaty of (2001)*

Treaty of Rome: see *Rome, Treaty of (1957)*

Treaty on European Union: see *Maastricht, Treaty of (1992)*

tribunal: a body that arbitrates in the case of disputes between individuals and between *citizens* and part of the *state*. It is a route by which citizens may seek *redress of grievances*.

Tribune Group: a left-wing *faction* within the *Parliamentary Labour Party*. Established in support of the socialist *Tribune* newspaper in the 1960s, it was influential between the mid-1960s and the 1980s. It declined in importance in the 1990s.

tripartism: an approach to governmental decision making that stressed the importance of cooperation between the *government*, employers and *trade unions*. See *corporatism*.

trustee model: the *Burkean model* of *representation* provided in a *representative democracy*. Contrast with the *delegate model* of representation.

TUC: see *Trades Union Congress (TUC)*

turnout: the percentage of *registered voters* who cast a *ballot* in a given election.
- Low levels of turnout at the 2001 and 2005 *general elections* (59.4% and 61.5% respectively) were taken by some as evidence of political *apathy*.
- Turnout at so-called 'second-tier' elections such as *local elections* and elections to the *European Parliament* is often even lower than that at general elections. See also the *Power Inquiry* and *voting context model*.

General election turnout (1945–2005)

Year	%	Year	%	Year	%	Year	%
1945	72.8	1959	78.7	1974 (Feb.)	78.8	1987	75.3
1950	83.9	1964	77.1	1974 (Oct.)	72.8	1992	77.7
1951	82.6	1966	75.8	1979	76.0	1997	71.4
1955	76.8	1970	72.0	1983	72.7	2001	59.4
						2005	61.5

two-line whip: an indication that the party's *chief whip* requires that party's MPs to attend the *Commons* and vote according to instructions in a *division*, unless they have made suitable arrangements under the *pairing* system. See also *whip*, *one-line whip* and *two-line whip*.

two-party system: a political system in which two fairly equally matched *political parties* compete for power, with smaller parties having no realistic prospect of breaking their monopoly. Most commentators characterise Britain as a two-party system.

> **TIP:** Some argue that extended periods of one-party dominance at *Westminster* in recent years have represented a series of *dominant-party systems* as opposed to a true two-party system. Others argue that the rise of the *Liberal Democrats* and *minor parties* has led to the UK being a *multi-party system*.

Example: is the UK a two-party system?

Arguments in favour:
- The Labour and Conservative parties are the only parties that have a realistic chance of forming a government at Westminster in the near future, or being the senior partner in a *coalition government*.
- Even at the 2005 general election, the Labour and Conservative parties secured 67.4% of the *popular vote* and 86% of the 645 seats contested.
- The Liberal Democrats (in third) are still a long way behind the second party (the Conservatives).

Arguments against:

- In recent years the UK has, in effect, operated under a series of dominant party systems.
- 32.6% of voters backed parties other than the big-two at the 2005 *general election*, suggesting that the UK now operates under a multi-party system.
- Though the Liberal Democrats are a third party at Westminster, they are often second to Labour in the North and West and to the Conservatives in the South and East.
- Any party that could mobilise non-voters (38.6%) could win the general election outright.

Aiming for a grade A*?

Don't forget to log on to **www.philipallan.co.uk/a-zonline** for advice.

UFF: see *Ulster Freedom Fighters (UFF)*

UK Independence Party (UKIP): a *political party*, founded in 1993, advocating a UK withdrawal from the European Union or, failing that, a renegotiation of the terms of the UK's membership.

Example: UKIP performance in European elections

While UKIP has generally performed poorly in elections to UK-based institutions, it has fared far better in elections to the European Parliament. Such success can be attributed to the party's policies on the EU, to high levels of *protest voting*, and to the introduction of the more *proportional* regional *party list system* in England, Scotland and Wales from 1999.

Election	Popular vote (%)	Seats won (total)
1999	6.96%	3
2004	16.10%	12
2009	16.50%	13

UKIP: see *UK Independence Party (UKIP)*

Ulster Freedom Fighters (UFF): a *loyalist* Protestant paramilitary group based in Northern Ireland.

Ulster Unionist Party (UUP): a *unionist* Protestant *political party* based in Northern Ireland.

Ulster Volunteer Force (UVF): a *loyalist* Protestant paramilitary group based in Northern Ireland.

ultra vires: from the Latin meaning 'beyond the authority' or 'beyond one's powers'. The process of *judicial review* can be used to determine whether or not *ministers* or other government officers have acted ultra vires, i.e. beyond the *authority* granted to them in *law*.

umbrella group: see *peak group*

uncodified constitution: where the rules that govern the relationships between the *state* and its *citizens*, and between the various institutions that comprise the state, are not set out in a single authoritative document.

- Uncodified constitutions are often said to be more evolutionary in nature and more flexible than those that are fully codified.
- Uncodified constitutions also lack the degree of *entrenchment* common to most codified constitutions. See also *constitution* and *codified constitution*.

Example

The UK constitution is said to be uncodified because it draws on a number of different sources, namely statute law, conventions, common law, EU law and treaties, and works of authority.

> **TIP:** It is better to describe the UK constitution as uncodified, as opposed to unwritten, because many of its sources are, in fact, written.

under-representation: see *resemblance theory*

unicameral legislature: a *legislature* consisting of a single chamber. See also *bicameral legislature*.

Example

The *Scottish Parliament* is a unicameral legislature, as is the Israeli Knesset. Nebraska is the only one of the 50 US states to have a unicameral legislature. Most legislatures adopt a bicameral model as the second chamber provides a further means by which legislative proposals and the actions of the *executive* branch can be subjected to effective *scrutiny*.

union: see *trade union*

unionist: a supporter of Northern Ireland's remaining part of the UK or, alternatively, a trade union member. See also the *Ulster Unionist Party (UUP)* and the *Democratic Unionist Party (DUP)*.

unitary authority: a way of arranging local government so that all local services are provided by a single tier of government as opposed to the two-tier system operating across most of the country, e.g. Southend-on-Sea. See also *district council* and a *county council*.

unitary state: a state where the ultimate power or *sovereignty* resides with the central government. Contrast with *federalism*.

Example

The UK is a unitary state with *Westminster* retaining the power to make or unmake any *law*. *Devolution* and the growth of *EU* power may appear to have made the UK 'more federal'. Indeed, some argue that the UK now practises *quasi-federalism*. In reality, however, Parliament retains the power to take back such power.

United Kingdom: collectively referring to the union of England, Scotland, Wales and Northern Ireland.

United States of Europe: a vision of a *federal* Europe along the lines proposed by Jacques Delors. See *Delors Plan*.

universal suffrage: the principle that the *franchise* should be extended to all adult *citizens*.

universalism: the principle that state benefits and services should be available to all, irrespective of means.

● Contrast with means testing, whereby an individual's personal circumstances are taken into consideration when determining the level at which a given benefit or service will be provided.

● Child benefit has traditionally been available as a universal benefit whereas the various forms of income support and housing benefit are means tested. See also *welfare state*.

unwritten constitution: see *uncodified constitution*

Upper Chamber: see *House of Lords*

usual channels: characterising the way in which parliamentary business in both the *House of Commons* and the *House of Lords* is managed by the two main political parties; more accurately, by the party *whips* and the leader and shadow leader of each chamber.

U-turn: a 180° turnaround in policy by a *politician* or *political party*. The term was mocked in a speech by *Margaret Thatcher* at the 1980 Conservative Party Conference, 'To those waiting with bated breath for that favourite media catch-phrase – the U-turn – I have only one thing to say: you turn if you want to; the Lady's not for turning.'

Example

In 2009, the Labour government announced a U-turn on its decision to deny some former Gurkhas and their families the right to reside in the UK. This change in *policy* came in the wake of an embarrassing defeat in the *Commons* at the hands of the two main *opposition* parties and a high-profile *pressure group* campaign led by actress Joanna Lumley.

UUP: see *Ulster Unionist Party (UUP)*

UVF: see *Ulster Volunteer Force (UVF)*

valence voting model: a model that holds that a party's chances of electoral success will depend upon its ability to convince voters that it can deliver on the key issues, e.g. 'national security', 'economic prosperity' and 'law and order'. A variant of the *issue voting model*. See also *spatial voting model*.

veto: the right of a single individual to block a course of action agreed by all others. From the Latin, meaning 'I forbid'.

Example

Prior to the introduction and extension of *qualified majority voting* in the *Council of Ministers* following the *Single European Act (1986)*, most important decisions were taken on the basis of unanimity. This meant that each member state retained a national veto over changes in *European Community* policy and organisation. EU member states still retain a veto over new states joining the Union.

volatility: see *electoral volatility*

vote: an indication of one's preference or the act of indicating that preference, whether for a *candidate* or party in an *election*, or for a particular course of action in a *referendum*.

- The term is used as shorthand for the *popular vote*; the total number of votes cast, as in 'the share of the vote'. It is also used to mean *franchise* ('adult men were given the vote in 1918').
- *MPs* and those who serve in other legislative bodies also have the opportunity to vote on legislative proposals or amendments to them.

vote of (no) confidence: see *no-confidence motion*

voter: someone who casts a *vote*, whether in an *election* or a *referendum*.

voter choice: one of the four criteria used by the *Jenkins Commission* when assessing the worth of alternative *electoral systems*.

voting behaviour: the ways in which different groups of voters respond to the various *long-term factors* (see *primacy model*) and *short-term factors* (see *recency model*) acting upon them.

- Reference to more general trends or patterns in the *electorate* is the usual explanation of an individual's voting behaviour.
- The science of studying voting behaviour is known as *psephology*.

voting context model: where the behaviour of voters is affected by the nature of the election being contested, the importance of the resulting institution and the workings of the *electoral system* in operation. See example overleaf.

Example

The behaviour of voters became apparent when comparing the results in the 2004 European elections with the general elections of 2001 and 2005. In the 2004 elections to the European Parliament, the Conservatives were the most popular choice with voters (with 26.7% of the vote), yet they were second to Labour in the general elections of 2001 and 2005. Similarly, UKIP was able to secure 16.1% of the vote, winning 12 seats, in the 2004 European elections, yet managed only 1.5% in 2001 and 2.2% in 2005.

voting model: a theory that attempts to explain patterns in voting behaviour.

Example

The *rational choice model* takes the view that voting is an intellectual, rather than simply an emotional, act; that voters weigh up the merits and demerits of each party or candidate before making their choice. This would go against the idea that people vote simply as a result of *long-term factors* such as their *social class*.

TIP: The attempt to explain voting behaviour scientifically through the development of voting models is problematic as the act of voting is, at least in part, an emotional as opposed to a purely rational, act. Many of the models advanced in recent years enjoy significant overlaps with existing models. Some models plainly contradict others. William Miller's *general voting model* seeks to overcome such problems.

voting system: see *electoral system*

Wakeham Commission: formally known as the 'Royal Commission on Reform of the House of Lords'.

- Established in 1999 and chaired by Lord Wakeham, the commission was charged with the task of proposing changes to the form and function of the second chamber in line with *New Labour*'s 1997 *manifesto* commitment.
- The commission's report was published in January 2000 (see *Wakeham Report (2000)*).

Wakeham Report (2000): the report of the *Wakeham Commission* on Lords reform. See also *House of Lords Act (1999)*.

- The report proposed a reduced second chamber of around 550, with a small proportion directly elected – possibly under a *party list system*.
- Appointed peers were to be selected by a new appointments commission, with a remit to provide a chamber that better resembled the population in terms of gender and ethnicity, as well as being balanced in terms of party ties. One fifth of the new chamber was to be *crossbenchers*.
- The power of the second chamber would remain largely unchanged. Established *conventions* such as the *Salisbury Doctrine* would remain in place and the new Lords would still be a *revising chamber* as opposed to a co-equal legislative chamber.

Walpole, Robert: *prime minister* (Whig), 1721–42. Widely regarded as the first prime minister.

war cabinet: a subset of the full *cabinet* that meets in times of war. Senior members of the military and intelligence services are often also invited to attend such meetings. See also *Civil Contingencies Committee*.

war powers: the power to take the UK to war and enter into treaties with other nations.

- War powers are formally held by the *monarch*, though in practice exercised by the *prime minister*.
- Under these *prerogative powers*, *John Major* was not legally required to present the *Treaty of Maastricht* to *Parliament* for its approval, and *Tony Blair* did not need to consult the *legislature* over his decision to invade Iraq in 2003.

> **TIP:** One of the central themes of the *Governance of Britain Green Paper (2007)* had been the effort to check the prime minister's prerogative powers. In no area have such prerogative powers provoked more controversy in recent years than in the case of the power to conclude treaties and commit the nation to war. The *Constitutional Renewal Bill (2008)* sought to address the former by establishing a procedure that

ward: a local government *constituency*.

wasted votes: those votes said to have served no purpose in an election because they have been cast either for a candidate who has been defeated or for one who had already secured sufficient votes to win the contest.

- This phenomenon is associated with *majoritarian electoral systems*, particularly *simple plurality* systems such as *first-past-the-post* – where candidates need only secure one vote more than their nearest rival in order to be elected.
- Other majoritarian systems such the *alternative vote system (AV)* and *supplementary vote (SV)* reduce the number of wasted votes by requiring the victor to secure more than 50% of the votes cast. *Proportional electoral systems* such as the *party list system* and the *single transferable vote (STV)* system virtually eliminate wasted votes when used in their purest form.

Example: St Albans (2005 general election)

In the 2005 general election, 29,869 of the 45,462 valid votes cast in the St Albans constituency were wasted (see table).

Conservative	Labour	LibDem	Other
16,953	15,592	11,561	1,356
A =	Total valid votes cast		45,462
B =	Winner's votes		16,953
Wasted votes (A − B)			28,509
Winning margin			1,361
Total wasted votes?			29,870

weapons of mass destruction: describing nuclear, biological and/or chemical weapons.
- The supposed presence of weapons of mass destruction (WMD) in Iraq was used in justification of the joint USA–UK invasion of that country in 2003. No such weapons were ever found.
- The controversial death of David Kelly, who had advised the government on Iraq's WMD programme ahead of the invasion, prompted the *Hutton Inquiry (2003–04)*.

Weatherill Amendment: an amendment to the *House of Lords Act (1999)* that saw 92 *hereditary peers* retain the right to sit and vote in the House of Lords. The amendment was named after the then leader of the *crossbenchers* in the Lords, Lord Weatherill. See also *Lords Reform (1997–2010)* and *Cranborne Compromise*.

welfare state: a universal system of healthcare, social security and education, provided free at the point of delivery and funded through taxation. See also *universalism*.

- The welfare state is said to support those in need 'from the cradle until the grave'.
- Often regarded as the main achievement of **Clement Attlee**'s postwar Labour administration.

welfare-to-work: a **policy** requiring those in receipt of state benefits to make themselves available for work, as directed by the relevant government **agency**.
- Originally associated with the presidency of Bill Clinton in the USA, it is now also advocated by most mainstream parties in the UK.
- Controversial because the policy recalls the kinds of compulsory public works programme introduced by Hitler in 1930s Germany.

Wellesley, Arthur (Duke of Wellington): the 'Iron Duke'. Commander-in-chief of British forces at the Battle of Waterloo (1815). Tory **prime minister** (1828–30). **Foreign secretary** (1834–35) in **Robert Peel**'s first administration. Subsequently **minister without portfolio** (1841–46) in Peel's second ministry.

Welsh Assembly: the National Assembly for Wales, the legislative part of the devolved institutions operating in Wales since 1999.
- The Assembly is based in Cardiff.
- It consists of 60 Members of the Welsh Assembly (MWAs), elected using an **additional member system (AMS)**: 40 members being elected to represent **single-member constituencies** under **first-past-the-post** and the remaining 20 members elected under a closed, regional **party list system**.
- In theory, the Assembly's legislative power falls some way short of the **primary legislative powers** granted to the **Scottish Parliament**. It also lacks the Scottish Parliament's **tax-varying powers**.
- The Assembly holds various administrative powers as well as secondary legislative powers. This means that it can make law in many areas of policy with the consent of **Westminster**: this consent has generally been forthcoming. The Assembly can normally also rely upon Westminster to legislate in those areas that are beyond the Assembly's **authority**.

Welsh Executive: referring collectively to the **first minister** of Wales and the **cabinet**, both of them drawn from the **Welsh Assembly**. It holds **executive** power under the devolved arrangements that came into force in 1999.

Wentworth, Charles (Marquess of Rockingham): **prime minister** (Whig), 1765–66 and 1782.

West Lothian question: referring to the fact that in many areas of policy, **MPs** representing Scottish constituencies at **Westminster** still have a say over policies that do not directly affect their own constituents, while having no say over most of the things that do, such powers having been devolved to the **Scottish Parliament**.
- It is particularly apparent in the areas of education and healthcare.
- The matter was first raised by the then Labour MP for West Lothian, Tam Dalyell, in the 1970s and was subsequently dubbed the 'West Lothian question' by fellow MP Enoch Powell.
- The reduction of the number of MPs representing Scottish constituencies from 72 to 59 ahead of the 2005 **general election** was aimed at lessening the problem identified in the question.

TIP: The creation of *regional assemblies* in England was supposed to address the problem of double representation, which had resulted from *New Labour*'s *devolution* programme. However, plans for such assemblies were shelved in the wake of the 'no' vote in the 2004 referendum on the creation of an assembly for the North East of England. The *Conservative Party* floated the idea of *English votes for English laws* as another means by which the West Lothian question could be addressed.

Westland Affair: the fallout from the decision of **Michael Heseltine** to resign from the post of Defence Secretary in 1986, over a bid to save the UK helicopter manufacturer Westland.

- The ailing Westland company was the subject of two rival rescue bids, one European and the other US-based.
- Heseltine favoured a solution that would see the creation of a new European consortium. The then prime minister **Margaret Thatcher** and her Trade and Industry Secretary, Leon Brittan, preferred a merger between Westland and the US helicopter manufacturer Sikorsky.
- Heseltine felt that Thatcher had prevented him from arguing his case properly within **cabinet**. He chose to resign so that he could speak openly on the question of Westland and on the broader issue of how cabinet was being run. See **collective responsibility**.
- Heseltine challenged Thatcher for the leadership of the Conservative Party in 1990, a move that ultimately precipitated her resignation.

Westminster: the seat of central government in the UK. A term often used to refer to *Parliament*.

Westminster model: a synonym for the system of **parliamentary government** operating in the UK and centred on the Westminster Parliament.

wets: a derogatory term applied to **one-nation Tories** such as Sir Francis Pym by **Margaret Thatcher** and her acolytes. Thatcher purged most of the wets from cabinet following the 1983 general election. See also **Thatcherism** and **dries**.

Whigs: see *Liberal Party*

whip: a legislator in the **Commons** or the **Lords** who is charged with the task of maintaining unity and **party discipline** within the parliamentary party, especially on key votes.

- Whips act as liaison between the upper echelons of a parliamentary party and the backbenchers. They also manage the **pairing** system, a way of limiting the damage done by the absence of MPs for key votes.
- Each party's whips answer to a **chief whip**.
- The term 'whip' also refers to the document in which the party communicates its priorities to MPs. See **one-line whip**, **two-line whip**, **three-line whip** and **withdrawal of the whip**.

whipless wonders: a term collectively applied to the eight Conservative **backbenchers** who had the party **whip** withdrawn in 1994 as a result of their voting against the European Communities (Finance) Bill.

whips' office: referring collectively to the **chief whips** and their assistant **whips**. See **usual channels**.

Whitehall: the geographical area of Londan where the offices of most government **departments** are located. The term 'Whitehall' is also used to refer to the **civil service**.

White Paper: a document setting out an area of *policy* in which the *government* intends to legislate. A firm proposal that commonly comes in the wake of the period of consultation that follows a *Green Paper*.

Example

In February 2007, the Labour Government published the White Paper, 'The House of Lords: Reform (Cm 7027)'. This paper set out the government's plans for the long-awaited second stage of the *Lords Reform (1997–2010)* – following on from the removal of most of the *hereditary peers* with the *House of Lords Act (1999)*.

Wilson, Harold: *prime minister* (Labour), 1964–70 and 1974–76.

windfall tax: a tax imposed on private companies that are seen to have benefited unfairly at the public's expense.

window of opportunity: a short interval during which it might be possible to achieve a particular objective. The phrase entered common usage at the time of the first Gulf War in the 1990s, when it was used to refer to the limited availability of satellite coverage.

winner's bonus: see *landslide effect*

winter of discontent: the period of widespread strikes and industrial unrest that spanned the winter of 1978–79 and which was said to have played a part in the then prime minister, *James Callaghan*, losing a *vote of (no) confidence* in 1979. Also said to have contributed to Labour's defeat in the subsequent *general election*.

withdrawal of the whip: the act of removing an *MP* from the parliamentary party. Most often applied as a temporary punishment when an MP has gone against the party *whip* on a key vote in the *Commons*. Although the removal of the whip is normally only a temporary and largely symbolic punishment, it can cause problems for the MP in question because it raises the possibility of *deselection*, should the member fail to resolve his or her differences with the party.

Example

Most memorably occurring at the time of a number of votes following the *Treaty of Maastricht* in 1994, when eight *Eurosceptic* Conservative MPs (later dubbed the *whipless wonders*) had the party whip withdrawn for voting against the party line.

women-only shortlists: a device used by the *Labour Party* whereby certain constituency Labour parties were required to draw up entirely female shortlists from which their parliamentary candidates would be chosen.

- The practice existed in its original form between 1993 and 1996. It was briefly outlawed in 1996 in the wake of a ruling under the Sex Discrimination Act – but the government subsequently amended the legislation, thus allowing women-only shortlists once more.
- The use of such shortlists in many safe Labour seats was largely responsible for the significant increase in the number of women MPs returned to Parliament in the 1997 *general election*. See *Blair's Babes*.
- In the 2005 general election, the independent candidate *Peter Law* was elected to represent the *constituency* of Blaenau Gwent, having been prevented from seeking selection as the official Labour Party candidate as a result of the party's imposition of an women-only shortlist.

W

working class: a collective term generally applied to those engaged in unskilled or semi-skilled manual work. See *social class*, *new working class* and *old working class*.

working-class Tories: those traditional *Labour Party* supporters in the lower *social classes* (primarily C1 and C2) who supported *Margaret Thatcher*'s *Conservative Party* in increasing numbers in the 1980s. See also *deviant voting*.

> **TIP:** The phenomenon was explained by a number of factors including *embourgeoisement*, the emergence of a *new working class*, and the Conservatives' 'right to buy' legislation, under which long-term council tenants could buy their homes at knock-down prices.

working peer: an individual who is elevated to the *House of Lords* as a *life peer* at the request of a *political party* to work on that party's behalf in the chamber.
- *New Labour* appointed a significant number of Labour life peers to the Upper Chamber following its victory in the 1997 *general election* as a way of redressing the inbuilt Conservative majority in the chamber.
- Such appointments and the fact that most *hereditary peers* lost their right to sit and vote in the Lords meant that Labour peers outnumbered Conservative peers by 216:197 by March 2009.

works of authority: scholarly texts that serve to codify constitutional practices not set out on paper elsewhere. Although these works have only a persuasive authority, the fact that many of them have been used as constitutional references for well over 100 years affords them a certain status.

Example

Key texts include *Walter Bagehot*'s *The English Constitution* (1867), Erskine May's *Parliamentary Practice* (first published in 1844) and A. V. Dicey's *An Introduction to the Study of the Law of the Constitution* (1885).

writ: a formal legal order issued by a judicial body. See also *subpoena*.

written constitution: see *codified constitution*, *uncodified constitution* and *constitution*.

written questions: where *MPs* seek detailed written answers to particular questions, as opposed to the point-scoring of *Prime Minister's Questions*. See *parliamentary questions*.
- The questions and the answers provided by ministers are recorded in *Hansard*.
- MPs often use written questions as a way of raising issues on behalf of their constituents.
- They also provide a way in which the *executive* can be held to account. See *scrutiny*.

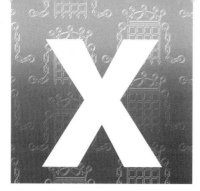

X: the mark voters make on the *ballot paper* in order to select their preferred *candidate* in an *election*, or their preferred course of action in the case of a *referendum*.

xenophobia: an extreme and irrational fear of foreigners.

Yes Minister: the long-running BBC situation comedy centring on the relationship between a government *minister* and the *civil servants* in his *department*. See *Theakston's models*.

- The series focused on the way in which the Machiavellian *permanent secretary*, Sir Humphrey Appleby, was able to outmanoeuvre the hapless minister, Jim Hacker.
- It was succeeded by the series *Yes Prime Minister*, with the leading protagonists in the original series relocating to *Number 10*.

zero-tolerance policing: an approach to policing that advocated the targeting of relatively low-level yet persistent and visible criminal activity such as vandalism, alcohol-related disorder and other antisocial behaviour.

- The approach was based on the principle that a failure to deal with such petty crime would create an environment in which more serious crime could take root and flourish.
- In the UK the zero-tolerance approach was pioneered by Ray Mallon, often dubbed 'Robocop', during his time at Cleveland Police. It was a significant issue in the 1997 *general election*.

UK government and politics revision lists

Using A–Z Online

In addition to the revision lists set out below, you can use the A–Z Online website to access revision lists specific to your exam board and the particular exam you are taking. Log on to **www.philipallan.co.uk/a-zonline** and create an account using the unique code provided on the inside front cover of this book. Once you have logged on, you can print out lists of terms together with their definitions, which will help you to focus your revision.

On the pages that follow, we have listed revision terms for the AS examinations for the three main awarding bodies:

- AQA, see pages 182–184
- Edexcel, see pages 185–187
- OCR, see pages 188–191

This is to help you use this handbook as effectively as possible. The areas of the subject that are covered in the following pages are summarised in the tables below.

AS Unit 1 UK politics and participation

AQA Unit 1 (GOVP1) People, politics and participation	Edexcel Unit 1 People and politics	OCR Unit 1 (F851) Contemporary politics of the UK
1 Participation and voting behaviour	1 Democracy and political participation	1 Political parties (mandatory)
2 Electoral systems	2 Party policies and ideas	2 Pressure groups (mandatory)
3 Political parties	3 Elections	3 Electoral systems and referenda
4 Pressure groups and protest movements	4 Pressure groups	4 UK parliamentary elections
		5 Voting behaviour in the UK

AS Unit 2 Governing the UK

AQA Unit 2 (GOVP2) Governing modern Britain	Edexcel Unit 2 Governing the UK	OCR Unit 2 (F852) Contemporary government of the UK
1 The British constitution	1 The constitution	1 The constitution
2 Parliament	2 Parliament	2 The executive (mandatory)
3 The core executive	3 The prime minister and cabinet	3 The legislature (mandatory)
4 Multi-level governance	4 Judges and civil liberties	4 The judiciary
		5 The European Union

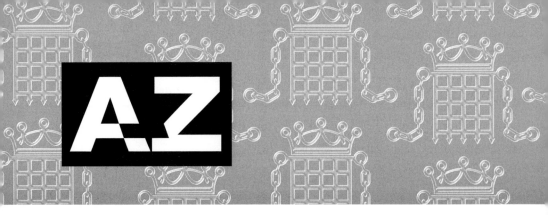

AQA revision lists

Unit 1 (GOVP1): People, politics and participation

1 Participation and voting behaviour

abstention	partisan alignment
apathy	partisan dealignment
churn	pluralist democracy
class alignment	political participation
class dealignment	politics
democracy	protest voting
dominant ideology model	rational choice model
elitism	short-term factors
gender gap	social structures model
general voting model	swing
identifier	tactical voting
liberal democracy	turnout
long-term factors	voting context model
media	

2 Electoral systems

additional member system (AMS)	landslide effect
Burkean model	party list system
direct democracy	majoritarian electoral system
electoral reform	proportional electoral system
electorate	quota
first-past-the-post	referendum
hybrid electoral system	representation
initiative	representative democracy
Jenkins Commission	single transferable vote (STV)

stable government

top-up

voter choice

wasted votes

3 Political parties

catch-all party

conservatism

constituency

dominant-party system

ideology

internal party democracy

minor party

multi-party system

National Policy Forum

neo-liberalism

New Labour

New Tories

Old Labour

party conference

party system

policy

Policy Forum

political party

single-party system

socialism

Thatcherism

two-party system

4 Pressure groups and protest movements

access points

attitude cause group

cause group

corporatism

direct action

ideological outsiders

insider group

insider/outsider typology

internal pressure group democracy

lobbying

outsiders by necessity

outsider group

policy network

political cause group

potential insiders

representation

sectional group

sectional cause group

sectional/cause group typology

single-issue pressure group

Unit 2 (GOVP2): Governing modern Britain

1 The British constitution

Bill of Rights

codified constitution

common law

constitutional monarchy

convention

European law

federalism

flexible constitution

fusion of powers

Human Rights Act (1998)

judicial activism

Judicial Appointments Commission

judicial independence

judicial neutrality

judicial restraint

judicial review

judiciary

parliamentary government

parliamentary sovereignty

rigid constitution

rule of law

separation of powers

statute law

uncodified constitution

unitary state

unwritten constitution

works of authority

written constitution

2 Parliament

accountability

backbencher

bicameralism

elective dictatorship

front benches

guillotine

House of Commons

House of Lords

legislation

legislative process

mandate

Ministers' Question Time

official opposition

parliamentary sovereignty

Prime Minister's Questions

representation

resemblance theory

scrutiny

select committee

standing committee

statute law

whips

3 The core executive

anonymity

bilateral meetings

bureaucracy

cabinet committee

cabinet government

Cabinet Office

civil service

collective responsibility

core executive

department

individual ministerial responsibility

permanence

prerogative powers

presidentialism

Prime Minister's Office

prime ministerial government

primus inter pares

sofa government

special advisor

spin doctor

4 Multi-level governance

democratic deficit

devolution

EU enlargement

European Commission

European Council of Ministers

integration

European Parliament

European Union (EU)

intergovernmentalism

local council

local democracy

Northern Ireland Assembly

qualified majority voting (QMV)

regional assemblies

regional development agencies

representative

Scottish Parliament

subsidiarity

supranational

Welsh Assembly

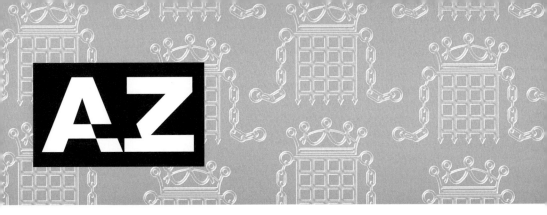

Edexcel revision lists

Unit 1: People and politics

1 Democracy and political participation

abstention

apathy

Burkean model

citizens' jury

compulsory voting

delegate model

democracy

direct democracy

e-democracy

elitism

franchise

initiative

legitimacy

liberal democracy

parliamentary democracy

pluralist democracy

political participation

politics

referendum

representation

representative democracy

resemblance theory

trustee model

turnout

2 Party policies and ideas

adversarial politics

catch-all party

consensus politics

conservatism

constituency

factionalism

ideology

internal party democracy

left wing

liberalism

National Policy Forum

neo-liberalism

New Labour

New Tories

Old Labour

party conference

party system

policy

Policy Forum

political party

right wing

socialism

Thatcherism

3 Elections

additional member system (AMS)

election

electoral reform

electorate

first-past-the-post

hybrid electron system

Jenkins Commission

landslide effect

majoritarian electoral system

mandate

party list system

party system

proportional electoral system

representation

single transferable vote (STV)

stable government

strong government

supplementary vote

voter choice

wasted votes

4 Pressure groups

access points

cause group

corporatism

direct action

elitism

Eurogroup

functional representation

insider group

insider/outsider typology

internal pressure group democracy

lobbying

outsider group

pluralist democracy

policy network

pressure group

representation

sectional group

sectional/cause pressure group typology

single-issue pressure group

Unit 2 : Governing the UK

1 The constitution

codified constitution

common law

constitution

constitutional monarchy

constitutionalism

convention

devolution

elective dictatorship

European law

federalism

flexible constitution

fusion of powers

parliamentary government

parliamentary sovereignty

pooled sovereignty

quasi-federalism

rigid constitution

rule of law

separation of powers

statute law

uncodified constitution

unitary state

unwritten constitution

works of authority

written constitution

2 Parliament

accountability

backbencher

bicameralism

elective dictatorship

front benches

fusion of powers

guillotine

House of Commons

House of Lords

legislative process

mandate

Ministers' Questions Time

official opposition

parliamentary government

parliamentary sovereignty

presidential government

Prime Minister's Questions

representation

representative democracy

resemblance theory

responsible government

scrutiny

select committees

separation of powers

standing committees

statute law

Westminster model

whip

3 The prime minister and cabinet

bilateral meetings

bureaueracy

cabinet committee

cabinet government

Cabinet Office

civil service

collective responsibility

core executive

department

government

individual ministerial responsibility

kitchen cabinet

patronage

prerogative powers

presidential prime minister

presidentialism

Prime Minister's Office

prime ministerial government

primus inter pares

sofa government

spatial leadership

special advisor

spin doctor

4 Judges and civil liberties

Bill of Rights

citizen

civil liberties

civil rights

European Court of Human Rights

European Court of Justice

European law

Human Rights Act (1998)

judge

judicial activism

Judicial Appointments Commission

judicial independence

judicial neutrality

judicial restraint

judicial review

judiciary

ombudsman

redress of grievances

rule of law

separation of powers

Supreme Court

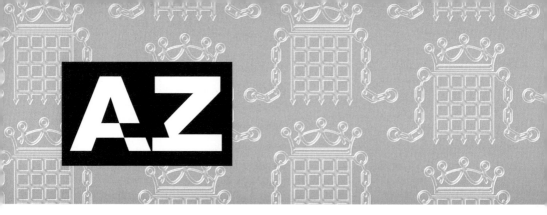

OCR revision lists

Unit 1 (F851): Contemporary politics of the UK

1 Political parties (mandatory)

catch-all party

conservatism

constituency

dominant-party system

ideology

internal party democracy

liberalism

multi-party system

National Executive Committee (NEC)

National Policy Forum

New Labour

New Tories

Old Labour

one-nation Conservativsm

party conference

party funding

party system

Policy Forum

representation

socialism

Thatcherism

two-party system

2 Pressure groups (mandatory)

access points

cause group

corporatism

democracy

direct action

elitism

insider group

insider/outsider typology

internal pressure group democracy

lobbying

media

outsider group

pluralist democracy

policy network

power

public opinion

representation

sectional group

sectional/cause group typology

single-issue pressure group

3 Electoral systems and referenda

additional member system (AMS)

democracy

direct democracy

election

electoral reform

electoral system

first-past-the-post

hybrid electoral system

legitimacy

majoritarian electoral system

mandate

party list system

proportional electoral system

referendum

representation

representative democracy

responsible government

simple majority

single transferable vote (STV)

wasted votes

4 UK parliamentary elections

by-election

campaign

candidate selection

coalition government

democracy

first-past-the-post

general election

landslide effect

legitimacy

majority government

mandate

manifesto

media

minority government

opinion poll

representation

representative democracy

swing

voting behaviour

wasted votes

5 Voting behaviour in the UK

abstention

apathy

campaign

class alignment

class dealignment

dominant ideology model

gender gap

identification (party)

identifier

long-term factors

media

partisan alignment

partisan dealignment

protest voting

rational choice model

short-term factors

social class

social structures model

tactical voting

turnout

voting behaviour

voting context model

voting model

Unit 2 (F852): Contemporary government of the UK

1 The constitution

codified constitution

common law

constitution

constitutional monarchy

constitutional reform

convention

devolution

European law

federalism

flexible constitution

fusion of powers

parliamentary government

parliamentary sovereignty

prerogative powers

rigid constitution

rule of law

separation of powers

sovereignty

statute law

uncodified constitution

unitary state

unwritten constitution

works of authority

written constitution

2 The executive (mandatory)

accountability

authority

bureaucracy

bilateral meetings

cabinet

cabinet government

civil service

collective responsibility

core executive

department

executive

individual ministerial responsibility

legitimacy

minister

parliamentary government

power

prerogative powers

prime minister

prime ministerial government

primus inter pares

special advisor

spin doctor

3 The legislature (mandatory)

accountability

backbencher

democracy

House of Commons

House of Lords

legislative process

legislature

Ministers' Question Time

opposition

Parliament

parliament debate

parliamentary government

parliamentary sovereignty

Prime Minister's Questions

representation

resemblance theory

scrutiny

select committees

speaker

standing committee

whip

4 The judiciary

Bill of Rights

citizen

civil liberties

civil rights

equality of opportunity

Human Rights Act (1998)

judicial activism

Judicial Appointments Commission

judicial independence

judicial neutrality

judicial restraint

judicial review

judiciary

justice

law

liberty

ombudsman

redress of grievances

rule of law

separation of powers

Supreme Court

tribunals

5 The European Union

co-decision procedure

democratic deficit

devolution

EU enlargement

euro

European Commission

European Council

European Council of Ministers

European Court of Justice

European Parliament

federalism

integration

intergovernmentalism

Lisbon, Treaty of (2007)

Maastricht, Treaty of (1992)

pooled sovereignty

qualified majority voting (QMV)

quasi-federalism

Rome, Treaty of (1957)

sovereignty

subsidiarity

supranational

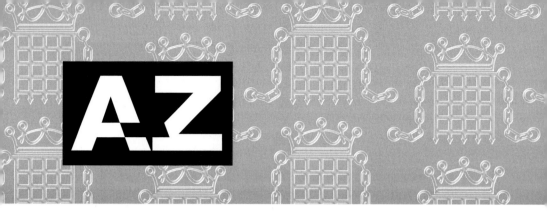

Hints for exam success

Revision is a very personal thing and the way in which you revise will, therefore, be guided largely by what works for you. That said, there are a number of things you probably need to take on board at an early stage if you are aiming for a top grade.

Knowing your specification

It is crucial that you familiarise yourself with the main elements of the specification you are studying – as well as the format of each examination you will face.

Specifically, you need to know:
- how the subject content is divided between the various units and sections within each unit
- precisely what you need to know and what you don't need to know in each section
- how many questions there are on each paper and how much time you have for each question
- how these questions relate to the sections in the unit content – one question per section of content or rather less predictable
- how much choice you will have when tackling each paper, i.e. are there any 'mandatory' (compulsory) questions or sections?
- what types of questions you will face

All this information is readily available direct from the websites of the three main examinations boards: AQA (www.aqa.org.uk); Edexcel (www.edexcel.com); and OCR (www.ocr.org.uk). These sites will allow you to download specifications, sample examination papers and other useful materials – free of charge. The examination papers are particularly useful as they will help you to become accustomed to the range and mix of questions you are likely to face in the real examination. They will also give you a chance to see the advice and the rules (the 'rubric') set out on the cover of the examination paper.

Five steps to effective revision

✓ **Step one:** as we have already established, first you need to get hold of the full subject specification (syllabus) for the examination board whose course you are following. You should also collect a selection of specimen papers or past papers, along with any other guidance available.

✓ **Step two:** you will need to work out a realistic revision timetable. This should incorporate all your subjects and be broken down into focused sessions of around 40 minutes, divided by breaks. These breaks are important. If you leave no time for relaxation, your revision will be less effective and you will also be less likely to keep to your timetable.

✓ **Step three:** using the specification, go through your folder and divide up your notes between the various areas of content identified. It might help you to photocopy the page of the specification that relates to each section of the course content and then put these sheets on top of each pile of notes. Alternatively, you could use subject dividers labelled with the various unit and section headings as a means of organising your notes. When this is done you should have several piles of notes – each one relating to a single topic – or one or more lever-arch files, divided and indexed in line with the specification content.

✓ **Step four:** the next task is to check your notes in order to make sure that you have covered everything on the specification. Look through each pile of notes checking each topic off against the content summary from the specification. Are there any big gaps? It may be that you have 'mislaid' some notes – or that you missed some lessons and failed to catch up. It is also possible that your teacher has left out certain sections for good reason: perhaps a lack of time if you are being entered for the Unit 1 examination in the January of Year 12. Check it out. Make sure that you are not missing something vital. If you find that there are gaps, you need to work quickly. If the exam is still some way off, you may have time to reinforce any particularly thin topics by expanding your notes. If the problem is largely down to a lack of understanding – rather than a lack of notes – you may be able to seek individual help from your teacher.

If the examination is only a few weeks away, however, something more drastic is probably called for. This book is aimed at helping you to familiarise yourself with the various terms and phrases you may encounter whilst studying the subject. You will need to look elsewhere for greater depth. There are, however, a number of books on the market that provide the kind of factual summaries that can help you to cut corners if time is short, e.g. Paul Fairclough (2009) *AS & A Level Government and Politics Through Diagrams* (OUP).

✓ **Step five:** look at the specification content and the available specimen papers or past papers for each module. Which questions do you feel fairly confident about tackling? Which make you want to cry or retreat to your bed with a packet of bourbons? However tempting it is to start your revision with the topics you feel happy with, it really is better to grasp the nettle and address your weaknesses first. Once you have identified these weaker areas, you need to go through making summary notes. Try – if you can – to get each small topic on a single page. This process of summarising should eventually leave you with a much less daunting set of memory-jogging revision notes. You could also try presenting your notes in different formats. Some books, for example, present the information in the form of diagrams. You could try turning these diagrams into prose or into bullet-pointed lists. Equally, try turning some of your own hand-written notes into diagrams or mind-maps. You will find that the very process of reformatting your notes in this way reinforces learning and develops a greater understanding of the material.

Five things to avoid

✗ **Leaving it too late:** though 'last-minute revision' may have served you well at GCSE, students who adopt this approach at AS and A-level rarely come away with the kinds of grade they are capable of. The depth of knowledge and understanding required at this level makes it difficult to find 'quick-fixes'.

✗ **Staying at home** when you should be attending in-school revision sessions. Though you may feel that you can do a better job yourself, the vast majority of students who adopt this approach do not achieve their potential. However pointless the school revision lessons may seem to you, they are probably helping you more than you realise.

✗ **Revising for hours on end** without a break or working for whole days on a single subject. A series of 40-minute sessions interspersed with 15-minute breaks can lead to more productive work and it is good to build some daily variety into your revision programme, by mixing and matching different subjects.

✗ **Question spotting:** although it is good to look at the kinds of question that have turned up in the past, question spotting (i.e. trying to guess what the examiners will put on the exam paper) is a dangerous game. Even if your 'banker' topic does turn up, there is no guarantee that it is going to be phrased in such a way that you want to tackle it.

✗ **Omitting major topics** from your revision. Leaving out major topics when you revise can be disastrous. It is not uncommon for examiners to face a script where an obviously able candidate has scored an A-grade equivalent mark on one question, only barely to scrape a C-grade in the other. Though the free choice of questions available on some AS papers means that you are less likely to be forced to answer a particular question, failing to revise one or more of the sections of content relating to a unit will seriously reduce your options if something really nasty appears in one of your preferred topic areas. An overly narrow approach when revising will also limit your overall (i.e. 'synoptic') understanding of the subject.

Examinable skills

The Qualifications and Curriculum Authority (QCA) identified the assessment objectives that are common to all three main government and politics specifications (see below). At AS level (i.e. Units 1 and 2), the assessment is weighted more towards AO1 (knowledge and understanding), whereas at A2 (i.e. Units 3 and 4), the emphasis shifts slightly. Though this shift in emphasis clearly reflects the greater emphasis on analysis and evaluation required at A2, you will obviously need to do more than simply demonstrate knowledge at AS level also.

| | | | AS weighting | |
Assessment objectives		AQA	Edexcel	OCR
AO1	Demonstrate knowledge and understanding of relevant institutions, processes, political concepts, theories and debates.	50%	50%	50%
AO2	Analyse and evaluate political information, arguments and explanations, and identify parallels, connections, similarities and differences between aspects of the political systems studied.	30%	30%	35%
AO3	Construct and communicate coherent arguments making use of a range of appropriate political vocabulary.	20%	20%	15%

Your AS examination answers will be marked according to these assessment objectives. Examiners will not simply give you a mark for every tick they have added to your script (a so-called 'penny points' mark scheme). Marks will be available against each assessment objective and the total mark for all but the shortest questions will therefore be arrived at by totalling the marks awarded for knowledge and understanding (AO1), analysis and evaluation (AO2) and communication (AO3) on each subquestion.

Writing good answers

The key to achieving a good mark when answering government and politics questions is fourfold:

1 **Take time to identify what the question is getting at:** i.e. what you are being asked to do. Look for 'command words' (see the examples below) and make sure you do what is being asked of you.
   - **Analyse:** break down the topic in question into its component parts, considering each in turn.
   - **Assess:** weigh up the merits of a particular argument or associate arguments.
   - **Discuss:** generally requires you to put both sides of an argument before arriving at your conclusion. Though in theory it is possible to discuss only one aspect of the debate in question, you are more likely to secure the higher grades if your answer is balanced.
   - **Evaluate:** weigh up the evidence in order to determine the extent to which a particular statement or viewpoint is valid.
   - **Examine:** look in detail at the argument or material provided, identify the issues or debates that surround it and arrive at a conclusion.
   - **Explain:** demonstrate an understanding of the meaning of a particular term or topic.
   - **Identify:** pick out one or more features of the topic under consideration.
2 **Try to write in an analytical style** as opposed to simply describing things. The latter may be rewarded on AO1, but you are unlikely to pick up many marks on AO2.
3 **Strike the right balance between theory and supporting examples** Ideally, each separate argument/point should be developed in a single paragraph and each point you make should be supported by at least one example.
4 **Try to use appropriate political vocabulary.** This will help you to score more highly on AO3.

What to do when the examination day finally arrives

Though many of your examination strategies will be shaped by the demands of the specification you are following, it is worth making some general points about how to maximise your chances in examinations once your revision is complete and the 'big day' has finally arrived.

Ensure that you know which exam is on which day. This might sound obvious but it is not uncommon for candidates inadvertently to miss examinations, or turn up having revised Latin Unit 1 only to find that they are in fact due to sit Politics Unit 2. It may be that you have an examination clash involving two or more subjects. If this is the case, make sure that you know which unit(s) you will be doing in the morning and which you will be sitting in the afternoon. It is your responsibility to make sure that you know which exam is on which day and whether exams are in the morning or afternoon. Even if you have revised for both subjects on the same day, it can be unsettling to be told that you are tackling them in a different order from that which you had expected. Such mistakes can cost grades.

Make sure that you arrive in good time for the examination. If you arrive at the last minute, or even late, you will probably not be in the best frame of mind to tackle the examination paper. Arriving far too early can be just as bad if you are nervous by nature, as you may well manage to get yourself into a complete state before you even enter the examination room.

Make sure that you arrive properly equipped. You should know what you need for the examination. Do not turn up without a pencil if you have spent your whole revision programme planning essays in pencil before you start. More importantly, think carefully about what pen you are going to use. Examiners frequently complain about the problems they have reading scripts written in faint biro. It makes far more sense to use a black roller ball pen, a black gel pen or a black ink pen in examinations. Why lose valuable marks simply because your words of wisdom are illegible?

Get the timing right. You must make a mental note of the total time available for the examination and the amount of time you have available to complete each question. It can be helpful to make a note at the start of the examination of the times at which you should be starting each question or subquestion. This will help you to make sure that you do not fall behind schedule. Remember, the number of extra marks you will gain by spending an extra 10 minutes on a question that you have already answered well will not make up for the marks you lose as a result of having only 15 minutes left to do the last question. Be strict with yourself!

Think before you commit pen to paper. Although it can be tempting to start writing as soon as you open the paper, particularly if everyone else is scribbling away, it is far better to have a good look at all the questions first to make sure that you haven't missed anything. It might be that the question on voting behaviour is there, after all, but that it is just worded in a less obvious way. It would be a shame to miss your 'banker' topic for the want of a pause for thought.

Make sure you do what is asked of you rather than simply writing what you want to write. If it says 'explain', do not simply 'describe'. If the question asks you to consider a particular period (e.g. the 1990s) then focus on that period rather than reeling off all of your pre-learnt examples from the 1960s; as a rule, take the word 'recent' to mean the last 20 years or so.

Strike the right balance between political theory and supporting examples. Answers that are overly theoretical or ones that simply describe recent events without any attempt to bring in theory are likely to fall short. Anyone can do the latter if they watch the news. You have been studying politics for at least a year and you should, therefore, be able to deploy political theory when evaluating events, as well as putting such events into their historical context.